The Psychology of Poverty Alleviation

In order to design, enact, and protect poverty alleviation policies in developing countries, we must first understand the psychology of how the poor react to their plight, and not just the psychology of the privileged called upon for sacrifice. This book integrates social and psycho-dynamic psychology, economics, policy design, and policy-process theory to explore ways to follow through on successful poverty-alleviation initiatives, while averting destructive conflict. Using eight case studies across Latin America, Southeast Asia, and South Asia, William Ascher examines successes and failures in helping the poor through affirmative action, cash transfers, social-spending targeting, subsidies, and regional development. In doing so, he demonstrates how social identities, attributions of deservingness, and perceptions of the policy process shape both the willingness to support pro-poor policies and the conflict that emerges over distributional issues.

WILLIAM ASCHER is Donald C. McKenna Professor of Government and Economics at Claremont McKenna College.

The Psychology of Poverty Alleviation

Challenges in Developing Countries

WILLIAM ASCHER
Claremont McKenna College

CAMBRIDGE
UNIVERSITY PRESS

University Printing House, Cambridge CB2 8BS, United Kingdom

One Liberty Plaza, 20th Floor, New York, NY 10006, USA

477 Williamstown Road, Port Melbourne, VIC 3207, Australia

314-321, 3rd Floor, Plot 3, Splendor Forum, Jasola District Centre, New Delhi - 110025, India

103 Penang Road, #05-06/07, Visioncrest Commercial, Singapore 238467

Cambridge University Press is part of the University of Cambridge.

It furthers the University's mission by disseminating knowledge in the pursuit of education, learning and research at the highest international levels of excellence.

www.cambridge.org
Information on this title: www.cambridge.org/9781108794572
DOI: 10.1017/9781108885775

© William Ascher 2020

This publication is in copyright. Subject to statutory exception and to the provisions of relevant collective licensing agreements, no reproduction of any part may take place without the written permission of Cambridge University Press.

First published 2020
First paperback edition 2021

A catalogue record for this publication is available from the British Library

Library of Congress Cataloging in Publication data
NAMES: Ascher, William, author.
TITLE: The psychology of poverty alleviation : challenges in developing countries / William Ascher.
DESCRIPTION: Cambridge ; New York, NY : Cambridge University Press, 2020. | Includes bibliographical references and index.
IDENTIFIERS: LCCN 2020002775 (print) | LCCN 2020002776 (ebook) | ISBN 9781108840361 (hardback) | ISBN 9781108794572 (paperback) | ISBN 9781108885775 (epub)
SUBJECTS: LCSH: Poverty–Government policy–Developing countries. | Poverty–Developing countries–Psychological aspects. | Developing countries–Social policy. | Developing countries–Economic policy.
CLASSIFICATION: LCC HC59.72.P6 A78 2020 (print) | LCC HC59.72.P6 (ebook) | DDC 339.4/6019–dc23
LC record available at https://lccn.loc.gov/2020002775
LC ebook record available at https://lccn.loc.gov/2020002776

ISBN 978-1-108-84036-1 Hardback
ISBN 978-1-108-79457-2 Paperback

Cambridge University Press has no responsibility for the persistence or accuracy of URLs for external or third-party internet websites referred to in this publication, and does not guarantee that any content on such websites is, or will remain, accurate or appropriate.

To the memory of Jennie Litvack, an extraordinary person

Contents

List of Figures		*page* ix
List of Tables		xi
Acknowledgments		xiii

PART I INTRODUCTION

1	The Challenges of Conflict-Sensitive Poverty Alleviation	3
2	Political Economy Considerations	24

PART II THE UNDERLYING PSYCHOLOGY

3	Identity, Attributions, Deservingness Judgments, and Hostility	51

PART III LESSONS FROM PRO-POOR POLICY INSTRUMENTS

4	Conditional Cash Transfers	91
5	Social-Sector Spending Targeting the Poor	103
6	Pro-Poor Subsidies and the Problem of Leakage	123
7	Affirmative Action	135
8	Regional Development Targeting the Poorest Areas	170

PART IV OVERCOMING OBSTACLES IN THE POLICY PROCESS

9	How the Wealthy React to Pro-Poor-Labeled Initiatives	193
10	Lessons and Conclusions	210

References		221
Index		243

Figures

2.1	Growth of the lowest quintile and overall growth	*page* 26
10.1	Attributions and perspective components	213

Tables

1.1	Share of national income of the bottom 20 percent and bottom 40 percent of the population, key cases, circa 1995–2015	*page* 17
2.1	Percent increase in GDP/capita in constant 2011 international dollars	42
2.2	Economic growth rates, case study nations, 1961–2015	43
2.3	Poverty head-count percent at less than $1.90/day and $5.50/day, key study countries, circa 1980–2015	45
2.4	Gini indices, key cases, circa 1995–2015	47
2.5	Gini indices across subnational units, key study countries	47
2.6	Tax capacity, selected countries including case study countries, 1994–2009	48
3.1	Judgments of laziness attributed to welfare recipients, six most populous Latin American countries, 2012	81
6.1	India: gross state domestic product (GSDP) ratio to the national average, 2017–2018	129
7.1	Poverty headcount by province, Sri Lanka, 1990/1991–2016	162
8.1	Regional per capita income ratios to Bangkok and vicinity levels, Thailand, 1995–2016	175
9.1	Agreement of the need for strong government policies to reduce income inequality, six most populous Latin American countries, 2014	195

Acknowledgments

This book grew out of a four-year-long working group at Claremont McKenna College. Impressive background research was conducted by Aleena Ali, Hannah Bottum, Audrey Breitwieser, Brian Chmelik, Byron Cohen, Syed Farooq, Sydney Flynn, Tania Alicia Gray, Michael Grouskay, Sydney Joseph, Katherine Krey, Isabel Laterzo, Chenyu Li, Xinzhu Li, Andrea Medina, Charlotte Reinnoldt, Paola Salomon, Tania Salomon, and Sanjana Sankaran. I am especially grateful for the research by Alejandra Vazquez Baur on Afro-Brazilian affirmative action, by Lauren Giurata on ideological polarization in Argentina, and by Shambhavi Sahai on affirmative action in India. Reactions by Robert Healy, Jin Sato, Lars Schoultz, and Aseema Sinha to earlier drafts were extremely helpful. Finally, hundreds of conversations with Barbara Hirschfelder-Ascher about the theories and cases, as well as her editing of dozens of versions, made this book possible.

PART I

INTRODUCTION

I

The Challenges of Conflict-Sensitive Poverty Alleviation

Over the past few years more than ten million relatively prosperous families in India gave up the right to buy fuel at subsidized prices so that poorer Indians could do so. On the other hand, some wealthy Indians have muscled their way into qualifying for affirmative action privileges, undermining an effective way of improving the prospects for deserving low-income students. In Brazil, the new millennium gave birth to a radical departure from the race-blind "racial democracy" myth to enact benefits for deprived Afro-Brazilians, despite the lack of a powerful pro-affirmative-action movement. Yet the affirmative action program has divided the Afro-Brazilian community, with recriminations and student expulsions for not being "black enough."

These contradictions are a small fraction of the puzzles encountered in the efforts to induce relatively prosperous citizens to sacrifice some of their income for the sake of the poor. And, other puzzles arise in efforts to protect poverty alleviation programs from efforts of more prosperous people to wrest away the privileges. In highly polarized Argentina and Brazil, the extremism of pro-poor populist programs provided the opportunity for serious retrenchments of the programs. In contrast, violence by a populist movement based in Thailand's poorest region following a coup d'état against its leader reduced the movement's formal government and electoral power, yet brought the region greater policy relevance. It also elevated the rural inhabitants' social and political status from subservient "villagers" to active participants in policymaking.

Poverty goes beyond simply the lack of income, to encompass deprivations in education, health, respect, and so on. Nevertheless, increasing the incomes of the poor typically provides them with greater capability to

3

4   *Introduction*

overcome these deprivations. Moreover, in accord with a core premise of this book, poverty alleviation is best served by overall economic growth that not only increases the incomes of the poor, but also increases a country's capacity to enhance social services for the poor.

If the ultimate objective is to address the broad spectrum of deprivations of the disadvantaged, then understanding how respect is enhanced or denied is also a key challenge. Pro-poor initiatives have to avoid the surprisingly common consequence of poverty alleviation programs that they strengthen the prejudices against lower-status people. In Bogotá, Colombia, residents of expensive neighborhoods accept much higher utility rates so that residents of poorer neighborhoods could pay less, yet the neighborhood designations add disrespect to the deprivations of poverty.

Further, it is equally challenging to understand how to minimize the damage caused by government leaders who institute self-serving initiatives masquerading as poverty alleviation programs. The Malaysian and Sri Lankan affirmative action programs not only have further undermined the international standing of affirmative action, but also have greatly exacerbated societal polarization and economic decline.

Understanding these complex interactions is crucial for advancing the well-being of the roughly two billion people living below the internationally recognized poverty line, of whom three-quarters of a billion people live in extreme poverty.[1] Despite the remarkable poverty reduction documented by Millennium Development Goals assessments, poverty alleviation remains the most compelling development challenge. If the policies *also* contribute to empowering the poor, the gains are more likely to be sustainable. And if prosperous and poor people can avoid sustained destructive conflict, the overall gains of the economy are highly likely to be shared by the poor.

The cases sketched above demonstrate why the parsimonious models most prominent in economics and political economy are insufficient. For example, will altruistic impulses be directed to the poor in individual towns, regions, or nations? Or to kinsmen or coreligionists? Will social identities be enhanced if members of other groups are seen as deserving or undeserving of assistance? Moreover, models attempting to predict whether people at particular income levels would favor redistribution fail to find empirical confirmation, in part because of the distorted views

---

[1] World Bank PovcalNet database; the poverty line defined as US$3.20 per day, the extreme poverty line as US$1.90 per day.

people have of their own standing within the income distribution (Gimpelson and Treisman 2018).

In addition, none of these models can tell us what the basis of income comparisons might be. Are people satisfied or dissatisfied with their perceived relative standing in relation to the entire nation, to another region, or in comparison with people of different ethnicity, language, religion, or other ascriptive characteristics? In many Latin American and Southeast Asian countries, the national income distribution is becoming more equal, according to the standard measures, and yet there is no indication that this has tempered the dissatisfaction about economic policies. In Southeast Asia, particularly in Thailand, a case especially highlighted in this book, dissatisfaction over regional inequality appears to be more important than perceived inequalities overall. The fact that the poverty in Thailand's poorest Northeast region has declined substantially has not reduced the antagonism toward the center, and may lead to growth-suppressing conflict in the future. The "revolution of rising expectations" undoubtedly is at play in some of these cases.

Furthermore, economics in isolation, with its emphasis on utility maximization, cannot address the central issues of sacrifice, as Simpson and Willer (2015, 44) ask:

Why do people cooperate in situations in which they could benefit more through selfishness? Why do people behave generously, often making great personal sacrifices in order to help others? Why do people behave in trustworthy ways, when they could profit more by exploiting dependent partners? In situations such as these an opposition exists between what is best for oneself versus what is best for others. Because of the fundamental nature of that conflict – reflecting the often-divergent consequences of egoism and sociality – answers to these questions offer important insights into understanding the microfoundations of social order.

Whether out of straightforward generosity or to maintain the social order, efforts to strengthen poverty alleviation outcomes require prosperous people to make some sacrifices by supporting, or at least acquiescing to, pro-poor policies. Of course, some prosperous people may perceive a pro-poor policy as benefiting themselves; such clear-cut scenarios are of little need for psychological insights to understand the behaviors of these segments. Thus, the first concern of this book is how to promote the willingness of the non-poor to make some degree of sacrifice for the sake of the poor. Their mindsets – their degree of empathy with the poor, the threat levels that they feel, their stereotypes as to whether the poor want or deserve greater benefits, and other psychological aspects – play a significant role in enhancing or deflating this commitment. Even if relatively prosperous individuals are predisposed to support pro-poor policies and programs, their expectations and identifications are crucial in establishing whether they believe that an initiative claimed to be pro-poor actually would have the claimed impact. This, in turn, depends on perceptions as to whether the government is truly committed to, and capable of, pursuing the initiative.

They would also ask whether the initiative freezes out better alternatives, and whether the beneficiaries are deserving of the benefits – clearly an attitude that goes beyond economic self-interest. In terms of protecting the individual's own interests, and others whom the individual wishes to protect, the obvious question is whether the initiative would lead to unacceptable harm. A less obvious but also important concern is whether the initiative would open the way to other initiatives that lead to unacceptable harm.

Of course, favoring pro-poor government policies and programs is not the only way to contribute to poverty alleviation. Philanthropy can be more direct. Many religions require charitability: tithing for many Christian denominations, zakat in Islam; tzadakah in Judaism; dāna in Hinduism, Buddhism, Jainism, and Sikhism. Yet, often the contributions are to be implemented by the religious institutions (particularly in Christian denominations). However, in most developing countries, private philanthropy that reaches the poor is modest. For example, in Mexico, one of the richest countries still considered to be "developing," philanthropy by individuals was estimated to be only .0014 of the GDP in 2012 (García-Colín and Sordo Ruz 2016, 339, 343). This is only one-fifth of the magnitude of nonprofit philanthropy from other sources, presumably international sources and domestic corporate contributions.

In addition, private philanthropy typically contributes less to poverty alleviation than do concerted government efforts. Dasgupta and Kanbur (2011, 1) argue: "Rich individuals often voluntarily contribute large amounts towards the provision of public goods that are intrinsically important for the well-being of poor individuals, but have limited impact on their incomes."[2] They point out that:

---

[2] The examples of public goods to which they are referring are support of "places of worship, ethnic festivals, literary and cultural activities, sports clubs, civic/neighborhood amenities (including parks, museums, theatres, community halls, libraries), facilities for scientific research, etc." (Dasgupta and Kanbur 2011, 2).

The earlier emphasis on state-organized redistribution of income and wealth has largely been supplanted by attempts to encourage the rich to voluntarily contribute to local public goods ... What appears to be of critical importance in assessing such claims is the magnitude of their direct impact on the private asset base of poorer individuals, i.e., on their private consumption ... [P]hilanthropic provision of public goods that are intrinsically valuable, but have negligible income-augmenting effects on the non-rich, may often be reasonably viewed as complementary to a policy of redistribution. The poor do benefit from such provision, but the rich benefit more.

(Dasguptaand Kanbur 2011, 3–4)

This book sides with Dasgupta and Kanbur in emphasizing the importance of government policies and programs dedicated to poverty alleviation.

Nevertheless, it is essential to recognize that the incomes of the poor, whether it is the bottom 20 percent or bottom 40 percent, typically grow in close relation to the overall growth of the economy (this crucial point is elaborated in Chapter 2). This is why actions that jeopardize overall growth, including profligate spending as well as disruption that scares away investment capital, is damaging to the poor. Yet in some countries the poor's income gains can be augmented with pro-poor policies that complement sustainable overall growth policies, just as cases do exist in which the incomes of the poor lag behind the others. Achieving poverty alleviation beyond the economy's overall growth requires recognizing that some governments, responding to their own objectives and the support of key stakeholders, do not adopt the most effective pro-poor policies. Moreover, governments often neglect the very poorest people, who typically live in remote areas and are not integrated into the economy in ways that can enhance their livelihoods.

Thus, understanding how to achieve poverty alleviation requires attention to the psychology associated with two tasks. The obvious task is to provide the resources for the poor to increase their incomes and other assets, ranging from health and education to respect and self-esteem. The second task is to avert high levels of sustained conflict, because the economic decline brought on by destructive conflict undermines the incomes of the poor along with the non-poor, often with greater deprivation for the poor. Unsurprisingly, the correlation between levels of conflict and economic decline are very strong (Blattman and Miguel 2010; Justino 2011). This means that policies that provoke high conflict levels risk undermining economic growth, and consequently undermine poverty alleviation. The Dollar and Kraay (2002) and Dollar, Kleineberg, and Kraay's (2016) analyses also reveal that the poor do worse than the rest of the population when the overall economy is in recession, but better than others when the overall economy is doing very well.

The bottom line is that for the bulk of developing countries, overall economic growth is necessary for the rise in the incomes and socio-political standing of the poor. Systemic factors that undermine overall economic growth, such as high levels of sustained conflict, hit the poor the hardest.

A very important caveat is necessary, however. In some instances, destructive conflict, including open violence, may have a positive effect of providing entrée to the poor to the policy process, such that their needs and wants would be taken more seriously. The case of so-called red shirt violence in Thailand seems to be such a case. Of course, the risk is that destructive conflict will escalate and become endemic, rather than stabilizing with the new, broader policy participation.

Growth-killing conflict does not necessarily entail overt violence, despite the fact that so many conflict studies presume that the predominant issue is violence, ranging from street violence to civil wars. While physical harm is obviously important, the focus on economic growth means that other forms of conflict are important as well. These include impasses over needed policy reforms, lack of intergroup cooperation, suppression of information, economic sabotage, and capital flight. Contentious relations between employers and employees can lead to paralyzing strikes; economic crises begging for urgent action go unaddressed due to such non-violent conflicts. When groups become so polarized that the economy is seen as a zero-sum game, hobbling economic growth, the poor lose out. We can conclude: *Poverty alleviation has the best chance when pro-poor government policymakers, relying on enough support or acquiescence by the non-poor, can effectively enact pro-poor, pro-growth policies in a context of low destructive conflict.*

It is true that poverty alleviation can occur even without a pro-poor commitment, if rapid economic growth pulls up the incomes of the poor. However, a pro-poor commitment by a sufficiently relevant set of the non-poor often can resist policies that would beggar the poor and support policies that are more directly pro-poor. Of course, some of the non-poor may favor pro-poor policies in order to preempt disruption by the poor. Even so, the pages that follow argue that less defensive support for the poor out of concern for their welfare and contributions to the overall economy is even more promising.

The politics of pro-poor initiatives has to take into account that the "non-poor," though a convenient summary term, masks a wide range of

The Challenges of Conflict-Sensitive Poverty Alleviation

income levels and circumstances. Thus, in some circumstances, the very wealthy may have no qualms about steering government programs more in the direction of the very poor than in support of middle-income families. Yet, in other circumstances, the very wealthy may feel threatened by more radical initiatives.

In short: *The primary challenge addressed by this book is to understand the psychology relevant to promoting and defending pro-poor policies, while minimizing destructive conflict and empowering the poor in the policy process.*

THE PROMISE – AND LIMITATIONS – OF SOCIAL PSYCHOLOGY

The field of social psychology has made great strides, through both theorizing and experiments. It has generated insights on the general patterns of forming identities, attributing traits to both "ingroups" and "outgroups," and developing empathy directed toward accepting sacrifices on behalf of the poor. Social psychology now offers the framework to understand how antagonisms arise that fuel destructive conflict. For citizens called upon to make sacrifices for the poor, these psychological dynamics also shape perspectives about income distribution and judgments of the deservingness of the poor, which in turn depend on stereotypes of the poor.

In addition, the non-poor's tolerance depends on the degree to which they identify with elements of the poor. The dynamics of identification, a major focus of social psychology, influence whether those called upon to make sacrifices for the poor identify with some of the poor. And even for those non-poor disposed to support pro-poor policies in principle, the heuristics (Kahneman and Frederick 2002) that shape views of government leaders' dishonesty or incompetence can generate skepticism toward sound initiatives.

However, the useful application of these psychological underpinnings requires meshing them with the realities of policies and actors' concerns about the fate of policy alternatives. People we might expect to be predisposed to either cooperation or conflict act differently because of their perceptions of policy motives and potential consequences. Predispositions to make sacrifices for less-fortunate people often founder on perceptions that government policy initiatives are insincere, or would have little success. These predispositions may be blunted by stereotypes of the poor as uninterested or unable to take advantage of additional benefits.

The theories are invaluable, but knowing how they will play out, and selecting policy approaches and enactment strategies, require knowing how to put the theories into appropriate political and socioeconomic contexts.

This book attempts to fill the gap in connecting distributionally relevant identifications to the stance regarding pro-poor policies. Part of the challenge is that the willingness to make sacrifices that entail income losses and other risks is often fragile, in light of the capacity to rationalize self-serving behavior. We must presume that compelling reasons – whether practical or ethical – are necessary for prosperous people to be willing to make sacrifices for people beyond those with whom they most immediately identify. Thus, to guide the formulation of pro-poor government policies, this book applies understandings of psychological dynamics to determine:

- circumstances in which the non-poor consider the relevant poor as deserving, which depends on stereotypes held about the poor, the overlap of the identifications of the non-poor with the poor, and understandings of why poverty exists.
- whether seeking individual or ingroup self-esteem can heighten the salience of more inclusive ingroup identifications.
- whether the desire for ingroup self-esteem results in denigrating the poor in order to affirm the superiority of the ingroup, or self-esteem is more potently reinforced by generosity toward the poor.
- whether those whose support is pivotal for an initiative doubt that it would help the poor, or believe that it would result in unacceptably high damage to the pivotal group; both depend on confidence in the intentions and competence of the government.
- whether polarization and resentment that threaten to bring about growth-paralyzing conflict can be reduced by altering mental scripts, rectifying misperceptions of income-distribution trends, diminishing negative stereotypes, broadening salient identifications, or reducing the perception of victimization.
- whether appeals based on raw impulse, instrumental rationality, and conscience can be directed to strengthen altruism applied to support pro-poor policy initiatives.

These understandings can be the basis for determining how to change perspectives, time new initiatives, select the tactics for publicizing them, and know which initiatives are unlikely to succeed.

As this suggests, scaling up from individual attributes associated with pro-social behavior to group behaviors in the policy process requires a

The Challenges of Conflict-Sensitive Poverty Alleviation

much broader set of considerations. Psychological insights must be folded into the real-world contexts of policy debates, intergroup confrontations, skepticism, effectiveness of government initiatives, and so on. Yet, these contexts are not engaged in the experiments that underlie much of social psychology. Our analysis, therefore, must incorporate assessments of how people understand and react to the socioeconomic and political circumstances of their countries.

HOW PEOPLE SHAPE POVERTY ALLEVIATION POLICIES

People influence the degree to which government policies address poverty alleviation in more ways than most people realize. Policymakers may have their own predispositions to assist the poor, from pro-social sentiments, from emotional or strategic linkages with the poor, from the motive to preempt disruption, or from a farsighted effort to improve overall productivity. Or it may come from pro-social predispositions held by a large enough segment of politically powerful actors to make the enactment of pro-social policies a political advantage. However, pro-poor commitment of government leaders by itself is rarely enough. Such policies require the forbearance of some of the non-poor. Even authoritarian leaders cannot enact policies without some fraction of the non-poor in favor of such policies: the groups on which authoritarian leaders depend politically, the bureaucracy, and other non-poor elements of the state.

Many actions by citizens can contribute to poverty alleviation:

- Supporting pro-poor political parties, movements, or factions, as long as they are not so extreme as to provoke growth-crushing destructive conflict and disinvestment.
- Supporting nongovernmental organizations or other movements that contribute directly to poverty alleviation or pressure government to adopt moderately progressive poverty alleviation measures.
- Supporting, or at least acquiescing to, policies that:
  - increase taxation to fund government expenditures targeting the poor
  - penalize discrimination against groups that have many poor members
  - direct government expenditures and favorable economic conditions to the areas with the greatest poverty
  - eliminate regulations that benefit others at the expense of the poor

12   *Introduction*

- o address environmental conditions that, if left unchecked, compel the
  poor to migrate in a manner that increases their vulnerability
- o reduce government provocations that could lead to destructive
  conflict
- o reform initially pro-poor programs that have been distorted through
  efforts of wealthier groups to capture benefits targeted to the poor
- Increasing some charitable contributions.
- Cooperating with people of other groups to reduce the potential for
  growth-crushing conflict.

The effectiveness of these actions may be limited by uncertainty of the
impacts of institutions and policies. No one is in a position to master and
react to the full set of existing policies and pending initiatives that will
shape the benefits of the poor. Some new initiatives will be explicitly
identified as pro-poor (e.g., cash transfer programs), yet one of the biggest
challenges for people predisposed to make sacrifices for the poor is the
difficulty of judging the genuineness of policy initiatives *claimed* to be
pro-poor. The genuinely promising initiatives may be difficult to distinguish from insincere or infeasible initiatives. Motivation to make sacrifices weakens when the effectiveness of an initiative is in doubt; the line
between healthy skepticism and cynicism is often fuzzy.

WHAT PRO-POOR POLICIES REQUIRE

Of course, awareness of widespread poverty is essential. So, too, is the
assessment that some sacrifice of income, social status, and/or loss of
current benefits could be tolerated. The next hurdle is whether the individual believes that the poor *deserve* more benefits through government
policies. Beyond that is the assessment of whether such initiatives could be
successful *if* implemented and are politically viable.

While thus far our focus has been on the actions of the relatively
prosperous, sustainable pro-poor policies also require particular commitments by policymakers and the potential recipients of pro-poor benefits.
To gain favor with poorer constituents, policymakers may press for
economically unsustainable policies. They may go beyond the tolerance
of other groups that could oust the government or otherwise undermine
the pro-poor policy. Both patterns can be seen in the cases examined in
some depth in this book. In Argentina and Brazil, excessive populist
measures undermined the prospects for growth, leading to economic
collapse and the electoral defeat of the populist parties, leading to a higher

priority on economic stability than poverty alleviation. As with the Thai military overthrow of a populist regime mentioned earlier, the populist "red shirt" movement engaged in considerable violence. Some degree of restraint is required to avoid jeopardizing economic growth directly, or generating destructive conflict that has the same effect.

It also must be recognized that a key challenge to channeling pro-poor predispositions into support for pro-poor policies is the alternative appeal of private philanthropy. First, private philanthropy is generally at individual discretion, although social pressures sometimes make this less discretionary. Second, private philanthropy can be a temporary and discretionary commitment, in comparison to government programs with long-term budgetary commitments. Third, while uncertainty exists as to whether charitable contributions will go to good purposes, this uncertainty is often much higher for the impacts of government initiatives. Fourth, private philanthropy can earn esteem directly. Finally, most pro-poor government policies do not provide the opportunity for prosperous individuals to select beneficiaries.

POVERTY ALLEVIATION POLICIES AND PROGRAMS

Because overall economic growth typically reduces poverty, there is no end to the policies that have some potential for poverty alleviation, ranging from strengthening the banking system to breaking up monopolies. Yet to explore pro-poor predispositions, it is more enlightening to examine reactions to initiatives that are explicitly associated with poverty alleviation. Five approaches put forth to address poverty alleviation have been prominent:

(1) increasing general social services favoring the poor,
(2) subsidizing goods and services for the poor,
(3) cash transfers to poor families,
(4) affirmative action programs for disadvantaged groups, and
(5) favoring poorer regions for regional development.

These approaches overlap to a certain extent, and yet the appeals, politics, and psychology are distinctive enough to warrant separate examination.

WHERE DOES INCOME DISTRIBUTION COME IN?

So much of the economic discourse on development fastens on income inequality, and the risk of destructive conflict clearly brings income distribution into the picture, even if not as a predominant concern. It may seem intuitive that progress toward a more equitable income distribution means higher income growth for the poor. However, as Beteille (2003) cogently points out, poverty and inequality are quite distinct concepts, and in many cases do not go hand-in-hand. The connection between the income distribution and conflict is not direct. It is mediated by the perception of income distribution, and the salience of different dimensions of the distribution. These dimensions include perceptions of national income inequality, regional inequality, inequality across ethnicity, and so on.

Four points must be understood regarding how poverty alleviation, conflict sensitivity, and income inequality are interwoven through psychological dynamics.

First, while a highly unequal income distribution certainly can reflect both the degree of poverty and, often, regressive policies, this book is not a lamentation about unequal income distribution. For readers who doubt the plausibility of rapid growth for both the poor and the wealthy, it is important to restate that the typical relationship between the poor's economic improvement and the overall growth of the economy is very tight (a point elaborated further in Chapter 2 of this book).

This may seem counterintuitive because the incomes of the poor are often cast in terms of their relation to the overall income distribution, with the implication that an unequal income distribution is the root of poverty. In some cases, it may have been, but in some countries overall economic growth and welfare improvements for the entire society have occurred alongside increasing income inequality. While an unequal distribution may be regrettable, and while overall economic growth with a larger share going to the poor would be preferred,[3] the normative position taken in this book is that even an increasingly unequal distribution is of secondary importance as long as the poor are advancing as rapidly as possible. If the strongest economic improvement for the poor comes from policies and circumstances that permit wealthier people to earn more at a faster rate, this outcome is preferable to lower economic advance of the poor

---

[3] It is conceivable that both maximum economic growth and maximum reduction of inequality could be achieved through the same set of policies. Dollar, Kleineberg, and Kraay (2016, 69) state that "if one combination of macroeconomic policies and institutions that supports a given aggregate growth rate also leads to an increase in the share of incomes accruing to the poorest quintiles, while another combination did the opposite, then the former would be preferable from the standpoint of promoting shared prosperity." The challenge, of course, is whether the aggregate growth rate target would be reached.

and greater income equality. This has been the case in China over the past two decades. Of course, policymakers and other citizens still have to be alert that policies responsible for enriching the wealthy do not beggar the poor.

Second, stark "us versus them" identifications may be too polarizing to maintain adequately peaceful interactions across segments of the poor and the non-poor. Common identity across income levels may be the most fruitful way to mobilize support for pro-poor policies.

Third, it is the *perception* of income distribution, rather than the technical estimates of income distribution, that drives reactions to distributive prospects and outcomes, and often the levels of conflict-provoking animosity. Thus, conflicts generated by perceptions of skewed income distribution or perceived threats of damaging redistribution undermine poverty alleviation. Strong evidence demonstrates that perceptions of the income distribution are typically heavily distorted, in the perceptions of the poor and the non-poor. In many nations, there is a low level of people's awareness of where they stand in the income distribution, the shape of the distribution, and its trends (Gimpelson and Treisman 2018). Some reluctance to support pro-poor initiatives, and some destructive conflicts, can be attributed to misperceptions of income distribution. It is important to ask, then, what determines the salience of alternative dimensions of income distribution. It also is important to ask what roles do (or can) governments play in determining the salience of these dimensions. Finally, what correctives to perceptions of income distribution and income levels could enhance poverty alleviation?

People can recognize abject poverty if they experience it directly, but prosperous people often know of less prosperous members of the groups with which they identify. Therefore, the more prosperous can discharge their altruistic impulse, even if the targets of their support are not very poor compared to many others. This could be because of lack of knowledge of poorer people, compelling reasons to help people within the identification group, or the desire to strengthen the identification group as a whole. The impulse to help one's own group, and resentment over people of similar income levels getting better treatment ("horizontal inequality"[4]) may propel an ingroup's relatively prosperous members to demand favorable treatment for their group rather than the poorest. It is reasonable to presume that very few relatively prosperous ascriptive

---

[4] Stewart (2002) has led a major research program on "horizontal inequality."

Introduction

groups have no members living in poverty. Group solidarity often is a compelling rationale for defending the economic rights of the group as a whole, which may entail a generally anti-poor policy stance. Vigilance regarding fraternal deprivation (concern for people within the ingroup) may be seen to legitimize actions that would be considered inappropriate for an individual's sake (Gino, Ayal, and Ariely 2013).

Fourth, contention over income distribution may actually draw wealth away from the poor. Some relatively well-to-do groups, viewing others as undeservingly wealthier, may press for benefits that divert resources away from alleviating poverty. Government officials concerned with placating a prosperous group that challenges the wealth of other groups may indulge the former by allocating resources that otherwise would be destined for poverty alleviation.

Finally, despite the concerns raised by Palma (2011) that growing shares of the rich are coming at the expense of the poor, this is not a general pattern in key "middle-income"[5] developing country regions.[6] Lustig, Lopez-Calva, and Ortiz Juarez (2014, 129) report that in the first decade of this millennium, income inequality declined in 13 of 17 Latin American countries. The most recent comprehensive inequality data base (Solt 2019) reports declining inequality in Cambodia, Malaysia, the Philippines, and Thailand. In contrast, Indonesia, Laos, and Myanmar exhibit increasing inequality. For the eight countries featured in this book, Table 1.1 demonstrates that for roughly the past two decades, the income shares of bottom 20 percent and bottom 40 percent of the populations rose in Argentina, Brazil, Colombia, Malaysia, Mexico, and Thailand. No discernable trend appears in Sri Lanka, and data are lacking for India.

POVERTY ALLEVIATION INITIATIVES AND THE IMPLICATIONS FOR DESTRUCTIVE CONFLICT

Avoiding high levels of conflict, especially open violence, is a crucial end in itself. Not only do the poor often directly bear the brunt of violence,

---

[5] This term is used to denote the countries that have not reached the level of "First World" countries: Western Europe, United States, Canada, Japan, Australia, and New Zealand. The World Bank, needing to classify countries in order to establish lending, granting, and other designations, has a different set of categories, in some cases classifying middle-income countries as "upper-income."

[6] Palma's conclusion that the income gains are greatest for the wealthy is due to aggregating across low-, middle-, and high-income countries. Many low-income and "First World" high-income countries do follow this pattern.

The Challenges of Conflict-Sensitive Poverty Alleviation

TABLE 1.1 *Share of national income of the bottom 20 percent and bottom 40 percent of the population, key cases, circa 1995–2015*

		1995	2000	2005	2010	2015
Argentina	Bottom 20%	3.8	3.2	3.6	4.6	5.0[i]
	Bottom 40%	12.2	10.8	12.0	14.1	15.1[i]
Brazil	Bottom 20%	2.4[b]	2.5[c]	2.9	3.3[h]	3.6
	Bottom 40%	8.2[b]	8.5[c]	9.4	10.8[h]	11.5
Colombia	Bottom 20%	2.4[b]	1.9	3.6	3.3	3.8
	Bottom 40%	9.4[b]	8.6	11.0	10.3	11.7
India	Bottom 20%	–	–	–	8.3[h]	–
	Bottom 40%	–	–	–	20.2[h]	–
Malaysia	Bottom 20%	4.5	–	4.7[c]	5.2[h]	5.8
	Bottom 40%	12.8	–	13.5	14.5[h]	15.9
Mexico	Bottom 20%	4.4[a]	3.9	4.4	5.1	5.7
	Bottom 40%	12.6[a]	11.8	13.0	14.5	15.5[i]
Sri Lanka	Bottom 20%	8.0	6.8[d]	6.9[f]	7.7[g]	7.0[i]
	Bottom 40%	19.7	17.0[d]	17.4[f]	19.2[g]	17.7[i]
Thailand	Bottom 20%	6.2[b]	6.2	6.0[f]	6.6	7.5
	Bottom 40%	16[b]	15.8	15.9[f]	17.0[h]	18.8

[a] Interpolated 1994 and 1996; [b] 1996; [c] 2001; [d] 2002; [e] 2004; [f] 2006; [g] 2009; [h] 2011; [i] 2016.
Source: World Bank database updated November 18, 2018

but widespread violence also undermines the overall economic growth that typically contributes strongly to the incomes of the poor. The likelihood of highly destructive violence depends on the degree of antagonisms across groups formed by ingroup identifications and negative outgroup stereotypes. Thus, while some occasions justify taking up arms against oppressors, aggressive redistributive efforts in favor of the poor often run a serious risk of highly destructive backlash. Frequently, the less dramatic factors that drive defensive shifts in domestic economic activities and policy paralysis also reflect psychological dynamics. Because some degree of contention that individuals feel toward others is essential for conflict, psychological explanations may not always seem relevant. Yet often they are useful for accounting for the origin of contention, as well as to account for the magnitude of animosity and hence the degree of conflict. In light of the fact that destructive conflict has three distinctive forms – physical destruction, policy stalemate, and economic withdrawal – it is useful to consider separately the dynamics associated with each.

The framing of pro-poor initiatives often shapes the income-relevant aspects of identity that increase divisiveness. Obviously, many political identifications, such as party affiliation, have strong commitments for or against significant redistribution, and the strength of these identifications often primes members to act aggressively. Insofar as mobilizing the poor depends on invoking negative attributions of the prosperous, the provocateur's tactic of denigrating opponents encourages aggressive stances. The same holds for leaders of prosperous groups vis-à-vis the poor. In addition, models explored below suggest that the animus over economic demands may be strengthened by exaggerated attributions of intentionality when the actions of others harm the ingroup, and an attribution of malice to those with opposing positions. Because it is common that most of the poor and most of the prosperous are of different ethnic or religious groups, the resentment over perceived economic injustice may exacerbate the animus among groups. These circumstances are ripe for "vicarious retribution" that targets the innocent.

The conflicts over a pro-poor initiative or its consequences may be provoked by psychological dynamics that reduce the assessment of deservingness. The belief that undeserving people are accepting benefits can heighten the moral indignation against them, whether by more prosperous people or by other poor people excluded from the benefit. Moreover, if a group is believed to benefit from government policies, those who do not benefit may conclude that the favored group is in league with the government. Therefore, if members of a group have negative views of the government, they are more likely to have negative views toward the groups believed to be associated with the government. If the transfers are seen as unfair, the stereotypes are likely to be negative, and more acute as they become more salient. If the groups are not believed to be sufficiently deserving, others – whether poor or prosperous – may become morally indignant.

Extreme demands made by ingroup leaders in policy debates with major distributive implications may induce their followers to believe that these demands are not negotiable, even if the leaders posed them as negotiating stances. Insofar as these demands become important for ingroup solidarity, the leaders may not be able to back off of them.

The belief that one or more groups are to be targeted for benefits, or already receive benefits, is likely to focus more attention on these groups and exaggerate the attitudes, positive or negative, toward these groups. Several models of rising mutual antagonism rest on the premise that provocative intergroup interactions increase mutual disrespect. Aggressive action against an outgroup is, of course, more likely if ingroup members believe that outgroup members dislike them. The Thai case study in Chapter 8 dramatically illustrates this pattern.

The Challenges of Conflict-Sensitive Poverty Alleviation

Also, the arguments invoked to press for redistributive demands may provoke destructive conflict. Claims of being original inhabitants ("indigeneity" – "sons of the soil"), often based on disputable historical understandings, can create rancor among competing groups whose very presence is under question, as they are denigrated as interlopers or even invaders.

Physical Destruction/Violence

Confrontations that begin peacefully frequently result in violence. Mass rallies to press for redistribution may result in aggressive actions beyond what individuals would do in isolation. Weakened inhibitions may be explained by reduced standards in witnessing the behavior of others, reduced fear of negative consequences, group cohesiveness, or emotional arousal.[7]

In addition to the social psychology that began to flourish in the 1980s, the earlier psychodynamic theories of Freud and other psychoanalytic theorists offer models of the impacts of raw impulses to understand destructive behaviors. While some of these impulses can be helpful in appeals to the prosperous, impulses such as dominance, aggression, and punitiveness also can account for escalations of conflict. In particular, the demand for dominance can provoke extreme measures to control others, with possibly equally extreme measures to fend off these efforts. Punitiveness can support vicarious retribution; and submissiveness can expose ingroup members to provocateurs' appeals to engage in destructive actions.

---

[7] Prentice-Dunn and Rogers (1989/2015, 94) argue that:

> anonymity and diffused responsibility reduce individual accountability for acts by making the individual less aware of the public aspects of himself. That is, he is less concerned with others' evaluation of him and has decreased expectations of reprisals, censure, or embarrassment for any actions. The resultant behavior may be explained in terms of expectancy-value theory: The individual is quite aware of what he is doing, he simply does not expect to suffer negative consequences for his conduct. Second, physiological arousal and group cohesiveness (i.e., perceptual immersion in the group) decrease awareness of private aspects of the self. The individual experiences an internal deindividuated state characterized by lowered private self-awareness, with concomitant altered thinking and altered emotional patterns. With a hampered capacity for self-regulation, the individual becomes more responsive to environmental cues for behavioral direction than to internal standards of appropriate conduct.

Policy Conflict

The policy impasses that are destructive of economic growth can be due to polarization over stances on distribution. This is especially polarizing when the salience of identifications is defined by perceptions of income disparities (as in the case of Argentina examined in Chapter 5). The attribution of malice that can precipitate violence also makes policy stalemate more likely. Skepticism that compromise can be reached with malicious adversaries is an obstacle to reaching effective agreements.

Economic Withdrawal

The withdrawal of capital or labor by disaffected citizens may reflect the perceptions of threat to existing wealth, and low expectations of viable economic opportunities in the future. People may feel compelled to regard themselves as an ingroup if they believe that they are regarded as such by others who pose an economic threat. Therefore, actions to wrest wealth from some members of the ingroup may induce much broader defensive economic actions by ingroup members, such as capital flight.

FOCUSING ON POLICY ADOPTION AND DEFENSE OF EXISTING PRO-POOR POLICIES

In examining concrete cases of pro-poor policies, it must be kept in mind that the receptivity to a pro-poor policy is by no means the same as its long-term consequences. Many policies that will be examined in Chapters 4–8 have a "shelf life" limited by efforts by the non-poor to capture some of the benefits initially more tightly targeted to the poor. Budget cutbacks and inflation that erodes fixed monetary transfers also erode benefits. Therefore, the factors explaining the commitment to defend the magnitudes and reasonable targeting of pro-poor programs also must be explored.

Cases

The cases chosen for this analysis, from Latin America, South Asia, and Southeast Asia, reflect four needs. First, the cases must reflect diverse enough policy experiences to illustrate some of the patterns of each of the five pro-poor approaches: increased social services, subsidies, cash transfers, affirmative action, and targeted regional development. Second,

The Challenges of Conflict-Sensitive Poverty Alleviation

the cases must reflect how identifications and attributions shape judgments of deservingness; and some of them need to demonstrate how the formal identification of "poor" beneficiaries evolves and changes the effectiveness of pro-poor initiatives. This requires sufficient evidence to permit in-depth analyses that go beyond the facts of the policies and programs. Third, the set of cases ought to cover some countries that have experienced credible improvements in poverty reduction and income equity. Fourth, the cases should be clustered within only a few world regions, so that both intraregional and cross-regional insights can be gained.

Four Latin American cases are featured. Argentina, having experienced strongly pro-poor policies through targeting the poor with social benefits, suffered from the extreme nature of these populist efforts in the context of extreme polarization. Brazil is one of the world's most prominent examples of cash transfers and affirmative action, as well as a commitment to earmarking budgetary resources to provide pro-poor services despite the enormous gaps in the availability of such services for the poor. Mexico's cash transfer program makes for a highly insightful comparison with Brazil's. Colombia is a highly distinctive case of subsidies targeted to the poor that largely avoid the leakage that plagues most subsidy programs, but at the cost of negative images of the poor.

For South Asia, India represents the longest standing affirmative action program, which reflects both the power of a well-defined set of criteria that can, however, be degraded in the struggle over defining eligibility. In contrast, Sri Lanka's affirmative action, targeting the majority Sinhalese ethnic group, has been an element of the tragic imposition of majority power over a minority.

The Southeast Asian case of Malaysia offers another caution of the abuses of a majority-targeted affirmative action program that degenerated into growth-inhibiting conflict and cynicism. Analysis of Thailand's subsidized health system helps to round out the breadth of price-subsidy variations. The Thai case is assessed in considerably more depth in exploring how regional development challenges can trigger physical violence fueled by mutually antagonistic attributions across regions.

Preview of the Chapters

It is useful to begin with the rudimentary economic aspects at stake in poverty reduction. Chapter 2, *Political Economy Considerations*, examines how the incomes of the poor typically depend on overall economic growth, and yet pro-poor policies can advance the incomes of the poor more rapidly than overall economic growth. It also presents the general patterns of how income distribution is shaped by development trends, and the linkages among economic growth, increased productivity of the poor, and inclusive participation.

The book then covers the bases of the psychology and the predispositions of the non-poor by mapping four interlinked sets of dynamics. Chapter 3, *Identity, Attributions, Deservingness Judgments, and Hostility*, establishes how people hold identifications, define themselves as members of "ingroups," and regard others as constituting "outgroups." It presents the psychology of how individuals develop their perceptions of both their ingroup(s) and others, which strongly shape the orientations toward poverty, the poor, and government overtures. The chapter then outlines the multiple bases of deservingness judgments, a subset of attributions, as to whether sacrifices for the poor are justified, and for which of the poor. It also links empathy and altruism to deservingness, and how theories of ingroup esteem and understandings of poverty may enhance or undermine pro-poor predispositions and provoke hostility.

Chapter 4, *Conditional Cash Transfers*, begins the exploration of direct pro-poor approaches by reviewing the logic of the rapidly growing number of government programs that require beneficiaries of direct government payments to comply with conditions. It then demonstrates through the Brazilian and Mexican programs how these programs may address the psychological needs of prosperous people, such as social-identity enhancement and the motivation to control.

Chapter 5, *Social-Sector Spending Targeting the Poor*, examines the motivations and political vicissitudes of redressing the imbalances and inadequacy of government spending on the poor through education, healthcare, and protection against unemployment. The populist experiences in Argentina and Brazil demonstrate the dynamics of intergroup polarization.

Chapter 6, *Pro-Poor Subsidies and the Problem of Leakage*, extends the analysis of pro-poor targeting through lower prices for goods and services. The chapter reviews strategies to reduce "leakages" – the results of efforts by relatively prosperous people to capture the benefits. It reports on the remarkable examples of leakage reduction in India's food and fuel subsidies, including millions of relatively prosperous people voluntarily relinquishing their rights to avail themselves of the subsidies. The willingness to sacrifice wealth in order for poorer families to have lower financial burdens is also demonstrated in the case of differential utility rates in

Colombian cities, permitting wealthier residents to have higher status as a tacit exchange.

Chapter 7, *Affirmative Action*, begins with two cases – Brazil and India – for which special privileges were extended, at least initially, to deprived groups. Yet the ambiguity of identifications led to eligibility that eroded the targeting of benefits. The chapter then reviews the Malaysian and Sri Lankan cases, where leaders of the majority ethnicity instituted affirmative action privileges for their own, ultimately leading to disillusionment and withdrawal by Malaysian minorities and civil war in Sri Lanka. All of these cases demonstrate that the creation of ethnically based affirmative action has made the ethnic identification more entrenched, contrary to the expectations that interethnic unity would emerge.

Chapter 8, *Regional Development Targeting the Poorest Areas*, explores the complexity and uncertainty of the challenge of directing government investment to low-income regions. The resentment of activists in poor regions, exacerbated by the status differences between the wealthier and poorer regions, is exemplified by the case of Thailand's Northeast ("Isaan"). The case illuminates both the potential for destructive conflict that perceptions of regional inequality can provoke, but also the potential of demonstrations of disruptive capacity to strengthen the voices of the poor.

Chapter 9, *How the Wealthy React to Pro-Poor-Labeled Initiatives*, focuses on the factors that determine whether prosperous people predisposed to support poverty alleviation in principle will support particular policy initiatives. They may reject initiatives presented as pro-poor if these initiatives are suspected to be insincere, unwise, or excessively damaging to particular elements of the non-poor. The psychology of cynicism toward the poor, as well toward the integrity of the policy process, is explored. The chapter thus examines how malfunctions of the policy process pose obstacles to accepting these pro-poor initiatives.

Chapter 10, *Lessons and Conclusions*, integrates the psychological insights on support or resistance to pro-poor initiatives, through the lens of the policy sciences framework's distinctions among identifications, demands, expectations, and attributions. This organizing principle permits a systematic recounting of the wide variety of potentially effective strategies to promote pro-poor initiatives and to reduce destructive conflict. It also outlines what psychological insights imply for the suitability of different classes of policy instruments in different contexts.

2

Political Economy Considerations

INTRODUCTION

Economic Growth of the Poor and the Prosperous

This chapter demonstrates how the economic prospects of the poor relate to overall economic growth, and how economic growth of both the poor and the non-poor relates to income redistribution. The reduction of poverty that has occurred in many developing countries is based on overall economic growth – and, in some countries, pro-poor policies. The conclusion, surprising to many, is that radical redistributive efforts, even if framed as helping the poor, frequently undermine their economic prospects by undermining overall economic growth. In the context of low destructive conflict, pro-poor policies, accompanied by overall pro-growth policies, tend to raise the incomes of the poor.

Development practitioners committed to conflict-sensitive poverty alleviation are confronted with both promising and troubling facts. As mentioned in Chapter 1, the first promising fact is that ample poverty reduction has occurred. It is obvious that the reduction of poverty in many countries has been stunning, even allowing for poor data.[1] The percentage of people living in extreme poverty dropped to 14 percent in 2015 from nearly 50 percent in 1990 (United Nations 2015).

According to the Dollar, Kleineberg, and Kraay (2016) and the World Bank (2016a) analyses, the incomes of the poor countries experiencing

---

[1] An assessment of the weaknesses of income estimates is covered under the appraisal function discussion in Chapter 9.

Political Economy Considerations

rapid economic growth generally have seen greater growth for the poor than the overall economy. This is all the more remarkable given that existing asset endowments can be invested to generate income, such that asset concentration can lead to income concentration. Moreover, typically the poor have greater difficulty saving money, and the poor often reside in areas with weaker physical and social-service infrastructure to take advantage of growth prospects.

Beginning in the 1990s, the improvements enjoyed by the poor have been propelled by overall economic growth. For countries still classified as low- or middle-income countries, the increase in constant-dollar per capita incomes rose by 120 percent. India's per capita income is 3.5 times higher today as in 1990 and China's is 9.4 times higher (World Bank 2018a).

Strong evidence demonstrates that the reduction of poverty is highly correlated with overall growth. In 2002, World Bank economists David Dollar and Aart Kraay examined economic growth and the incomes of the poorest quintile in ninety-two developing countries. They concluded that, overall, the incomes of the poor rise in lockstep with the rise in per capita income. Figure 2.1, which represents these growth rates,[2] illustrates the striking correlation.

In a 2016 publication, Dollar and Kraay, along with Tatjana Kleineberg, updated this analysis, expanding the definition of "poor" to the bottom 40 percent. The broader definition may be considered as more reliable than narrower ones that depend on sorting out who is quite poor, very poor, or desperately poor. With this broader definition of the "poor," and with even broader set of 121 countries, they reach the same conclusion:

Average incomes in the poorest two quintiles [i.e., the poorest 20 percent plus the next poorest 20 percent] on average increase at the same rate as overall average incomes. This is because, in a global dataset spanning 121 countries over the past four decades, changes in the share of income of the poorest quintiles are uncorrelated with changes in average income. The variation in changes in quintile shares is also small relative to the variation in growth in average incomes, implying that the latter accounts for most of the variation in income growth in the poorest quintiles. In addition, we find little evidence that changes in the bottom quintile shares are correlated with country-level factors that are typically considered as important determinants for growth in average incomes or for changes in inequality. This evidence confirms the central importance of economic growth for improvements in living standards at the low end of the income distribution.

(Dollar, Kraay, and Kleineberg 2016, 68)

---

[2] As is typical, the log of per capita income is used rather than the absolute per capita income.

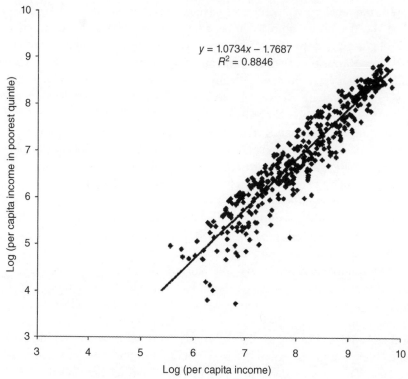

FIGURE 2.1 Growth of the lowest quintile and overall growth
Source: Dollar and Kraay (2002, 45)

Therefore, because poverty reduction is closely related to overall national income growth, whatever factors influence *overall* economic growth, including the global economy and internal conditions such as destructive conflict or natural disasters, will affect poverty reduction beyond the direct actions by the state and citizenry. Although the policy recommendations proposed by Dollar and Kraay in their original 2002 article have been criticized on methodological grounds (e.g., Amann et al. 2006), what is not in dispute is that overall economic growth is necessary for poverty alleviation. Amann et al. (2006, 23) point out "that it would be difficult to find a reputable development economist who would deny the primacy of economic growth in poverty alleviation. It has generally been taken for granted that economic growth was a necessary but not a sufficient condition for the achievement of generally agreed upon development objectives, among which poverty reduction has a high priority."

Political Economy Considerations

The outliers seen in Figure 2.1 (the points above the diagonal line in the upper right) indicate that when countries are growing very rapidly, the growth of the incomes of the poor generally outstrips the growth rates of the economy as a whole. The countries that experience greater income growth for the poor than the average income have been among the fastest growing countries. On the negative side of the ledger, when an economy is doing poorly, the poor tend to lose more than the rest of the population. The Dollar and Kraay (2002) and Dollar, Kleineberg, and Kraay (2016) analyses demonstrate that the "outliers" for the countries with the lowest growth entail even slower growth for the poor than for the rest of the income earners. This typically reflects the decreased flexibility of the poor to shield themselves from income declines.

Growth and Distributional Dynamics

The persistence of poverty does not have a single cause. Obviously, many countries lack physical or social assets to bring everyone out of poverty. Some would argue that the structure of the international system is stacked against particular countries or particular populations within those countries. Some have questioned the wisdom of prevailing development approaches. And it is entirely possible that for many countries, a substantial portion of poverty reduction occurs for reasons other than government policies or charitable behavior. This last point is consistent with the classic theory proposed by Simon Kuznets (1955) that the shift from agriculture to industry increases the incomes of those who have made the transition. This seems to be borne out in the reduction of poverty in two of the regions of focus of this book, Latin America and Southeast Asia. Even beyond the transition out of agriculture, the transition from the lower-productivity informal sector to the more highly capitalized, higher-productivity formal sector also brings a larger proportion of the population out of deep poverty.

Yet, it is crucial to understand that the high cross-national correlation between overall growth and the fate of the poor leaves room for variation in the degree of poverty reduction. The possibility of greater growth of the incomes of the poor than of the overall economy is illustrated by the fact that some countries have experienced substantially greater income growth for the poor than the rest of the population. In Latin America, for example, during the 1995–2015 period the poorest two quintiles in Argentina, Bolivia, Brazil, Ecuador, Peru, and Uruguay gained from 1.5 to 5 percentage points of the national income. Even in the very difficult

2009–2014 period, the growth rates of the bottom 40 percent were at least two percentage points higher than the rest in these countries, as well as in the Dominican Republic and El Salvador.[3]

The fact that reductions in poverty and trends in income distribution are only loosely coupled rests on the complicated relations between impacts of not totally and the structural changes in the economy. Where both growth and a more equitable distribution of income occur, the temptation of analysts is to try to separate out how much the reduction of poverty can be attributed to growth, to pro-poor policies, and to redistribution. For example, a 2016 World Bank analysis argued that, for Peru,

The contributions of the growth of the economy and improvements in the distribution differ considerably. The World Bank's decomposition of the drivers of poverty reduction suggests that the growth effect explains about 61 percent of the reduction in poverty, while the remaining 39 percent is explained by the improvements in the distribution of income across households .... .

(World Bank 2016b, 115)

For Brazil, Costa (2018, 67) notes:

Among analysts of Brazilian social structure, there is a broad consensus that the reduction in inequalities between 2003 and 2015 is rather a consequence of economic processes (such as increasing prices for commodities in international markets and moves in domestic labour markets) than of social policies. Accordingly, social policies based on cash transfers have a crucial impact on poverty reduction, but they are seen to be less effective for promoting redistribution ...

Yet, one should recognize that these drivers are interdependent. Economic growth can enhance the capacity of the poor to compete more effectively in the labor market. Lustig, Lopez Calva, and Ortiz Juarez (2014, 5) conclude that both labor-market changes and pro-poor policies account for Latin America's greater income equality: "Existing studies point to two main explanations for the decline in inequality: a reduction in hourly labor income inequality, and more robust and progressive government transfers ...." The point made above that progressive transfers can also increase the productivity of the poor to make relatively greater labor-income gains holds here as well.

The capacity of robust economic growth to reduce poverty in many developing countries does not mean that policies inducing maximum

---

[3] The 1995–2015 figures are from World Bank database, recalculated to estimate the income growth of the three top quintiles. The available starting figures for Chile and Colombia are 1996. The 2009–2014 figures are from World Bank 2016.

Political Economy Considerations 29

growth will do the most for poverty alleviation. Many policies can be pro-growth and will help to alleviate poverty, but they will not necessarily alleviate poverty *as much as possible*. Dollar, Kleineberg, and Kraay (2016, 69–70) note

> that some policies that are good for growth in average incomes will also lead to increases in inequality, while others will lead to decreases in inequality. Similarly, other policies that might reduce inequality will lead to faster growth, while others to slower growth. The challenge for policymakers who often find themselves under pressure to "do something" about inequality is to avoid choosing combinations of policy interventions that reduce inequality but that might decrease "shared prosperity" if these policies at the same time undermine growth.

They add that the absence of correlation between inequality and growth "suggests that some policies that are good for growth in average incomes will also lead to increases in inequality, while others will lead to decreases in inequality. Similarly, other policies that might reduce inequality will lead to faster growth, while others to slower growth."[4]

This may require policies that allow the non-poor's incomes to rise faster than those of the poor. Thus "shared prosperity," which the World Bank currently defines as high overall economic growth *and* a growing income share for the poor, may not *maximize* poverty alleviation. The balance implied by "shared prosperity" leaves this objective vulnerable from both sides. For the prosperous, the prospect of an income-share reduction, even if accompanied by promises of prosperity for all, may be seen as a threat. For the poor, the constraints imposed by the objective that all need to prosper may be seen as insufficient progress. The normative position that poverty alleviation is the overarching objective means that growing income inequality, even if regrettable, may be necessary to

---

[4] Perhaps the biggest disappointment for practitioners of cross-national statistical studies of poverty reduction and income-distribution trends is explained in Dollar, Kleineberg, and Kraay (2015, 371):

> These findings indicate that the historical experience of a large set of developed and developing countries does not provide much guidance regarding the set of macroeconomic policies and institutions that might be particularly conducive to promoting growth in social welfare beyond their effects on aggregate growth. This of course does not imply that there are no policies that can influence inequality in ways that raise social welfare – it is just that our cross-country empirical tools are too blunt to clearly identify what such policies might be.

Dollar, Kleineberg, and Kraay (2016, 69) also conclude that "a reasonable interpretation of our empirical findings ... is that cross-country regressions such as those we estimate are too blunt a tool to conclusively identify systematic correlates of inequality changes."

30 *Introduction*

help the poor to the maximum degree. China's "economic miracle" spanning the 1990s and 2000s is a clear case in point: the overall income distribution has become more unequal, yet the reduction of poverty among hundreds of millions of people has been astonishing.[5]

DESTRUCTIVE CONFLICT AND GROWTH

Aggressive redistributive efforts are generally counterproductive for the poor because of the capacity of the targets of redistribution to safeguard their assets at the cost of the economy's overall growth. Capital flight is very difficult to track, but Johannesen and Pirttilä (2016, 5) cite estimates of capital flight from developing countries, from US\$150 to \$200 billion annually, with total estimates of "missing wealth" of developing countries amounting to \$500 billion for Africa, \$700 billion for Latin America, and \$1.3 trillion for Asia. Capital flight can occur for multiple reasons, including tax evasion and straightforward diversification. Yet, many economies have a fairly constant pattern of capital flight that accounts for damping the *baseline* levels of investment, consumption, and growth; the growth *disruptions* result from new threats: far higher taxes, withdrawal of

---

[5] Dollar, Kraay, and Kleineberg (2015, 2):

> In China, for example, between 1990 and 2009 average incomes grew at 6.7 percent per year. At the same time, inequality increased in the sense that the income share of the bottom 40 percent declined from 20.2 percent to 14.4 percent, corresponding to an average annual rate of -1.7 percent per year. Combining these two observations, average incomes in the bottom 40 percent grew more slowly than overall average income, at 5 percent per year. From the standpoint of promoting shared prosperity, therefore, the growth "cost" of the increase in inequality in China over this period is about 1.7 percentage points of growth per year. Or put differently, had inequality not increased in China during this time, a growth rate of 5 percent per year (instead of the 6.7 percent that actually happened) would have generated the same improvement in social welfare according to the "shared prosperity" metric of the World Bank.

Yet, this presumes that the growth rate of 5 percent per year could have been sustained over that time period. This, in turn, presumes that some set of policies could have accomplished this overall growth rate while redistributing to the poor. The plausibility of this scenario is highly questionable. Broader evidence that high poverty alleviation can coincide with high levels of poverty reduction is provided by the Dollar, Kleineberg, and Kraay (2016, 10) report that in East Asia in general,

> spells with faster growth in average incomes were more likely to also have decreases in the income share of the poorest quintiles. However, this does not imply that those in the poorest quintiles fared particularly poorly in such spells ... [I]ncomes in East Asia grew fastest among all regions at 3.4 percent per year, and incomes in the poorest 40 percent rose at 3.2 percent per year on average, faster than in any other region.

privileges, or direct expropriation provoking unusually high capital flight. The decline of economic activity also leads to a decline in government revenues, often leading to cutbacks in services for the poor.

In addition to the withdrawal of domestic capital, foreign direct investment often suffers as well, as foreign investors may be even more skittish than domestic businesspeople about redistributive efforts, frequently framed as redressing the unfairness of the relations between developed and developing countries. In short, if overly aggressive income redistribution, or its perceived prospects, does occur, economic dislocations often follow.

THE POLITICAL ECONOMY OF GROWTH AND STABILITY

In light of the fundamental finding that the incomes of the poor generally rise with overall economic growth (Dollar, Kleineberg, and Kraay 2016), the obvious question is how to enhance this growth without damaging the economic and sociopolitical standing of the poor. What accounts for higher growth? What accounts for uneven growth that typically puts the poor into greater jeopardy? What are the modal interactions among economic growth, political alignments, institutions, and the socioeconomic distribution?

For low-income countries, by definition with large proportions of very poor families, very rapid growth is possible with sound economic policies and institutions strong enough to prevent corruption or less blatant forms of rent-seeking from drawing resources away from productive investments. Canuto (2019, 4) describes the archetypical pattern:

In most cases of successful evolution from low- to middle-income per capita in recent history, the underlying development process has been broadly similar. Typically, there is a large pool of unskilled labor that is transferred from subsistence-level occupations to more modern manufacturing or service activities that do not require much skill upgrade from those workers, but nonetheless employ higher levels of capital and embedded technology. The associated technology is available from richer countries and easy to adapt to local circumstances. The gross effect of such a transfer – usually happening in tandem with urbanization – is a substantial increase in "total factor productivity", i.e. an expansion of the value of GDP that goes beyond what can be explained by the expansion of labor, capital and other physical factors of production to the economy.

For these low-income countries, the "poverty trap" comes about when the poor lack (or reject) the opportunities to engage in higher-productivity work. This can occur for a host of reasons. Some reasons are physical:

natural disasters, poor soils and climate, and so on. Some reasons are sociocultural: unwillingness by the poor to take advantage of opportunities that do exist, or discrimination by potential employers. Yet, some problems can be laid to government failings: insufficient skill-development resources or physical infrastructure to permit people to move into more productive employment and policies that obstruct the expansion of employment opportunities. In short, the transition from subsistence-level employment to more productive manufacturing or service sectors stalls, leaving a large segment of the population very poor (Sumner 2018).

It is important to understand that in countries far wealthier than the extremely poor countries of most of sub-Saharan Africa and South Asia, major regional disparities persist. Thus, among the cases examined in this book, particularly Brazil and Thailand, the poverty trap exists in certain regions. Regional disparities grow, increasing polarization, and, in some instances, provoking secessionist movements.

Once the "easy" gains of bringing low-productivity workers into the modern sector – accounting for extraordinary growth rates in countries like China and India – have been achieved, growth rates typically falter dramatically. Very few countries that have absorbed most of the very low-productivity workforce into more productive employment have been able to converge with the long-standing "First World" countries. Although the existence of a "middle-income trap" has been contested,[6] it is clear that very few "middle-income" countries – no matter how the boundaries among low-, middle-, and high-income countries are defined – have advanced to high-income status.[7]

The Damage due to Economic Volatility

The inability of middle-income developing countries to go beyond modest sustainable growth rates has profound political implications. With a

---

[6] Canuto (2019, 2), the author of many publications on the so-called middle-income trap, nevertheless acknowledges: "Overall, the evidence on the supposed middle-income trap is mixed. While [several authors] ... find evidence that countries are more likely to slow down at middle income than at high or low income, others – e.g. [several authors] – do not find growth patterns conforming to one clear pattern that can be characterized as a 'trap.'"

[7] Agénor (2017, 773) lists the following as the only countries classified as middle income in the 1960s that advanced to high-income status by 2008: Equatorial Guinea, Greece, Hong Kong, Ireland, Israel, Japan, Mauritius, Portugal, Puerto Rico, Singapore, South Korea, Spain, and Taiwan. Equatorial Guinea is of high income only because of oil revenues; two are city states; Mauritius has a population of only 1.3 million and Puerto Rico is hardly an economically separate nation.

modest economic-growth baseline, external shocks or problematic domestic policies can cause negative growth, with all of the disappointment and recriminations that recession brings. Unlike China, for which adverse conditions reduce growth from, say, 9 percent to 6 percent, countries like Argentina (with a per capita real purchasing power increasing only 1.4 percent *in total* from 2007 to 2018[8]), some negative growth years are virtually inevitable. Among the countries examined at length in this book, recessions in Argentina, Brazil, Malaysia, Mexico, and Thailand have led not only to dramatic changes in top governmental leadership, but also to increasing intergroup antagonism.

For the sustainability of poverty-alleviation measures, the negative growth experiences are particularly damaging, as governments drop or emasculate poverty-alleviation programs and policies. Ravallion (2002) demonstrates that during the Argentine economic downturns of the 1980–1997 period, poverty-alleviation programs took the brunt of budget reductions. Then the 2000–2001 financial disaster decimated the incomes of the poor, with unprecedented unemployment. Chapter 5 recounts how the 2015 Argentine financial collapse led to a sharp reversal of pro-poor spending in order to stabilize a disastrous economic situation. It also reports on how Brazil's populist regime was ousted in 2016, in part because of the recession caused by the commodity slump, giving way to right-wing presidents bent on severely curtailing pro-poor programs. The question, then, is how to achieve equitable economic growth without the damaging volatility that often besets developing countries.

"Hollow" Growth, "Hollow" Democracy, Institutions, and Organizing

One perspective on the growth bottlenecks blames the failure of institutions to provide incentives to develop new technologies and to improve human capital (Acemoglu and Johnson 2007; Agénor, Canuto, and Jelenic 2012). Acemoglu and Robinson (2009, 679) assert that:

Institutional factors – in particular, those related to security of property rights and constraints on political power – play a powerful role in shaping technological developments and economic growth ... and account for the ability and willingness of different nations to adopt and develop new technologies and create entrepreneurial dynamism. Such a role explains the strikingly divergent trajectories of modern nations in an age where technology is largely global and is available for those who wish to adopt it.

---

[8] World Bank Database (2019).

34   *Introduction*

The concern with constraints on political power highlights the relevance of democratic checks. Similarly, the need for "entrepreneurial dynamism" in turn presumes the existence of a broad range of human skill – not just technical expertise – to respond to entrepreneurial initiatives. The countries that have strong authoritarian practices despite formally democratic institutions, such as Sri Lanka, do not provide fertile ground for dynamism. Sri Lanka has suffered significant brain drain of scientific and entrepreneurial talent (Anas and Wickremasinghe 2010).

The "supply-side" logic of leaving wealthy firms and individuals with lower tax burdens, in the hope of greater domestic investment, typically neglects social safety nets and other directly pro-poor measures. This approach has been characterized as "hollow" – the GDP increases, but long-term capability does not increase, and the gains accrue to the wealthy.[9]

An important equivalency exists between "hollow democracy" and "hollow economic growth." Democracy that does not provide sufficient participation of low-income groups to secure reasonable levels of benefits undermines both poverty alleviation and the opportunity for low-income groups to become more productive. Hoff and Stiglitz (2001, 249) argue:

> Although poverty has declined in many countries – a significant achievement – the rise in inequality is profoundly disturbing. This rise is leading to a growing gap between affluent middle and upper classes and a relatively disadvantaged majority that is falling further and further behind, even though per capita incomes may be increasing. The disadvantaged often feel politically marginalized and lacking in voice. This breeds apathy, an unwillingness to participate, and, ultimately, anger. Democratic politics is hollowed out, and institutions have little chance of securing legitimacy. As a result, political change and the desirable transition from centralized government to a more participatory governance can stall.

In contrast to the supply-side economic strategy, Evans (2004, 39), reflecting a widespread perspective on more inclusive development, argues:

> Although the overall relationship still remains contested ..., the debate [on the impact of progressive redistribution on growth] has produced support for arguments connecting egalitarian policies with growth that are quite consistent with

---

[9] Fetni (2009, 181) labels as "hollow development strategies" the concentration on a few turnkey industries with no significant human-development or poverty-alleviation benefits in Algeria, Egypt, Iran, and Iraq: "These policies had negative tactical and strategic impacts on agricultural production. They fueled a redirection of investments from agriculture to industry, thereby intensifying rural-urban asymmetries and leading to a major slowdown in national socioeconomic development."

Sen's capability approach. Greater equality is associated with higher general levels of health, nutrition and education, which in turn make for a more productive population. Likewise, more egalitarian distribution of assets (land and credit being the archetypal examples) makes productive contributors out of people previously unable to use their energy and ideas because they lacked complementary inputs. Overall, the arguments that egalitarian strategies can enhance growth are as compelling as the arguments that such strategies might impede it.

Evans (2004, 32) sees embedded institutions protecting vested interests as the obstacle to enacting this approach:

Questions of power and distributive conflict further complicate the problem. Any set of institutions entails a distribution of gains and losses. The "institutional winners" are likely to gain political power along with economic benefits and ... they are unlikely to support institutional changes that diminish their gains relative to other participants, even if the change would result in greater productivity that would increase their returns in absolute terms. Vested interests in the distributive results of "bad" institutions make them harder to change and help keep poverty traps firmly in place.

"Thick" Democracy. To address the problem, Evans (2004, 31) asks (and answers affirmatively): "Could deliberative institutions founded on a 'thick democracy' of public discussion and interchange improve developmental performance?" With Amartya Sen, Evans distinguishes between "thin" and "thick" democracy – the latter featuring "meaningful" deliberation that includes the participation by non-elite citizens.

A key implicit premise of these defenses of deliberation is that such "thick" interactions will moderate policies. Rodrik (2000) invokes the potential of democracy to limit social conflict and induce compromise, to account for the lower volatility (if not more rapid growth) that appeared to be the case among democracies in the 1970s. He posits that three factors reduce the overall economic losses and damaging volatility that conflict and retaliation would produce: (a) democracy entails more deliberation and thereby increases the value of moderation and the common interest, reducing the losses due to conflict; (b) separation of powers and limits to the majority's power to expropriate assets from the minority; and (c) through continual interaction, today's winners will moderate their demands and actions because they have to anticipate power reversals and the risk of escalation. Perhaps these dynamics would produce the happy result of greater equity and stability.

Unfortunately, many democratic countries have not enjoyed moderation, and many have lacked stability despite considerable deliberation. To be sure, severe economic instability in democratic countries can reflect

36 *Introduction*

exogenous shocks: commodity collapses, the Great Recession, natural disasters, and so on. Yet, one must wonder why the formal democracies in the countries featured in this book (with Thailand being sporadically democratic) do not reflect moderation of demands or policies. Extreme, unsustainable policies in Argentina and Brazil have led to sharp policy reversals compelled by the collapses. The elections in Malaysia and Sri Lanka do little to reduce the cynical discrimination against the ethnic minorities. In India, the democratic system has fallen prey to intimidating pressure by undeserving beneficiaries of affirmative action that should be reserved for much needier people. In contrast, Thailand, the only country that has not had democratic continuity in the past two decades, has shown remarkable moderation in maintaining the benefits of the rural people who have posed the greatest security risk.

Do these results defy the premise that "thick" democracy of "meaningful deliberation" improves developmental performance and reduces volatility? The question is how "meaningful" is conceived. For "meaningful deliberation" to accomplish conflict-sensitive growth, it would have to mean inclusiveness in accommodating the broad range of interests, not just interaction in policymaking. In all of the cases prominently covered in this book, "deliberation," if that means debates, lobbying, issue-focused election campaigns, and so on, has been abundant. The limitation is that "deliberation" per se without accommodating the preferences of out-of-power groups is hollow. In addition to formal, explicit restrictions on confiscation, interactions should be marked by informal "mutual adjustment" or "mutual accommodation" that support a self-fulfilling expectation that everyone's losses will be limited. Lindblom (1965, 1977) argues that this expectation reflects understandings within the political culture, based on a range of policymaking institutions, as well as the history of interactions among groups.

Widespread skepticism exists toward the prospects of meaningful inclusive participation without organized power of the poor to ensure that their genuine preferences are taken into account. Hickey and Mohan (2008) critique the superficiality of many top-down efforts to stimulate stakeholder participation through techniques designed and administered by development practitioners, such as the consultations behind the Poverty Reduction Strategy Papers for each World Bank-funded country. They point out that the selection of participants often excludes potentially obstructionist organizations, such as labor unions. The implication of this critique is that low-income people have to find means to assert their own modes of effective participation. In the featured case of Thailand, this was accomplished through the potential for disruption. Beyond that, at least in principle, the interests of segments of the poor can be reinforced by the need of others to depend on discretionary actions of the poor. However, it is questionable as to whether the poorest populations could enter into such exchanges.

Stewart (2000, 256) argues that formal state power-sharing is the only way to achieve full inclusiveness:

The most universal requirement is for political inclusivity because it is monopolization of political power by one group or another that is normally responsible for many of the other inequalities. Yet achieving political inclusivity is among the most difficult changes to bring about. It is not just a matter of democracy, defined as rule with the support of the majority, as majority rule can be consistent with abuse of minorities, as, for example, in the recent history of Rwanda, Cambodia and Zimbabwe. In a politically inclusive democratic system, particular types of proportional representation are needed to ensure participation by all major groups in the elected bodies. For inclusive government, representation of all such groups is essential not only at the level of the cabinet, but also other organs of government. For political inclusivity members of major groups also need to be included at all levels of the civil service, the army and the police.

However, this consociational approach of reserving state positions to representatives of different groups is not only a rarity among democracies, whether presidential or parliamentary, but also disregards the point that the formal organizational structure does not ensure that inclusiveness will operate in practice. Barron (2018) notes that

it is important to recognize the trade-offs involved in consociational democracy and to differentiate between power-sharing and inclusivity. Power-sharing agreements, such as Lebanon's, tend to oversimplify the interests of religious constituents while disregarding shared policy issues unassociated with religious identity. As a result, issue-based politics becomes difficult and inclusivity limited ... [C]onsociational power-sharing agreements have a tendency to calcify and institutionalize, leading to trade-offs between good governance and the maintenance of stability; the strengthening of elites at the expense of transparency, accountability, and public participation; and interference from outside actors.

The problem, then, is that "mutual adjustment" is in short supply, with no simple institutional fix possible. High polarization might result in the temporary winners neglecting the interests of the temporary losers. Instead of moderating in order to avoid retribution when no longer in power, current leaders may assume retribution would occur no matter what they do. Thus, they may conclude that it is best to maximize their own gains now while they can. It is also possible that even if newly empowered leaders wish to reduce the polarization, this may not be

38   *Introduction*

possible if preexisting policies are so destabilizing that restoring economic stability requires policies highly adverse to the constituency of the previous leaders.

Persistence of "Winners"?

Rodrik's hope that winners would moderate their policies in order to avoid adverse policies against them when they lose power also might be dashed because current winners may expect to remain winners. Highly salient ethnic divisions that place one group in a permanent majority could result in this scenario, if the characteristics of that majority group are served by policies that largely favor that group in the aggregate. Malay dominance in Malaysia and Sinhalese dominance in Sri Lanka are clear cases.

When will winners believe that they will continue to win? In the cases where distributive politics is dominated largely by a single dimension, the probability of a permanent majority depends on whether the dimension is essentially class or ethnicity. A dominant class dimension, as in Argentina despite the correlations with ethnicity and regional differences, the continuous rather than dichotomous nature of income levels means that the strength of either the relatively wealthy or the relatively poor will vary, according to the policy initiatives at play and the economic context. Winners and losers will change over time. If mutual adjustment is weak, polarization and extreme policy swings are likely to be high.

Where a relatively stable ethnic division is characterized by the dominance of one ethnic group, as in Malaysia and Singapore, the power balance among ethnicities is less likely to change regardless of the policies and economic context, although factions within the dominant group may jockey for power. The minority ethnic groups must develop strategies to cope with their lower power. One strategy is to be a partner in a multi-ethnic coalition, as in the Malaysian case with multiethnic parties, or Chinese and Indian parties within Malay-led electoral coalitions. In contrast, Sri Lanka has no heritage of multiethnic parties (Horowitz 1989). In 2015 a glimmer of multiethnic hope emerged when a multiethnic electoral coalition defeated an increasingly authoritarian and corrupt President Mahinda Rajapaksa, who had been strikingly punitive vis-à-vis Tamils and even Sri Lankan Muslims (DeVotta 2016). Yet by 2018 Rajapaksa's successor was compelled to try to bring Rajapaksa back in as prime minister (Fernando and Singh 2018). Though this was blocked by the courts (Freedom House 2019), it does reveal the fragility of the commitment to greater democratization.

Political Economy Considerations

Organizing and Mutual Adjustment

If mutual adjustment is to prevail over polarization and retribution, regardless of the permanence or impermanence of the politically dominant political elite, the question is how such an institution can be established and sustained. Leftwich and Sen (2011, 321), following North's (1998) definition of "institutions" as "rules of the game," conceive of institutions "as predictable and stable patterns of interaction ... as durable social rules and procedures, formal and informal, which structure – but do not determine – the social, economic and political relations and interactions of those affected by them." The essential point of this perspective is that the institutions per se do not determine the relations and interactions; various organizations must push both formal and informal institutions to support more inclusive outcomes. Hoff and Stiglitz (2001, 389) posit that "[d]evelopment is no longer seen primarily as a process of capital accumulation but rather as a process of organizational change." North (1998: 15) emphasizes that "[t]he continuous interaction between institutions and organizations in the economic setting of scarcity, and hence competition, is the key to institutional change." Clearly, this must go beyond state organizations.

What kinds of organizations might these be? The efforts to establish unity, expand numbers, and instill commitment to pursue a "campaign" to counter vested interests, in this case for sustainable inclusion, are the hallmarks of a social movement, as Tilly (1998b, 467) would define it. Tilly (1998b, 455–456) notes that

on the whole social-movement analysts have ended up thinking that movements depend intimately on the social networks in which their participants are already embedded, that the identities deployed in collective contention are contingent but crucial, that movements operate within frames set by a historical accumulation of shared understandings, that political opportunity structure significantly constrains the histories of individual social movements, but that movement struggles and outcomes also transform political opportunity structures.

For mutual adjustment to benefit the poor when they are not effectively represented by a dominant group, organizing becomes crucial to overcome the disadvantages of scarce economic resources. Lindblom (1977, 141) argues that even in a democratic system, "[w]hile a proliferation of public and private groups engaging in mutual adjustment brings a remarkably wide range of interests and considerations to bear on public policy, the same process tends also to take gains for the organized at the

40   *Introduction*

expense of the unorganized: gains for union labor at the expense of nonunion, gains for organized agriculture at the expense of smaller unorganized farmers, or gains for producer groups at the expense of consumers."

As elaborated in Chapter 3, taking advantage of the "embedded" identities that Tilly calls for is one reason why ethnicity, insofar as it often encompasses large numbers of people with an obvious identification, has strong potential as the basis of social movements. The belief of shared economic status can also be the basis for social movement mobilization, as reflected by labor movements. Yet, the striking uncertainty as to where people fit within the income distribution (Gimpelson and Treisman 2018) creates a challenge for such mobilization. In short, the question is whether organizations built on different potential dimensions of identification can be effective in compelling policymaking institutions to engage in inclusive mutual accommodation.

TAXATION

The willingness to accept higher taxes is an important basis of the potential for poverty alleviation. While increasing taxes is not the only way to increase government spending for pro-poor initiatives, in most developing countries a stronger tax effort is key to increasing benefits for the poor without incurring long-term problems of inflation, indebtedness, excessive natural-resource depletion, or – of typically great political risk – reducing spending for more prosperous people. Therefore, when pro-poor initiatives are debated, the possibility of higher taxes is typically a central concern.

Determining the success of efforts to collect sufficient taxes, reflecting both formal tax rates and compliance, is difficult. While the goal is not maximum tax burden, most developing countries fall short of the *optimal tax effort*, which measures how close the tax effort comes to the optimal "tax capacity."[10] Across developing and developed countries, this tax

---

[10] Le, Moreno-Dodson, and Bayraktar (2012, 3) define tax capacity as follows:

> Taxable capacity refers to the predicted tax-to-GDP ratio that can be estimated with regression analyses, taking into account a country's specific macroeconomic, demographic, and institutional features. Tax effort is defined as an index of the ratio between the share of the actual tax collection in GDP and the taxable capacity. The concepts of taxable capacity and tax effort are also extended to measure total fiscal revenue capacity and revenue effort.

Political Economy Considerations

effort varies from just under 50 percent to nearly 100 percent.[11] Developing countries, whether low- or middle-income, have lower tax efforts, averaging 65 percent and 64 percent respectively; developed countries average 76 percent (Pessino and Fenochietto 2013, 16), even though developed countries have higher tax capacity. If countries lack very large revenues collected by the government from natural-resource exports – this is not guaranteed even for resource-rich countries – government spending on pro-poor social services requires higher tax effort in most developing countries. Of the fifty-four developing and forty-two developed countries covered in the Pessino and Fenochietto (2010) tax effort study, forty-two of the forty-eight countries below the 50 percent level are developing countries. Resource-dependent countries, in particular, typically have particularly a weak domestic tax effort (Devarajan, Le, and Raballand 2010), which makes social-service spending especially vulnerable to the volatility of resource prices.

Weak tax collection can reflect government leaders' worries that raising tax rates or tightening tax administration would reduce their support. To be sure, low tax collection can reflect administrative weakness (Keen and Slemrod 2017), and overcoming some aspects of weakness can be prohibitively expensive, but government leaders typically have opportunities to overcome some of this weakness.

According to the analysis by Le, Moreno-Dodson, and Bayraktar (2012), for 110 developing and developed countries in the time period 1994–2009, Brazil had the second-highest tax effort among Latin American countries, at 1.26 (only Uruguay has a higher level, at 1.35). Brazil had a far higher tax effort than other major Latin American countries (Argentina's .95; Colombia's .78; Mexico's .75).[12] This is an important indicator of both the aspirations and the commitment to expand the state's role.

---

[11] Singapore is a notable outlier, with a ratio of .33 (Pessino and Fenochietto 2010, 15).

[12] Some sub-Saharan countries have very high tax effort ratios – e.g., Namibia (1.54) and Zimbabwe (1.36) – but the high ratios largely reflect the very low taxing capacity. If a country has low tax capacity, low tax collection can still constitute a high ratio to tax capacity. For example, Zambia's optimal tax capacity is only 16.9 percent of GDP, such that the fact that tax collection is a paltry 16.6 percent of GDP still yields a very high tax effort. In contrast, the total revenue as a proportion of GDP for Brazil is nearly 30 percent and for Uruguay 26 percent, both on a par with many developed countries. Therefore the Brazilian and Uruguayan tax efforts are not simply artifacts of a low GDP, as they are with the sub-Saharan African countries.

THE TRENDS IN THE FEATURED CASES

To put the country case studies into context, this section briefly summarizes the trends in economic growth, poverty, and income distribution. However, it is important to keep in mind the problems regarding both the accuracy and relevance of the data. Estimates of poverty headcounts are subject to distortions of undercounting the poor, particularly in Sri Lanka and Colombia, because of large-scale, violence-provoked displacement. National income-distribution estimates may be distorted for the same reason, in addition to the likelihood of underreporting of income by the wealthy. Moreover, national income distributions may be less relevant than perceived regional disparities, particularly in the case of Thailand (see Chapter 8). Those caveats notwithstanding, the more robust patterns are revealing of the contexts and consequences of relevant policies.

Economic Growth Trends

The economic growth patterns beginning in the 1960s, with relevant comparisons from the 1990s to the present, confirm the slowdown associated with middle-income countries. As Tables 2.1 and 2.2 demonstrate, the more-advanced Latin American cases over the past nearly

TABLE 2.1 *Percent increase in GDP/capita in constant 2011 international dollars*

Country/region	Percent increase, 1990–2018 (%)
Argentina	61
Brazil	38
Colombia	73
Mexico	33
Latin America total	49
Malaysia	167
Thailand	154
Other Southeast Asia[a]	207
India	262
Sri Lanka	231
South Asia total	221
Bangladesh/Pakistan avg	127

[a] Simple average of Cambodia (1993), Indonesia, Laos, Philippines, and Vietnam.
Source: World Bank database, August 2019b

TABLE 2.2 *Economic growth rates, case study nations, 1961–2015*

	1961–65	1966–70	1971–75	1976–80	1981–85	1986–90	1991–95	1996–2000	2001–05	2006–10	2011–15
Argentina	4.0	4.0	3.1	3.0	−2.4	−0.3	6.7	2.7	2.3	5.1	1.5
Brazil	4.6	7.8	10.3	6.7	1.2	2.3	3.1	2.1	2.9	4.5	1.2
Colombia	4.7	5.9	5.7	5.4	2.2	4.9	4.1	1.3	3.6	4.6	4.6
India	3.5	4.6	2.9	3.2	5.2	6.0	5.1	6.1	6.7	8.3	6.8
Malaysia	6.9	6.1	8.0	8.6	5.2	6.9	9.5	5.0	4.8	4.5	5.3
Mexico	7.4	6.3	6.3	7.1	2.0	1.7	2.1	5.3	1.4	1.6	3.0
Sri Lanka	2.6	5.8	3.6	5.3	5.0	3.5	5.4	5.0	4.0	6.4	6.2
Thailand	7.2	9.2	5.8	8.0	5.4	10.3	8.2	0.9	5.5	3.8	3.0

Source: World Bank database, 2019b updated November 14, 2018

44   *Introduction*

thirty years have had the lowest increases in GDP per capita. Malaysia and Thailand, the two most economically advanced Southeast Asian countries (excluding Singapore and Brunei), benefited from the absorption of low-productivity labor in the rather rapid industrialization until the late 1990s. Both were severely affected by the East Asian financial meltdown but even thereafter the lower growth rates reflect their middle-income status. This is reinforced by the greater average growth of the less advanced Southeast Asian countries. Low-income countries such as India and Sri Lanka have had the highest growth rates, again consistent with the potential to increase productivity from a very low base.

Regarding the *volatility* of economic growth, the striking pattern shown in Table 2.2 is that the Latin American countries demonstrate great variation, even after averaging over five-year periods. Argentina, in particular, has had highly disappointing periods, fitting in with the policy impasses and sociopolitical polarization featured in Chapter 5. Yet, Brazil, Colombia, and Mexico also have had dramatic swings. Of course, not all fluctuations are due to domestic actions; nearly all Latin American countries suffered during the 1980s "Lost Decade," caused by, among other things, U.S. monetary policy that saddled borrowers with crushing international debt and the commodity-price collapse that hobbled Brazil in 2011–2015. Even so, these fluctuations accentuate the disappointments when high growth levels are followed by economic stagnation or recession.

Poverty Trends

Official statistics, despite spotty reportage and suspiciously low rates of poverty reported for Argentina in the 1980s, indicate considerable progress in reducing extreme poverty in all of the case study countries. Table 2.3 demonstrates a steady improvement in all of the countries, with the exception of the spike in Argentina during the financial meltdown at the beginning of this millennium. Yet India's extreme poverty rate around 2010 still demonstrated considerable absolute poverty.

At a US$5.50 per day poverty threshold, which World Bank analysts (World Bank 2018d, xi) posit is a more appropriate standard for countries at the upper-middle-income level or higher, Malaysia and Thailand have made the most progress. Argentina is close behind, with Sri Lanka, Mexico, and Colombia lagging further behind.

TABLE 2.3 *Poverty head-count percent at less than $1.90/day and $5.50/day, key study countries, circa 1980–2015*

	Per capita income 2017 In'tl PPP ($)		1980	1985	1990	1995	2000	2005	2010	2015
Argentina	20,785	$1.90	0.4	0.0		4.1	5.7	3.9	1.1	0.6[b]
		$5.50	5.5	4.9[c]	14.2[d]	20.5	26.3	21.7	11.1	8.4[b]
Brazil	15,484	$1.90	21.0	23.1	21.6	13.0	12.5[b]	8.6	5.0[b]	3.4
		$5.50	60.4[a]	61.5	57.8	45.0	43.6[b]	38.1	25.7[b]	19.4
Colombia	14,473	$1.90				16.5	16.4	9.7	7.8	4.5
		$5.50				55.2[f]	53.7	46.7	38.4	28.7
India	7,059	$1.90		57.8[b]				38.2	26.2[b]	
		$5.50		95.0[b]	95.4[b]			92.6[g]	88.8[b]	
Malaysia	29,449	$1.90		2.9	1.6	1.8	0.4[b]	0.4[b]	0.1	0.0
		$5.50			32.4[c]	29.4		12.1[g]		2.7
Mexico	18,273	$1.90		8.1		8.9[b]	8.9	6.2	4.2	3.3[b]
		$5.50				49.3[b]	45.1	41.0	37.1	37.6[b]
Sri Lanka	12,835	$1.90		13.3	8.7	8.8	8.5[b]	3.8	2.4	0.7
		$5.50		81.0	80.6	75.2		58.3[h]	55.7[i]	39.2[j]
Thailand	17,872	$1.90	20.0		9.4	2.7[b]	2.5	0.8[b]	0.1	0.0
		$5.50	69.6[a]		64.7		48.9	30.5[b]	17.8	7.1

[a] 1981; [b] interpolated; [c] 1986; [d] 1989; [e] 1991; [f] 1996; [g] 2004; [h] 2006; [i] 2009; [j] 2016.
Source: World Bank database, 2019b updated November 18, 2018

Introduction

Income-Distribution Trends

Nationwide. The other component of Kuznets' theory, that the incorporation of low-productivity workers into the modern sector would finally lead to a reduction in income inequality, is largely borne out in Latin America and Southeast Asia, which have advanced farther economically than South Asia. Thus, after the increasing inequality of the 1980s and 1990s, the trend of greater inequality has been reversed in the bulk of Latin America and the more-advanced countries of Southeast Asia. Simson (2018, 36–38), synthesizing several data bases, judges all Latin American countries as having "strong evidence" of declining inequality, except for Honduras (no clear pattern) and Costa Rica (increasing inequality).[13] Among Southeast Asian countries, Thailand exhibits strong evidence of declining inequality, and Malaysia displays plausible evidence of declining inequality. Both India and Sri Lanka are judged as experiencing increasing inequality.

The formal statistics, displayed in Tables 1.1 (referenced in Chapter 1) and Table 2.4, largely bear this out. The Gini coefficients (Table 2.4), as overall indicators of inequality, are still higher for the Latin American countries, but are declining, as are the coefficients for Thailand and Malaysia. The Sri Lankan trend is inconsistent, but inequality is low. The sole data point for India also indicates relatively low inequality. More concrete measures of the national income shares are important, because the Gini coefficient trends may reflect changes in the income of the relatively prosperous. Even so, as mentioned in Chapter 1, the national income shares of the bottom and fourth quintiles (Table 1.1) confirm the Gini trends.

Intrastate Regional Distribution

Regional inequalities can be examined by comparing the magnitude of differences across subnational units. Table 2.5 reveals the greatest

---

[13] The patterns are, of course, more complicated if assessed dynamically. For Latin America, a World Bank assessment (2016b, 83) concludes:

> Latin America and the Caribbean stands out as a region that has been successful in narrowing inequality in the last 10 to 15 years, also driving the decline in the global average. ... However, these declines occurred after a prolonged increase during the 1980s (not shown) and 1990s, such that, by 2012, the average Gini in the region had returned to the level of the early 1980s. Hence, the long-run progress in the reduction of inequality in Latin America and the Caribbean has been limited. Furthermore, the downward trend has slowed, and inequality recently stagnated.

Political Economy Considerations

TABLE 2.4 *Gini indices, key cases, circa 1995–2015*

	1995	2000	2005	2010	2015
Argentina	48.9	51.1	47.7	43	42.4[h]
Brazil	59.6	58.4[b]	56.3	52.9[g]	51.3
Colombia	56.9[a]	58.7	53.7	54.8	51.1
India	–	–	–	–	35.1[h]
Malaysia	48.5	–	46.1[d]	43.9	41
Mexico	48.2[a]	51.4	48.9	45.3	43.4[h]
Thailand	42.9[a]	42.8	41.8[c]	39.4	36
Sri Lanka	35.4	41.0[c]	40.3[c]	36.4[f]	39.8[h]

[a] 1996; [b] 2001; [c] 2002; [d] 2004; [e] 2006; [f] 2011; [g] 2009; [h] 2016.
Source: World Bank database updated November 18, 2018

TABLE 2.5 *Gini indices across subnational units, key study countries*

	Argentina provinces (2008)	Brazil states (2016)	Colombia districts (2017)	India states (2017)	Mexico states (2016)	Sri Lanka provinces (2016)	Thailand provinces (2013)
Excluding the capital district	.416	.238	.266	.278	.196	–	.387
Including the capital district	.426	.289	.273	.291	.219	.091	.395

Source: World Bank database

regional differences in Argentina and Thailand, although an important caveat is that the magnitudes may be sensitive to the different number of units from one country to another.[14]

Other dimensions of inequality are considerably more difficult to capture through straightforward statistics. Urban vs. rural inequality is difficult to capture because of the lack of sharp boundaries between urban and rural, and because in some countries the urban–rural distinction is an administrative designation having to do with the provision of services, rather than population density. Inequalities across ethnic groups are challenging to measure because some ethnic categories are not crisply bounded, e.g., the "degree of African ancestry." In some cases, however,

[14] That is, Argentina has 23 provinces; Brazil 26 states; Colombia 32 departments; India 33 states; Malaysia 13 states; Mexico 32 states; Sri Lanka 9 provinces; and Thailand 76 provinces.

TABLE 2.6 *Tax capacity, selected countries including case study countries, 1994–2009*

	1994–2001	2002–2009		1994–2001	2002–2009		1994–2001	2002–2009
Argentina	–	0.95	Indonesia	1.01	0.81	Bangladesh	0.83	0.80
Brazil	1.16	1.33	Malaysia	0.84	0.80	India	0.85	0.91
Colombia	0.73	0.79	Philippines	0.98	0.85	Pakistan	1.31	1.03
Mexico	0.75	–	Thailand	–	0.97	Sri Lanka	1.13	0.98

Source: Le, Moreno-Dodson, and Bayraktar (2012)

at least for Sri Lanka and Thailand (as indicated in the cases), regional differences are useful indicators of ethnic disparities.

Tax Effort

Finally, although the data are incomplete for Argentina, Mexico, and Thailand, the differences in tax effort are clear. Brazil has the most ambitious tax effort; the tax efforts in Argentina, Sri Lanka, and Thailand are also high, although the effort in Sri Lanka declined in the 2002–2009 period compared to the 1994–2001 period. The Malaysian and Indian tax efforts have been less impressive, and Colombia and Mexico even less so. Of course, relatively high tax revenues do not guarantee that the funds will be allocated to pro-poor programs, but they do provide greater budget resources ("fiscal space") to do so by government committed to such programs.

PART II

THE UNDERLYING PSYCHOLOGY

3

Identity, Attributions, Deservingness Judgments, and Hostility

INTRODUCTION

This chapter presents the fundamental psychological links between identity and attributions. Among these attributions are the crucial perceptions of deservingness, as well as the potential for intergroup antagonism. As individuals identify with particular ingroups for their own esteem and security, the esteem and security of that group as a whole becomes compelling. To a certain degree, this shapes the attributes assigned to the ingroup and the outgroups. The contrast between characteristics attributed to the ingroup and an outgroup would serve the drive for esteem if the ingroup is perceived as superior to a particular outgroup or to outgroups in general.

Pro-poor commitment on the part of relatively wealthy people depends on the salience of the attributes that ingroup members hold toward their own group. These may include attributions of ingroup social and economic vulnerability or neediness – even of groups that outside observers would regard as among the "prosperous."

The dimensions of superior ingroup attributes can promote pro-poor commitment (e.g., the ingroup is highly charitable, pro-social, etc.) or discourage pro-poor commitment (e.g., the ingroup is vigilant and powerful enough to defend its economic and social advantages). The lesser quality attributed to the outgroup also can promote either pro-poor commitment (e.g., the outgroup's lower capability warrants supporting them – "noblesse oblige") or discourage pro-poor commitment (e.g., less hardworking outgroups do not deserve coddling).

Intergroup antagonism depends on self-attributions, as well as attributions held for both the salient ingroup and outgroups. Perceived self or ingroup attributes of vulnerability and neediness arouse defensiveness.

The Underlying Psychology

Attributions of negative characteristics of outgroups might heighten the feelings of vulnerability and serve as a rationalization for hostile actions against them. Perceptions that an outgroup holds negative attributions toward the ingroup can inflame antagonism, especially if this attribution challenges the ingroup's self-esteem and feelings of security.

Each of the concepts and dynamics outlined above has considerable complexity and variation. The rest of the chapter clarifies key concepts. It also introduces additional conditioning factors that are important for understanding how pro-poor predispositions can be promoted and intergroup hostility reduced.

SOME SIMPLE DEFINITIONS AND CONCEPTS OF IDENTITY

Defining Group Membership

The ingroups to which people regard themselves as belonging are based on one or more common characteristics, which may be ascriptive (essentially given at birth, such as ethnicity, mother tongue, etc.), acquired social status, circumstances (such as geographic displacement), or adopted beliefs (such as political affiliation). This constitutes the multidimensional social identity of each individual as the potential basis for individual and group action.

Tajfel notes that only two criteria are essential for considering a set of individuals as an identification group – awareness and relevance.[1]

He adds, however, a "third component [that] consists of an emotional investment in the awareness and evaluations" (Tajfel 1982, 2), even if it is not a necessary criterion to define a group. Actions on behalf of an identification group rely on an emotional investment.

Every individual holds a bundle of identifications with various sets of people expressed through thought, speech, or action,[2] many of which

---

[1] A "group" can be defined as such on the basis of criteria that are either external or internal. External criteria are the "outside" designations such as bank clerks, hospital patients, members of a trades union, and so on. Internal criteria are those of "group identification." In order to achieve this stage of "identification," two components are necessary, namely, a cognitive one, in the sense of awareness of membership, and an evaluative one, in the sense that this awareness is related to some value confrontations (Tajfel 1982, 2).

[2] Lasswell and Kaplan (1950, 11) define "identification" as "the process by which a symbol user symbolizes his ego as a member of some aggregate or group of egos (X identifies with the Y's if X symbolizes X as a Y)." They go on to emphasize that these acts of "symbolizing" can be internal as well as external; individuals "tell" themselves the groups to which they regard themselves as members.

Identity, Attributions, Deservingness Judgments, and Hostility 53

involve emotional investments. Therefore, individuals often confront trade-offs in deciding who ought to be considered as part of one's "ingroup." However, sometimes individuals have identifications imposed upon them. Identifications may arise from circumstances – common history, the need for interaction, being treated as members of a group by others, and so on. Circumstances may impose identifications upon individuals, rather than the individual's desire to affiliate. The most prominent example was the persecution of Christian converts of Jewish ancestry in Nazi-controlled areas. Imposed identifications may compel individuals to engage in collective action that would not have occurred to them before. Currently the Rohingya ethnicity in Burma is obviously of enormous salience because of the persecution directed specifically at that group.

This insight also accounts for cases in which simple ingroup esteem-seeking is absent or quite attenuated. "The" ingroup may not be well defined in people's minds when several salient identifications do not define the same ingroup. A Malay industrialist may identify with the wealthy cohort of industrialists, including Chinese Malaysians, or with the relatively poor Malay population. In Siberia, an ethnic Korean convert to Christianity may identify with fellow ethnic Koreans, with fellow Christians, or, in relation to resentment against Moscow's neglect of Siberia, as a Siberian (Anisimova and Echevskaya 2012).

In addressing the question of who is regarded as a group member, it is important to note the strong possibility of discrepancies between how individuals define the boundaries of their ingroups and how they are defined by outsiders. Light-skinned Brazilians with darker-skinned grandparents may regard themselves as Afro-Brazilian, but other Brazilians may not regard them as such.

Defining Membership Meaning

The salience of identifying with a particular group depends on not only group membership but also the beliefs and other identifications associated with the ingroup. Reicher, Spears, and Haslam (2010, 50) point out that to analyze the possible outcomes of the Social Identity Theory dynamics, "the specific behavioural outcomes … require one to understand the specific belief systems (and hence the valued dimensions of comparison) associated with the specific groups of interest." This is particularly true for partisan and other loyalty identifications. For example, Argentine Peronism, once center-right, is now populist leftist. In simple terms, if a

54 *The Underlying Psychology*

Malay identifies strongly as a Malay, or a wealthy Argentine identifies as a wealthy Argentine, the question is, "What does it mean to be a Malay, or to be a wealthy Argentine?" Put another way, the internal symbolization is "Being Malay is important to me because ...."

The meaning of both individual and group identity is shaped by the actions of the individuals and other group members. Bem (1967, 185) reports that, "Several studies have shown that an individual's belief and attitude statements can be manipulated by inducing him to role-play, deliver a persuasive communication, or engage in any behavior that would characteristically imply his endorsement of a particular set of beliefs." In other words, when people engage in pro-poor activities, they are more likely to define their identity as pro-poor.

A crucial possibility of the meaning of identity among the poor is that the state of poverty may have normatively positive implications. One of the problems encountered in formulating and enacting poverty-alleviation programs is the possibility of a gulf between the outlook of people designated as the poor by the measures and the outlook of pro-poor government officials and NGO activists trying to address poverty. The dominant perspective of pro-poor decision-makers and activists is that socioeconomic disadvantage needs to be overcome through policies that would increase the productivity and access to social services of the poor, so that they could rise above poverty. This perspective runs the risk of disregarding how the poor relate their modes of production, or even the very status of struggling with poverty. In short, treating poverty as a failure may be an assault on the pride of the poor. Bourdieu (1990, 190) notes that for native Algerian men, "The more vulnerable a family is, the more *nif* [honor] it must possess to defend its sacred values, and the greater are the consideration and esteem it enjoys. Thus poverty, far from contradicting or prohibiting respectability, only enhances the merit of a man who manages to win respect although he is particularly exposed to outrage." In Northeast Thailand, as Chapter 8 argues, the farmer's poverty becomes a virtue as the struggle against harsh conditions is contrasted with the corruption of central Thai business people who manipulate rather than engage in hard work.

Emotive vs. Non-emotive Identifications

Emotive identifications entail a positive affect toward other group members, such that an individual member would be willing to act on behalf of other group members even if the individual does not benefit.

Identity, Attributions, Deservingness Judgments, and Hostility   55

A non-emotive identification may entail recognition of commonalty of interests, vulnerabilities, and so on that could lead to cooperation without emotional connections. Wealthy individuals may have to recognize their identification with other wealthy people, even if they disdain these people, perhaps because of the belief that other wealthy people are selfish and corrupt. The distinction is important because emotive identifications are more likely to involve the development of beliefs that serve psychological needs.

Ascriptive vs. Non-ascriptive Identifications

Identifications based on inborn characteristics, such as ethnicity, mother tongue, region of origin, gender, and religion at birth, are particularly relevant insofar as these characteristics are associated with the perception of a common history, common risks, and so on. The possibility of common plight vis-à-vis other groups, and the more-or-less invariant basis of ascriptive identifications, often can provide powerful bases for within-group cooperation. To be sure, some attributes considered to be ascriptive can be altered; people can learn other languages, and they can change their religions.

Even so, the ascriptive characteristics at any point in time frequently define the bases of both cooperation and conflict. The standard presumption is that individuals who do not share salient identifications with other individuals (their differences are "overlapping cleavages") are more likely to engage in conflict than individuals who share at least one salient ascriptive characteristic (crosscutting cleavages). For example, the cleavages in Tanzania are crosscutting, in that Christian and Muslim Tanzanians may share the same ethnicity (Heilman and Kaiser 2002). In Nigeria, the most-salient cleavages are overlapping, in that the Muslim Hausa-Fulani are of different ethnic groups than the Christians within the same northern region and in other regions of the country (Bormann, Cederman, and Vogt 2017).

Non-ascriptive identifications are based on achievements, current circumstances, or attitudes. Non-ascriptive identifications by definition are in principle alterable. Thus, one can seek to "escape" the reputation of ascriptive characteristics by trying to affiliate with people of other ascriptive characteristics. People convert to religions of more "respectable" or powerful people; some change their nationalities.

The distinction between ascriptive and attitudinal identifications is fuzzy (Brady and Sniderman 1985) insofar as some ascriptive identifications,

56 *The Underlying Psychology*

such as religion, can be changed through individual choice. Yet ascriptive identifications are generally less flexible, as people typically interact continuously with kin, engaging in ethnically or religiously specific practices, speaking their language, and so on. Reinforcing this rigidity is the common occurrence that others may treat people according to an ascriptively defined category, regardless of whether people within that category want to be treated that way. Thus, these people may have to react according to this identification.

Individuals may deny their ascriptive backgrounds, although an outside observer would regard the ascription as correct – denying partial black African ancestry in the United States is perhaps the most common example. Sometimes ascriptive denial has ideological significance, such as renouncing citizenship of one's country of origin.

Two points are crucial here. First, attributions regarding a group's standing, and the benefits and burdens, may not correspond closely to reality. The tendency to minimize the range of differences within an ingroup is common. Tajfel (1981, 133) notes that "when a classification is correlated with a continuous dimension, there will be a tendency to exaggerate the differences on that dimension between items which fall into distinct classes, and to minimize these differences within each of the classes."

Second, the salience of the self-identification will vary depending on the issue. For example, the residents of Siberia, in the face of their belief that the Russian government is denying them the benefits they deserve, identify as "Sibiryak" (i.e., Siberian as a quasi-ethnicity) rather than as Russian, Korean, and so on (Anisimova and Echevskaya 2012). In contrast, debates over the policies *within* the Siberian Federal District may increase the salience of more conventional ethnic distinctions, insofar as people of different ethnic groups may live in different parts of the vast Siberian area. Similarly, the migrants from many areas in Southeast Asia who migrated to Jakarta, shorn of their own culture of origin, formed the Betawi "creole" ethnicity with distinctive if syncretic cultural beliefs and practices (Knörr 2010, 740–744). Therefore, we need to understand which ascriptive characteristics are likely to have high salience with respect to particular types of policy initiatives, and how these identifications influence attitudes toward people with benefits and burdens that depend on the policy initiatives.

Continuum of Degrees of Boundedness

The boundaries of the set of people that any individual regards as within a group are subject to varying degrees of openness. Obviously, attributes such as "wealthy" or "poor" are fuzzy, but so are categories such as "Muslim" (ISIS fundamentalists have been explicit about their view that Shia are apostates [Hawley 2017, 161]); or "native Thai speakers" (as opposed to speakers of Northeast Thailand's "Isaanese").

Dimensions of Economic Bases of Identification

The primary basis of collective action could be perceived economic-status similarity, possibly the only salient identification engaged in individuals' orientations toward economic distribution. The top economic elite might see a common threat that unites them regardless of ethnicity or other distinctions. However, it is very common that economic status is just one basis of ingroup identification, coupled with occupation, ethnicity, region, or other bases of identification.

The other complication is that economic status may shape two quite distinct bases of identifications. First, people who share an occupation may identify as such because of common interests, common threats, opportunities for collective action, or pride derived by the association. However, seemingly straightforward occupational identification is actually quite complicated. Farmers with different-sized holdings may or may not regard themselves as a relevant ingroup. Workers in small, informal-sector repair shops may not feel kinship with industrial workers in large, unionized factories. Occupational census figures often fail to capture these differences.

Second, although a given level of income or wealth may also present common opportunities and threats, divisions among people of similar economic status may be at odds with one another (Stewart 2000). This could entail competition among sectors; for example, industrial magnates and large-scale farm owners are often on opposite sides of policies ranging from food price controls to exchange rates. Or it could pit people of different ethnicity or other ascriptive categories against one another.

Overlap of Wealth and Other Dimensions of Identification

The identifications most relevant to reactions to redistributional policy initiatives are the most-salient ascriptive self-identifiers such as ethnicity, language, religion, region, and so on, in contrast with other groups likely to be benefited or burdened by the initiatives. This contrast may encompass a very narrow or very broad set of relevant groups. For example, "I am an Iranian Arab, much poorer than Iranian Persians"; "I am a

Hindu, wealthier than the Muslims in my city of Calcutta"; "We Mapuche are poorer than other Chileans."

Different countries or subnational regions have different degrees of overlap between the wealth dimension and other highly salient bases of identifications. Sometimes the bases of identification of the non-poor do not include characteristics that they perceive of the poor, and the poor do not perceive much in common with the non-poor. It is reasonable to expect that if the poor and non-poor identify to a certain degree with one another, the willingness of the non-poor to tolerate policies that are more favorable to the poor will be higher.

It is plausible that pro-poor predispositions will be greatest when the strongest identifications are with people from *across* the income range. Prosperous people are more likely to empathize with co-ethnics, coreligionists, and so on; they are also more likely to feel a sense of obligation that might translate into a more general pro-poor predisposition.

Conversely, the scenario of both similar economic status and common ascriptive characteristics among the prosperous may yield the weakest pro-poor predisposition. For identity groups based on shared economic status, loyalty toward the poor per se lacks grounding in ingroup identifications, although this does not preclude the possibility that the non-poor would support pro-poor policies out of pro-social impulse, enhancing ingroup esteem, or self-interest.

THEORIES OF THE FORMATION OF IDENTIFICATIONS

Common history, common fate, and close interaction can all be bases for highly salient ingroup identifications. If the government or other powerful organizations classify a set of people as the same, these people may come to see themselves as such, or they may have to. Many members of the disparate groups labeled as "Dayaks" in Indonesia's Kalimantan now regard themselves as Dayaks; they have adopted the identification as a means to unite for self-protection and to press for rights (Davidson 2003; Fanselow 2015).

Although individuals thus may identify with groups for a broad range of practical reasons, such as being able to cooperate with other group members, identifications may be "internally" developed to serve psychological needs. What dimensions are commonly prominent in defining distinctiveness? If ingroup members have established positive reputations for particular attributes or accomplishments, the contrasts with others may be anchored by these characteristics. Masai are likely to emphasize their bravery in contrast to other Kenyans or Tanzanians. Groups reputed to be hardworking, such as Malaysian Chinese, are more likely to highlight the contrast with others, such as the supposedly indolent Malays. Yet, in the context of issues of the distribution of income and wealth, the dimensions defined by occupational roles are often extremely important. Individuals' attitudes toward pro-poor policies are shaped by both the self-attributes they regard as important and their identification with others they believe share these attributes. Basing identity on "respectable" economic roles, such as farming rather than moneylending, can enhance self-esteem in contrast to historically disdained occupations.

Formation of Attitude-Based Identifications

One rather comprehensive approach to categorizing the formation of *attitude-based* identifications is the functional approach offered by Katz (1960). He distinguishes among attitudes serving

- the "adjustment" function (maximizing rewards from the external environment);
- the "knowledge" function (making sense of complexity);
- the "ego-defensive" function (defending against unacceptable impulses and reducing anxiety); and
- the "value-expressive" function (positive expression of central values).

In taking on attitudes serving one or more of these functions, the individual may identify with others presumed to share these attitudes. Striving to maximize rewards from the external environment defines allies. Taking on beliefs to understand complexity – establishing a worldview or ideology – promotes identification with "like-thinking people," and stereotyping makes the complexity seem manageable. Ego-defensive attitudes, such as reaction formation against "impure" impulses (Baumeister, Dale, and Sommer 1998), may lead to identifications with other puritanical people who would denigrate the poor presumed to be promiscuous.

Value-expressive attitudes, in particular, can provide the individual with self-esteem and other gratifications. Such attitudes conveying a humanitarian self-conception may lead an individual to identify with philanthropists and pro-poor advocates in general. This identification requires the individual to believe that he or she supports pro-poor policies or engages in philanthropy. However, the reluctance to make sacrifices

60 *The Underlying Psychology*

might to rationalized by cynicism that existing initiatives actually would help the poor.

Identifying with others who are believed to hold admirable value-expressive attitudes enhances the emotional attachment to these admirable people. The evaluative attributions of others who are believed to lack these attitudes are likely to be negative. The presumption that the poor within an individual's ingroup are doing worse may indulge the individual's self-esteem by demonstrating the concern over fraternal deprivation (Huddy 2013, 518), while also reinforcing moral indignation against those believed to be responsible for the deprivation. Individuals may allow themselves to presume that the income distribution is becoming more unequal as a rationale for aggressive impulses against the government, the wealthy, and competing groups.

The prominent social identity theory takes up two of the four aspects of Katz's attitude-function framework – understanding complexity through stereotyping dynamics and value-expressive attitudes – and combines it with the objective of enhancing the individual and ingroup esteem. Following Katz, this goes beyond the premise that individuals pursue material self-interest.[3] Al Ramiah, Hewstone, and Schmid (2011, 44) note that "Group members are motivated to protect their self-esteem and achieve a positive and distinct social identity, and preference for one's own group is a way of achieving this." The convergence of attitudes and practices is strengthened further by the likelihood that an individual will share the beliefs, emotions, and commitments of that group (Haslam, Powell, and Turner 2000, 326–327).

The dynamic premise of the identification process is that whatever attributes can enhance an individual's self-esteem may heighten the identification with groups regarded as strengthening the claim to that attribute. The self-categorization theory that grew out of social identity theory (Turner and Oakes 1986; Turner et al. 1987, 1994; Turner and Reynolds 2012) posits that individuals not only strive to gain esteem for the groups with which they identify, but also choose to identify with groups that enhance self-esteem. Sindic and Condor (2014, 45) note "that social identity processes come into play when people categorise themselves

---

[3] The "realistic conflict theory" (Sherif 1962) posits that intergroup behavior, particularly conflictual behavior, can be based on self-interest. It is important to note that social identity theory does not dismiss this possibility, but rather adds another set of motivations behind intergroup behavior. It is often difficult to determine whether a pro-social behavior is regarded as also having a self-interested aspect.

Identity, Attributions, Deservingness Judgments, and Hostility 61

(and others) as group members. SCT focuses on the nature, antecedents and consequences of this psychological process of self-categorisation." For example, Iraqi Kurds may feel an even stronger affinity with other Kurds insofar as they regard Kurds as brave and loyal, diminishing the relative salience of identification as Iraqi. Reinforcing this tendency is that an identity may become more attractive through a stronger perception that ingroup members are admirable. This is common when a group comes to be perceived as more prosperous, sophisticated, powerful, and so on.

Esteem-seeking may also *restrict* the identification within an ascriptive category. Many moderate Sunnis do not identify with all Sunnis, but rather with other moderate Sunnis, rejecting the broadest range of Sunnis that would include ISIS Sunnis. Insofar as people define their ingroup so as to identify with others they regard as pious, religious identities may be prominent, particularly in contrast with other religions regarded as heretical (e.g., many Sunnis' views of Shia).

Thus, it is misleading to presume that social identity is fixed, or that it is straightforwardly determined by individuals' ascriptive characteristics. Individuals may change the degree to which they regard themselves as belonging to a multitude of sets of other people, including inborn attributes such as race, gender, or home language, but also attitudinal attributes such as political party preference.

The social identity and self-categorization theories further maintain that esteem of the ingroup is often in contrast with other groups. Hogg and Abrams (1998, 21) note that, "The social identity approach proposes the existence of a fundamental individual motivation for self-esteem ..., which is satisfied in an intergroup context by maximizing the difference between ingroup and outgroup on those dimensions which reflect positively upon ingroup."

This is a fundamental basis of attributions to outgroups. However, because of the multiplicity of potential motivations, social identities may reflect far more than the quest for self-esteem, ranging from seeking solidarity for socioeconomic advantage to physical protection. The sociology literature addresses both the malleability of identifications in the interactions among people of different groups, as well as the advantages that particular identities have in these interactions. Tilly (1998b) emphasizes the mobilization of identity to press for benefits through the political process, and the changes in how identities are conveyed as this process makes some claims more compelling than they had been before. Tilly (1998b, 457) argues that "the identities people deploy in political

62   *The Underlying Psychology*

claim-making (including identities of religious affiliation, nationality, and citizenship) consist of contingent relationships with other people rather than inbuilt personal traits; they therefore alter as political networks, opportunities, and strategies shift."

An application of Tilly's insight regarding the political relevance of identifications is his emphasis on the potential to mobilize social movements through the bonds of shared identifications that reflect maltreatment. He notes (1998a, 212) that

Social movements create or activate paired and under equal categories, with an important twist: they deliberately emphasize the unjust treatment of people on the weaker side of a categorical line and/or the improper behavior of people on the stronger side. The "we" referred to by social-movement activists comprises a whole category (composite or homogeneous) of unjustly treated persons or organizations. The "they" consists of others (industrialists, officials, immoral persons, sometimes competing groups) whose action or inaction allegedly causes the condition that activists are protesting in the name of their presumably aggrieved constituency.

The socioeconomic advantages of social identities that convey sophistication in the eyes of the ingroup and at least some fraction of outgroups are important insofar as sophistication implies mastery, higher class, and even greater intelligence. Bourdieu's (1986, 17–21) conception of "cultural capital," typically accumulated in the modern era through lengthy and the most well-respected education, can be parlayed into economic and other advantages over those considered to be less sophisticated. Of course, other origins of perceived sophistication and mastery may exist in other contexts. For example, religious adepts have had such advantages in many cultures, as the dominance of Brahmins in India attests.

It also must be understood that a positive self-image does not require holding negative attributions toward others; charitability toward groups disadvantaged through no fault of their own can be a source of pride for the ingroup (e.g., being helpful for victims of floods, earthquakes, etc.).

Plasticity of Identifications

The plasticity or malleability of identifications provides crucial openings for influencing pro-poor predispositions. Baruah (1986, 1185–1186) argues that

In Assam, ethnic categories cannot be viewed as primordial givens that take determinate political forms. They are better thought of as political projects: attempts at organizing particular forms of ethnic solidarity .... Ethnic boundaries

Identity, Attributions, Deservingness Judgments, and Hostility   63

therefore are fluid. For instance, at certain times linguistically defined ethnic solidarity may be salient; at other times religiously defined solidarity may become salient; and at other times neither form of ethnic solidarity may be salient. Nor are the boundaries of particular forms of loyalty, say, of language loyalty, determinate.

Previously cherished identifications may be rejected because they no longer provide esteem. Not infrequently, migrations that bring people of more advanced economic status leads to feelings of inferiority on the part of members of the local community, leading to a partial or full rejection of their prior identity.

Leaders of groups that attract prosperous people have the potential to inculcate pro-poor predispositions (e.g., high-caste Indian leaders instilled commitment among other high-caste Indians to embrace the affirmative action programs that favor Dalits ["untouchables"] and Adivasis [hill tribes]). Yet, as mentioned earlier, ingroup identifications can limit pro-poor impacts if the most salient identifications of the prosperous include some poor, who are not among the poorest. Ingroup favoritism, as Whitt and Wilson (2007, 658) assert, is backed by "extensive research in social psychology." Brewer (1999, 437) argues that "many forms of discrimination and bias may develop not because outgroups are hated, but because positive emotions such as admiration, sympathy, and trust are reserved for the ingroup and withheld from outgroups." A static assessment of individuals' most-salient identifications with respect to pro-poor policies or antagonism toward other groups ignores the multiple potential bases of identifications.[4] Identifications are malleable: in the scope, salience, and meaning of ingroups. For example, the flexibility of identity of people of Isaan, examined at length in Chapter 8, provides choice in their relations with other people. Some Isaanese opt to minimize their Isaanese identity when interacting with non-Isaanese by abandoning their distinctive Isaanese linguistic patterns, regarding themselves as Thais in relation to Laotians, while in other contexts celebrating their own Laotian heritage. As McCargo and Hongladarom (2004, 234) argue, "alternative modes of identity appear to be resources on which individuals could draw. Conscious choices were made to foreground particular aspects of identity in particular contexts."

---

[4] The early focus of social identity theory (Tajfel 1969/1981, 1981, 1982; Tajfel and Turner 1979) entailed defining a set of people suffering from negative stereotyping and therefore discrimination as the "outgroup," with the psychology centered on trying to determine why the "ingroup" holds these attitudes. For this purpose, taking the ingroup identifications as given is serviceable.

The literature on identifications notes that identifications can bring about the "emergence of social norms" (Turner and Oakes 1986, 242). Norms can change when identifications change in scope or salience. Broader identifications may encompass the norms held by the additional members of the identity group. A more salient identification could elevate the norms associated with that identity group over conflicting norms held by alternative identities. For example, if an industrialist's identification with an ethnic group of mixed-income levels becomes more salient, the norm more favorable to pro-poor sacrifice may replace the norm of protecting fellow industrialists.

In addition, the relevance of each social identity depends on the specific *temporal* context. As the prospects of redistribution change over time, the salience of ingroup identifications that face the greatest opportunities or risks from potential redistributive policies are likely to change accordingly. As a group's prestige changes over time, the attractiveness of stronger association with the group is also likely to change. In addition, as people become aware of policy initiatives, different identifications become more engaged. An Arabic-speaking Sunni Muslim physician residing in France may have an identification with Sunni Muslims in general, among many other identifications including physicians and other Arabic speakers. In the operating room, the Sunni identification may not be engaged, but if that individual hears of Shiite attacks on Sunnis, the Sunni Muslim identification is likely to gain in salience. Malaysian Chinese feel more "Chinese" insofar as the Malays treat Malaysian Chinese as Chinese, rather than simply as fellow Malaysians. An identification also can be weakened if other ingroup members come to be seen in a negative light, perhaps through poor treatment of other ingroup members or people in other groups.

Given the malleability of ingroup affiliations, the size and nature of the ingroup may not be stable. People of the same ascriptive heritage may redefine the ingroup boundaries to exclude members seen as of different economic status, or even lifestyle. This is stunningly exemplified by Kuwait's nomadic desert Bedouins, who no longer consider sedentary Bedouins as part of the same ethnicity. Longva (2006, 171–172) notes that "barriers ... being raised between hadhar [sedentary] and badu [nomadic] [Bedouins that] contribute to turning them into mutually exclusive identities."

Identifications are also shaped by the very interactions regarding pro-poor initiatives and/or anti-poor initiatives. Instead of assuming that pro-poor initiatives succeed or fail based on the preexisting predispositions, it

Identity, Attributions, Deservingness Judgments, and Hostility   65

must be recognized that the receptivity to the initiative can change as the initiative unfolds. Its impacts may become clearer, and revelations about the characteristics and plight of the poor may induce broader or narrower identifications of some of the prosperous. Identifying the potential beneficiaries may reveal that some of the poor share characteristics with some of the prosperous, thereby expanding the ingroup. In addition, if a pro-poor policy has been successful, its supporters could take on a stronger pro-poor identity if the initiative it is seen as successful; possibly weaker if the initiative is seen as a failure. If a pro-poor initiative is deemed threatening by several groups, they may form a broader identification group. Wealthy Venezuelans, regardless of ethnicity or political party affiliations, clearly share the solidarity of being victimized by the blatant confiscations by the Chavez and Maduro governments.

Ingroup Influences on Individual's Attributions

While an individual's self-evaluation shapes the identification with one or more ingroups, a strong ingroup identification in turn shapes the individual's attribution. This dynamic has been labeled, perhaps unfortunately, as "depersonalization of individual self-perception." Turner and Oakes (1986, 242) explain that "It is hypothesized that depersonalization is the basic process underlying group phenomena such as social stereotyping, in-group cohesiveness and ethnocentrism, intragroup cooperation and altruism, emotional empathy and contagion, social influence processes and the emergence of social norms."

Insofar as the individual regards a particular belief as part of this identification, that belief will become more firmly held; for example, "As a Bedouin, I am proud to extend hospitality to strangers."[5] Note that while some of the attitudes may be negative – which was the original concern of social identity theory – other attitudes, such as intragroup cooperation, altruism, and empathy, are positive. The "depersonalization" is by no means necessarily the suppression of individuality; an individual may choose to identify with a particular group because the groups' beliefs coincide with those of the individual, as well as embrace the group's norms as appropriate.

The identification may also increase the individual's commitment to favor and defend other members of the ingroup, for example, "As a loyal

---

[5] See, for example, Paradise (2016).

66   *The Underlying Psychology*

Bedouin, I have an obligation to defend my clan." Whitt and Wilson (2007, 658) note that experiments on allocating rewards to oneself or to others "support the extensive research from social psychology: ingroup favoritism is the norm and outgroup members are treated less favorably." Mohamad (2012, 179) explains that "[a]n identification of membership belonging within a group reinforces relative self-esteem or self-deprivation, hence fashioning behavior that further reinforces the saliency of group-based exclusionary politics." Thus, favoritism may provide fertile ground for perceived conflict and antagonism toward outgroups.

Moods, Crises, and Identities

The social identity and self-categorization theories are largely silent with respect to the impact of most affects. They typically focus on long-standing challenges of prejudice and discrimination, yet the opportunity to enact a pro-poor initiative often arises at a critical point in time. Therefore, it is important to take into account the influences of shifts in widespread mood.[6] In particular, the reactions to crises can shape unity or divisiveness, expand the sense of deservingness or limit it, and reduce or exacerbate conflict. Characterizing crises in terms of the emotions they arouse provides insights into mood swings.

Consider Brazil, a case featured prominently in this book. Brazil has had the highest tax effort in Latin America, and a ratio of tax revenues to GDP at a level comparable to developed countries (Pessino and Fenochietto 2010, 2013). This has reflected the extraordinary *Bolsa Familia* conditional cash transfer program (see Chapter 4) and constitutionally mandated investments in education. How to explain the willingness of prosperous Brazilians to finance all of this, followed by a dramatic backlash? The dramatic mood shift is taken up in Chapter 5.

Identifications and Pro-Poor Predispositions

The mechanisms and considerations presented above clarify the factors that determine how identifications can shape the pro-poor predispositions of relatively prosperous people.

---

[6] Lasswell (1965) used two terms: "moods" are generally considered to be more limited than "climates" in terms of the population involved. However, to avoid the confusion over the term "climate," the term "mood" is used here to refer to both narrowly and broadly shared prolonged emotional states.

Identity, Attributions, Deservingness Judgments, and Hostility 67

First, the prosperous may fear that policies presented as pro-poor would be too threatening to the identification group with which they have a positive emotional attachment. Of course, some pro-poor policies may be presented as benefiting all in the long run. For example, higher purchasing power in the hands of the poor can expand the economy in general. Successful conditional cash transfer programs would produce the better educated, healthier workforce. However, prospect theory offers the chilling insight that the prospect of loss looms larger than the anticipation of gain.[7]

Second, even a largely prosperous ascriptive identification group inevitably has a range of wealthier and poorer people, though the magnitude of ranges vary greatly. The awareness of the range also varies greatly, although ingroup members typically are more aware of the range than are others. For example, wealthy Chinese Indonesians are aware that some Chinese Indonesians are poor, contrary to the stereotype that they are all rich. In theory, knowing that some members of the ingroup are poor may increase the likelihood of tolerance toward poverty alleviation.

However, the income disparities within an identification group can weaken the identification. Stewart (2000, 253) suggests that "it may be more difficult to get group cohesion where there is high intra-group inequality ... because elite members may identify more with members of the elite from other groups than with lower-income members of their own group." In terms of conflict, though, the potentially greater identification with prosperous people of other groups means that "[s]trong intra-group vertical inequality may actually reduce the potential for inter-group conflict for any given degree of horizontal inequality" (Stewart 2000, 253).

Third, a different problem can arise if the wealthier members of an ingroup indeed do care for the poorer members of the group. In supporting pro-poor policies for these poorer ingroup members, the resulting policies may not benefit far-needier people.

Fourth, the prosperous may be proud that their identification group is known for its pro-poor attitudes and actions (e.g., Indian Jains are gratified with Jains' philanthropy to both Jains and non-Jains). Acting altruistically can enhance this pride.

---

[7] Tversky and Kahneman (1991, 1039–1040) assert that "the outcomes of risky prospects are evaluated by a value function that has three essential characteristics. Reference dependence: the carriers of value are gains and losses defined relative to a reference point. Loss aversion: the function is steeper in the negative than in the positive domain; losses loom larger than corresponding gains. Diminishing sensitivity: the marginal value of both gains and losses decreases with their size."

68 *The Underlying Psychology*

BASES OF ATTRIBUTIONS

Attributions are attitudes, and therefore Katz's attitude-function framework is quite useful. To begin, interactions with ingroup and outgroup members lead to attributions of characteristics of both, out of pragmatic concerns, amply covered by Sherif's (1962) realistic conflict theory, consistent with Katz's adjustment function.

These attributions, no matter how established, typically are exaggerated through stereotyping mechanisms. Overly generalized attributions are inevitable in characterizing any large group, because of the cognitive limits of what is known about all members of any group beyond the defining characteristic. This is even true of attributions of ingroups: Fritz Heider's "unit relation" over-simplifies the understanding of others believed to be within a category by assuming they have the same characteristics, consistent with Campbell's "entitativity" (i.e., belonging to the same entity).[8]

The dominant cognitive premise is that the mental effort to comprehend how to react in a given circumstance is aided by regarding any given case as the same in one or more respects as other members of a set. Thus, particular common characteristics are attributed to the set, and these characteristics shape actions vis-à-vis members of that set. Relevant to social psychology are the "aggregates of persons" as social entities.

Heider (1958) emphasizes the cognitive need to understand more about a set of people with one or a small number of shared attributes, by positing that individuals regard sets of people as being of a "unit." Whereas entitativity in itself is not stereotyping, it is an essential assumption of "unit relation" that particular people share relevant characteristics *beyond* the labeling definition – Armenian, southern, Catholic, and so on – in order for the individual to decide on actions vis-à-vis those people. Along with considering a set of people as an entity according to one or

---

[8] Perspectives on attributions have considerable overlap, although the underlying models are of different scope. Unlike the Tajfel and Heider models that are limited to ingroup and outgroup perceptions, the heuristics and biases framework is employed to explain not only perceptions of other individuals and groups, but also of circumstances, events, and so on. Campbell's "entitativity" was developed as both an empirical and subjective assessment of any set of objects as constituting an entity (Campbell 1958), but its contemporary applications do focus on intergroup perceptions (Denson et al. 2006; Lickel et al. 2000, 2006a, 2006b; Lickel, Hamilton, and Sherman 2001). The cognitive simplifications that can be labeled "heuristics" fit not only within the "heuristics and biases" framework of Kahneman and Tversky (1972), but also conform to Heider's "unit relation" and Campbell's "entitativity."

more defining characteristics, the individual attributes other, often strongly evaluative, characteristics to these sets. Armenians are shrewd; southerners untrustworthy; northerners uneducated; and so on. Even ingroup identification, insofar as members presume multiple commonalities among fellow members, can be considered as "entitative" (Effron and Knowles 2015).

The very prominent "heuristics and biases" approach also assumes that attributions entailing simplification are motivated by the basic drive to comprehend (Kahneman and Frederick 2002). The heuristics are cognitive simplifications applied to new events, circumstances, or people, in that the attributes of the new case are assumed to share one or more important attributes of one or more earlier cases. For example, a new acquaintance may be presumed to be typical of previously encountered dishonest people of the same ethnicity (an example of the representativeness heuristic). Or a new tax reform initiative will be regarded as having the same attributes and perhaps the same outcome as certain previous tax reform initiatives. The heuristics and biases theorists have offered up many different reasons why previous cases may be the basis for assumptions about the current case. McGraw (2000, 820) "discovered more than 50 distinct heuristics (or, at least, heuristics given distinct names by researchers)," ranging from complicated "deservingness heuristics" to simpler cognitive heuristics based on prior cases.

Stereotypes can arise simply by the presumed characteristics of individuals in particular socioeconomic roles. If contact has occurred, the roles involved in ingroup–outgroup interactions will increase the likelihood that the outgroup stereotype will be dominated by perceived attributes of the outgroup members of greatest contact. Clearly positive or clearly negative personal interactions can have a stronger influence on shaping the attributions toward others.

These stereotypes may arise without prior contact, in contrast to the scenario of individuals developing beliefs about merchants, laborers, bankers, and so on, following interactions. Occupational stereotypes include the attribution that farmers or herders are of low income and sophistication, and that merchants are grasping and exploitative. Similarly, informal-sector workers (i.e., those beyond the state's business regulations and associated benefits) are presumed to be of low income, even though some informal-sector workers earn a lot through incomes enhanced by being free of some regulations and some taxes. These attributions may reflect what the individual regards as typical of people within the occupation, corresponding to the representativeness heuristic

(Kahneman and Tversky 1972). Related, but not identical to occupational attributions is the degree to which perceived income and wealth levels define the attributions, sometimes but not necessarily associated with ethnic stereotypes. Koenig and Eagly (2014, 371–372) posit that

Social role theory postulates that social perceivers' beliefs about social groups in their society derive from their experiences with group members in their typical social roles – that is, in roles in which these group members are overrepresented relative to their numbers in the general population .... The behaviors enacted within these roles influence the traits that perceivers assume are characteristic of the group, a process enabled by correspondent inference.

The strength of occupationally based attributions, in turn, is often based on the strength of rewards or deprivations in the relationship. For example, if harsh supervisors of indigenous Latin American workers are identified as "Europeans," the characteristic of harshness might be attributed to "Europeans" in general.

Attributions based on economic roles are likely to be particularly strong for individuals who have contact to one or just a few people seen as representing a particular outgroup. For example, farmers in remote areas may come into contact with members of a different ethnic group only through the commodity merchant (such as ethnic Chinese rice merchants in Southeast Asia) who purchases their crops. Insofar as the interaction is perceived as exploitive, members of the ethnic group may be tarred with the same brush. The attributions may reflect particularly acute experiences, corresponding to the availability heuristic (Kahneman and Tversky 1972; Tversky and Kahneman 1973), such as feeling that one has been cheated in a business transaction or unfairly gouged by a price increase.

In contrast, through proximate interactions involving economic transactions (employment, renting, buying and selling, etc.) or more casual interactions (frequenting the same shops, attending the same meetings, etc.), the exposure to *multiple* members of an outgroup may weaken simplistic stereotypes.

Insofar as ingroup members interact and respect one another's views, ingroup members' attributions of outgroup characteristics converge, heightening stereotypes of the outgroups. Although attributions are individual beliefs, communication within groups often yields shared attributions of outgroups. That is, when people in a group communicate with one another, their views about other groups converge. Tajfel (1969/1981, 116), on the basis of "minimal intergroup" experiments, concludes that "[a] stereotype about an ethnic group is generally defined in terms of a consensus of opinion concerning the traits attributed to that group."

Identity, Attributions, Deservingness Judgments, and Hostility 71

However, it should not be taken for granted that stereotypes are coherent or commonly shared within one group toward other groups. For example, according to Chauvel (1990), the Butonese people, who have migrated from small, infertile Indonesian islands southeast of Sulawesi over the past century to the more prosperous Ambon Island, are regarded by Ambonese as entrepreneurial, hardworking, and frugal. Yet Mearns (1996) reports an Ambonese stereotype of the Butonese as drunkards and prone to violence.

Some cognitive theories[9] emphasize the tendency to characterize outgroups through the simple contrasts with the ingroup, accentuating the differences (Tajfel 1982; Upmeyer and Layer 1974). Insofar as the ingroup defines itself according to attributes that enhance its esteem, the sharp contrasts are likely to exacerbate the negativity of the outgroup stereotype.

The stereotypes may be further strengthened insofar as stereotypes expressed by ingroup leaders, whether regarding ingroup or outgroup characteristics, are likely to be broadly accepted by other ingroup members.

It is also possible that higher cognitive/emotional load will increase stereotyping. Experimental findings suggest that a group members' calm, deliberative interactions with other groups will yield a relatively nuanced assessment.[10] In contrast, in tense, complex situations, for example, encounters over income distribution or mobilizing ingroup members for confrontations, the presumed increase in cognitive and emotional load would heighten the preexisting stereotypes.

Once a stereotype is established, often it is difficult to alter, even if contrary evidence is made known. A "disconfirmation bias" (Edwards and Smith 1996; Taber and Lodge 2006) avoids or rejects information that clashes with preexisting beliefs, frequently favoring particular key

---

[9] These theories rely on experimental evidence. Krueger and Clement (1994, 35) clarify that "According to this theory, people's perceptions minimize the differences between stimuli falling into the same category (assimilation effect) and maximize the differences between stimuli falling into different categories (contrast effect)."

[10] Biernat, Kobrynowicz, and Weber (2003, 2064) propose that "cognitive load should increase the use of stereotypes." Experiments by Rothbart et al. (1978, 250) found that exposing subjects to hypothetical information about members of a group with favorable or unfavorable traits "demonstrated that under conditions of high memory load, subjects in effect treat multiple presentations of the same group members as if each presentation were a different group member, whereas under low memory load, subjects are able to adjust for multiple presentations of the same group member in their group impressions."

hypotheses that negate alternative knowledge (Nickerson 1998). The pervasiveness of overconfidence in existing beliefs (Dunning et al. 1990) reinforces this rejection of new information. In addition, people are often prone to selective exposure that favors sources consistent with previous beliefs (Frey 1986; Nickerson 1998; Taber and Lodge 2006).

Ethnic Stereotypes

It is remarkable that evaluative ethnic stereotypes can arise both with direct and indirect experiences. Some stereotypes of other groups are positive: Japanese are industrious, Armenians are shrewd, and so on. Yet many stereotypes carry negative attributions in that simply learning that an outgroup has characteristics different from the valued attributes of the ingroup gives rise to a negative evaluation. Insofar as one focuses on the positive attributes of one's ingroup, contrasting attributes of outgroups may be judged negatively. Thus, Fanselow (2015, 142–144) partly attributes the conflicts between Madurese migrants and indigenous Dayaks in Indonesia's West Kalimantan to the disdain that the Dayaks hold for the Madurese as irreligious, greedy, and overly aggressive; and the Madurese stereotype of the Dayaks as lazy and primitive.

Much of the problem of interethnic conflict arises from the connections between occupational and ethnic stereotypes. If a group is believed to have typical occupational roles, then the characteristics attributed to those roles may be attributed to the group. Thus, the possibility is that ethnic groups presumed to be in more remunerative occupations will be stereotyped as wealthier. For example, Lebanese in Senegal and other West African countries were reviled (and had their property confiscated) because of their roles as merchants, although many Lebanese in Senegal were involved in a host of other occupations (Leichtman 2005). Again, the experiences need not be direct interactions; they may be from perceptions – accurate or inaccurate – about the exercise of these roles. Campbell (1967, 286) noted that

An ethnic group specializing in physical labor ends up being stereotyped as strong, stupid, pleasure-loving, improvident (note, for example, the United States stereotypes of the Irish as of 1890). A group specializing in trade is stereotyped as grasping, deceitful, clever, sophisticated, domineering. When bureaucratic and technical occupations develop, groups so specializing are seen as ambitious, hard-driving, industrious, and aggressive.

Consequences of Enhancing Ingroup Esteem

Just as ingroup esteem is a powerful driver of ingroup affiliation, it frequently is a potent driver of attributions as well. Social identity theory offers the possibility that self-esteem may be enhanced if group members attribute admirable qualities to themselves, often in comparison with perceived less-admirable attributes of others. Tajfel (1982, 11) notes that "Social comparisons made by an individual may focus toward the ingroup or the outgroup. In the former case, the ingroup may provide a basis for the building up of a positive self-image, if it managed to preserve a system of positive evaluations about its 'folkways,' mode of life, social and cultural characteristics." Brewer and Kramer (1985, 224) summarize the links among identifying with a group, attributing positive characteristics to that group in contrast with others, and personal self-esteem. They stress "the role of social category membership, and of social comparison between categories, in the maintenance of a person's positive social identity, a role which leads individuals to seek distinctiveness between their own group and others, particularly on dimensions that are positively valued." Thus, insofar as positive self-regard is strengthened by believing that one's own group is superior to others, social identity theory is employed to account for negative stereotyping of outgroups.

The attribution of more favorable characteristics to ingroup members is not only consistent with the yearning for ingroup esteem, but also emerges from the fact that individuals can, at least to a certain degree, select and strengthen their identification with groups that are attractive because of their perceived positive attributes (Turner and Reynolds 2012). The emotional attachment to the ingroup is reinforced by the fact that the identification is favorable to individual self-esteem (Turner and Oakes 1986).

However, sometimes ingroup members hold negative self-attributions, whether or not espoused by outgroup members. Although the social identity framework emphasizes the attractiveness of focusing on positive ingroup attributes, it also recognizes that ingroup members might acknowledge the superiority of other groups, attributing to them greater economic achievement, technical skill, educational success, physical prowess, bravery, and so on. Tajfel and Turner (1986, 11) state that some groups "often seem to internalize a wider social evaluation of themselves as 'inferior' or 'second class.'" For example, for some Irulas, an Adivasi group in southern India, feelings of inferiority are reflected in linguistic behavior: "Irulas of Siruvani Hills are bilinguals and can also speak Tamil. Generally, they do not speak Irula in the presence of non-Irulas. Strikingly, due to their social insecurity and inferiority complex, they think that their speech is not a language" (Das 2013, 2). For the Indian Dalits, Nagamadhuri (2015, 111) notes that "The Dalits in India have long been suppressed to such an extent that they have been made to feel 'ashamed' of their own ancestors, history, values, and themselves. This sense of 'inferiority complex' has worked on their minds and influenced them to the core."

These negative ingroup attributions may be accepted by the ingroup insofar as the acceptance enhances their feelings of security that they live in a legitimate society. System justification theory explains accepting a lower status as a way to feel secure and validated as members of a legitimate society (Jost, Banaji, and Nosek 2004). The degree of conflict between groups of higher or lower status rests, in part, on whether instead of this reciprocal attribution of positive characteristics, one or both groups hold the other in contempt. Cambon, Yzerbyt, and Yakimova (2015, 142–143) note that

Research suggests that the coupling of perceived illegitimacy and instability of a given status system provides the most influential impetus for the rejection of the status hierarchy and, as a way of consequence, has a negative impact on inter-group relations and likely prompts competition …. Only if some difference between two groups is thought to be stable and legitimate will group members be inclined to refrain from competing with the outgroup …. The members of the high-status group should feel positive and securely positioned at the top of the social hierarchy. As a result, they should manifest ingroup bias on the dimension pertaining to the status difference (e.g., competence) and magnanimity towards the low-status group on the dimension unrelated to the status difference (e.g., warmth).

The distress of feeling inferior may be offset by highlighting their positive attributes, which might denigrate outgroups for being inferior with respect to these attributes. For example, "They are better at business, but we are more generous in our business dealings." Or, "They are brave – in a foolhardy way."

Attribution Biases

Several rather prevalent patterns exacerbate intergroup relations through distorted perceptions. Vorauer et al. (2000) and Techakesari et al. (2015) emphasize that ingroups may attribute characteristics to outgroups in reaction to what the ingroup believes are the outgroup's attitudes toward the ingroup. One particularly insidious bias rests on the ego-defensive tendency to disdain outgroup members whom the individual believes disdains the ingroup, whether correct or not. The psychological distress of believing that others hold negative attitudes toward the ingroup can be relieved by rejecting the worthiness of the outgroup.

Biases of causal inference can account for the belief that outgroup actions damaging to ingroup members are intentional, and therefore are motivated by malice. For Heider (1958) and other Gestalt theorists, the cognitive bias of focusing on individuals' actions rather than the situations that shape their actions accounts for the "fundamental attribution error" of overemphasizing *traits* of these people in contrast to situational factors in accounting for outcomes. Among (but not confined to) these traits are intentions. Insofar as individuals share circumstances and interact more intensively with ingroup members, they are likely to have more knowledge of the constraints that other ingroup members face.

In addition, it is psychologically comforting to believe that ingroup actions that do harm are due to circumstances rather than to ingroup discretion. Therefore, intentionality (rather than circumstances) is less likely to be attributed to ingroup members than to outgroup members, particularly in accounting for negative outcomes. Kelley (1973) reinforces this premise, arguing that "individuals tend to attribute responsibility for positive outcomes to themselves, and negative outcomes to others. This can be extended to group responsibility as well. A positive ingroup attribution is likely to induce a belief that competent and well-meaning ingroup members are unlikely to perform badly; less capable outgroup members are more likely to act badly deliberately, or simply to fail." This may lead ingroup members to deny responsibility, and the presumed contrast between malicious outgroup members and blameless ingroup members would increase intergroup antagonism even more.

Similarly, negative attributions of an outgroup's overall character may be generalized on the basis of holding the "wrong" beliefs and engaging in the "wrong" practices. Insofar as individuals regard their religioethical beliefs as uniquely correct, people of other beliefs and practices may be regarded as ignorant, morally less worthy, or both. The speakers of the standard form of a dominant language typically regard people who speak other variants as unsophisticated. This is especially true if the education system heavily emphasizes "proper" speech and writing.

Attributions of Policy Characteristics and Success

Attributions pertain to policy initiatives as well, in terms of both whether policy initiators are seen as truly committed to the policy as presented and whether the stated goals of the policy are likely to succeed. Part of the evaluation of a policy initiative is an extension of the evaluation, positive or negative, of the motivations of those responsible for enacting the policy.

Two models of how motives are inferred have been suggested. One is that individuals begin with the premise that the initiators have the same motives that the individuals would have in the same situation (as perceived), then adapted in accordance with additional available information (Epley et al. 2004). The other is the application of existing stereotypes, positive or negative, to infer a benevolent or malevolent motive to the initiative. Ames (2004) and Mitchell (2009), each summarizing several laboratory experiments, report that, unsurprisingly, the closer that individuals identify, or at least believe they share characteristics with, an actor, the more likely the first model will be employed.

Special attention must be paid to the scenario of prosperous people suspecting that the installed leftist leader will engage in the provocative populist model of challenging the constitutive arrangements of governance. Not all leftist "populists" pose this risk; some simply employ strongly redistributive rhetoric, or engage in strong pro-poor policies. The worry that prosperous people typically find most concerning is that redistributive policies will be linked with initiatives to weaken policy-making institutions that provide checks and balances to the populist leader trying to monopolize policymaking authority, typically denouncing the governance elite as much as the economic elite.

JUDGMENTS OF DESERVINGNESS

Apart from acceding to pro-poor policies out of self-interest, supporting pro-poor initiatives that require one's sacrifice requires a strong enough sense that the policies would provide sufficient benefit to sufficiently deserving people. This requires encouraging pro-poor predispositions, but only if validated by perceptions of deservingness. To promote perceptions of deservingness requires understanding the dynamics of these perceptions; rejection of pro-poor appeals can arise from negative attributions (Oorschot 2000; Wilkins and Wenger 2014).

Identity, Attributions, Deservingness Judgments, and Hostility   77

An individual's predisposition to make pro-poor sacrifices rests on a general commitment to make sacrifices for at least some of the poor and attributions of deservingness of these segments of the poor. If the self-attribution is that the individual's own assets are inadequate or under threat, perhaps no commitment would exist. Yet when a commitment does exist, the attributions regarding the poor in general or different segments of the poor become crucial. It is likely that many different categories of people could be regarded as needy to different degrees, and deserving to different degrees as well.

Policy initiatives vary in terms of impacts on different segments of the population, including differences among low-income people. For example, an initiative to pour resources into a particular province may well have a very different reception than an initiative to increase resources for a broad multiprovince region. Similarly, increasing the minimum wage would benefit people employed in firms required to adhere to the minimum wage, but may disadvantage those not covered by the regulation.

Beliefs of deservingness have multiple dimensions, shaped by attributions and behaviors of both the poor and the prosperous. Understanding the bases of deservingness requires insights across four aspects: the foundation of empathy required for sympathy, levels of deservingness judgments, criteria for judging deservingness, and deservingness in the context of aggressive actions by the poor.

A crucial point is the surprisingly large number of dimensions that can be invoked as the basis of deservingness, or rejected because of judgments that one or more aspects of deservingness are not present. Therefore, outlining the full range of possible deservingness criteria illustrates the broad potential variation in stances taken about the poor.

Criteria for Judging Deservingness

It is useful to distinguish ten dimensions of deservingness criteria, although substantial overlap is common.

High Need

An obvious criterion for the focus of benefits is the degree of perceived need. Whether need is sufficient to motivate a pro-poor sacrifice depends not only on whether the poor are seen as morally worthy, but also whether their distress is believed to be serious enough to warrant sacrifice by the prosperous.

Of course, people on the verge of starvation are likely to be considered as more deserving of assistance than well-fed people who cannot afford to send their children to school. Nevertheless, knowing whether a particular set of people is neediest, or even highly needy, is a different matter. For example, knowing the degree of poverty of a group targeted for an affirmative action initiative is difficult insofar as the interactions between the relatively wealthy and the group targeted for the initiative are limited. The degree of poverty in remote areas that might be prospects for poverty-alleviative regional development similarly may be speculative, as would the degree to which the regional development targeting would assist the neediest. The degree of neediness is also relevant in determining whether the benefits justifying the sacrifice are directly addressing their material needs. Pro-social predispositions that prompt charity to museums, concert halls, and other good works may be laudable, but they do not alleviate poverty directly.

Need has the perplexing status of being both objective and subjective, complicating the attribution of neediness even more. One obvious correlate of judgments of need is the perception of the depth of poverty. However, the lack of awareness of the magnitude of poverty, what resources are going into pro-poor programs, and other policies that impact the poor, means that people cannot comprehensively assess overall fairness. The exception, of course, is for people who have clearly suffered horrible fates, accounting for the groundswell of sympathy and assistance that typically follows major earthquakes and other natural disasters.

Given the often convenient presumption that the poor are not needy because they are accustomed with their low-income livelihoods, or that their work provides intrinsic rewards even if it relegates them to poverty, it is important to emphasize the other vulnerabilities that low incomes create. Indeed, some people do not want greater material wealth. For example, desert Bedouins, proud of their self-sufficiency and disdain for material accumulation beyond what is needed, feel superior to sedentary descendants of desert Bedouins (Paradise 2016). Yet such cases are rare. As a policy challenge, the question is how to improve the lives of such groups. It may be that health-care safety nets are the only social-service provision that government programs can provide. When the poor need cash for medical care, or for coping with natural disasters or forced dislocation, it should be obvious that presuming "contentment" with poverty is a thin excuse for neglecting the poor.

High Want

The relevance of the criterion of high need, as defined by societal standards, may be undermined by the belief that some of the poor, especially the very poorest, are living in a nonmaterial-oriented world. The most isolated Adivasi ("tribals") in India, or the Amazon-dwelling indigenous peoples, might be regarded as content with their "simple" folkways. However, high want by itself is difficult to determine and is not particularly compelling as a criterion of deservingness. Quite wealthy people may have very high levels of "want."

Helplessness

Among the poor who are seen as both needy and desiring benefits (need and want), those who have the least chance without assistance may be regarded as even more compelling than other needy people. The attribution of helplessness rests on an overall conception of the context in which this segment of the poor live.

Current Discrimination

One cause of helplessness is discrimination in employment, eligibility for benefits, or social exclusion. Current discrimination, insofar as it is recognized by more prosperous people, is often a compelling reason for the "reverse discrimination" of affirmative action or other targeted help. Some aspects of the perception of current discrimination include the difficulty of knowing whether the poor are excluded for legitimate reasons and recognizing subtleties of social discrimination suffered by others.

Rights

An increasingly prominent view is that all citizens deserve a minimum level of benefits simply as citizenship rights. Of course, many constitutions and laws pay lip service to the rights to education, health, and so on. Yet, the idea that material benefits actually would be adopted as an obligation of the state through transfers to the poor to ensure at least a "basic income" (Murray and Pateman 2012) as a citizenship right is much more radical.

The belief that a *particular* individual or group is entitled to benefits may rest on the premise that they are simply entitled apart from other considerations of deservingness. In some cases, this may beg the question as to why the group is deserving of this right. Yet, in other cases the basis of the right may be separate from other aspects of deservingness, such as constitutional or other legal guarantees, religious precepts, preexisting enjoyment of the benefits, and so on.

The justification that because a group had preexisting enjoyment of benefits, such as natural-resource user rights over land or water, is the basis for the so-called "sons of the soil" demands. Such demands are commonly based on claims of indigeneity, although these claims are often disputable. For example, Malay claims that they preceded Chinese migration into Malaysia are problematic insofar as many Malays are more recent immigrants from what is now Indonesia and other areas. Siddique and Suryadinata (1981, 666) report, "In British Malaya there was a general tendency for the diverse ethnic groups which represented the category called 'Other Malaysians' (for example, Javanese, Baweanese, Sundanese, Buginese, Minangkabau) to be assimilated into the Malay category, which was used to refer to Malays native to British Malaya."

Past Discrimination ("Reparations")
A group that is believed to have suffered grievous maltreatment in the past may be regarded as deserving special care in the present, out of simple fairness or expiation by those (or their forebears) who could be held responsible. The connection of reparations with the acknowledgment of guilt or at least past failure often blunts the motivation to provide reparations. In addition, nearly every group can refer to its own past maltreatment that reduces any sense of responsibility to make up for the past deprivations of others. The case is stronger insofar as has discrimination has residual impact on current capability and opportunities.

Righteousness
People perceived as righteous, in desisting from unacceptable behavior or beliefs, are likely to be regarded as more deserving than others. These others may be seen as criminals, substance abusers, and so on. For example, Doron (2010) asserts that in India, public opinion and public policies toward the poor are shaped by stereotypes of the poor that link their alleged excessive alcohol use to criminality and inability to progress. Moreover, insofar as negative stereotypes reduce the commitment to make sacrifices for the poor, the impulse to be selfish could be indulged with less feelings of guilt.

A more rarified aspect of perceptions of righteousness is favoritism toward people believed to be highly religiously observant, or even holy.

Identity, Attributions, Deservingness Judgments, and Hostility 81

They may be regarded as deserving to reward them for their sacrifices, for resisting temptation, or because the beliefs of the more prosperous call for supporting people who are deeply engaged in religious practices. The living "saints" in Mali and other West African countries receive gifts from devout Muslims (Soares 2004).

Diligence and Blamelessness for Poverty

Because people may be regarded as undeserving due to their unwillingness to earn or retain wealth, holding poor people blameless for their poverty has often been cited as a sine qua non for the willingness of others to sacrifice for those poor (Sniderman, Brody, and Tetlock 1991; Wilkins and Wenger 2014).

One of the few well-studied aspects of blame leading to low-assessment deservingness concerns judgments of laziness. Attitudes in Latin American countries – the developing region with the most advanced attitude surveys, indicate that the dynamics of such judgments are not as straightforward as one might think. As Table 3.1 demonstrates, the Latin American Public Opinion Project 2012 reported that Argentines, whether above or below the dividing line between less and more prosperous, are strikingly skeptical about the willingness of welfare recipients to work; and the less prosperous are even more skeptical than the more prosperous. In four of the six countries, the less prosperous respondents are, expectedly, less skeptical. Brazilians are the least skeptical, particularly among the less

TABLE 3.1 *Judgments of laziness attributed to welfare recipients, six most populous Latin American countries, 2012*

	Percent of less prosperous respondents attributing laziness to welfare recipients (%)	Percent of more prosperous respondents attributing laziness to welfare recipients (%)	Ratio of less prosperous to more prosperous respondents attributing laziness to welfare recipients
Argentina	74	69	1.07
Brazil	27	39	0.69
Chile	53	68	0.78
Colombia	44	39	1.13
Mexico	51	59	0.86
Peru	46	53	0.87

Source: Latin American Public Opinion Project 2012

prosperous respondents. In short, attitudes as to whether at least some of the poor are to be blamed for their own poverty are not straightforward.

These surveys, while illuminating, do not tap into differentiated judgments of different *segments* of the poor. Often the stereotypes undermining the assessment of deservingness are held about the poorest group. For example, other groups of Northeastern Luzon in the Philippines view the hunter-gatherer Agta as lazy (Page et al. 2018, 40). If the Agta are held up as "typical" of the poor, the impetus to make sacrifices will be undermined.

Potential for Improvement

Judging the value of benefiting some of the poor to relieve neediness also rests on whether the benefits would have a sustainable impact. Making sacrifices without being able to expect a sustainably positive effect is obviously questionable. The individual's preconceptions of the poor's capabilities are the key attributions. Another perspective is that the poor are wedded to modes of production that keep them poor, despite opportunities to adopt more productive modes. This perspective is a fairly common reaction to the frustrations of trying to train and provide incentives to farmers or artisans who then do not change. DeWalt and DeWalt (1980, 292) noted that "change agents" who had set up poorly attended schools to train Mexican farmers in modern agricultural and livestock technologies cited the lack of interest "as another example of how peasants in the region were resistant to change and content with their poverty." While this attitude may ignore rational risk aversion on the part of the non-adopters, nevertheless it is a widespread presumption.

Ingroup Priority

The relatively poor members within an individual's ingroup may be regarded as more deserving than others if they meet minimal standards of worthiness (e.g., they are not criminals), and the more prosperous members feel a fraternal responsibility. The poverty of ingroup members may diminish the self-esteem and external standing of the more prosperous members, dreading being disdained for "not taking care of their own." Therefore, many groups establish charities and foundations to support needier members of the ingroup, through direct financial support, scholarships, and so on. The appeals of within-group poverty-alleviation efforts include the opportunity to relieve the distress of fraternal deprivation. These efforts can also elevate ingroup esteem in demonstrating the achievements of its members and its capacity to look after its own, and

Identity, Attributions, Deservingness Judgments, and Hostility   83

possibly the greater sociopolitical standing of the group with its more uniformly prosperous membership.

In some circumstances, the revelation that some members of an otherwise prosperous ingroup are languishing in poverty could mobilize the prosperous members to support pro-poor policies that benefit all of the poor. However, because relatively poor members of an otherwise prosperous ingroup often are not be among the poorest people within the jurisdiction of potential policies, ingroup deservingness can divert pro-poor impulse away from supporting assistance for the neediest people. Bhavnani and Lacina (2015) highlight the "sub-national nativism" in India – the discrimination against migrants from other states. Insofar as states are defined by home language, and home language strongly correlates with other cultural aspects, identification with the state (e.g., Tamil Nadu, Karnataka, Kerala), the identification with people native to the state will be a closer ingroup identification. If it is believed that each state has native populations living in dire poverty, favoritism toward these peoples – and resulting discrimination against migrants from other states – does not mean that migrants are undeserving, but that they are less deserving than native state members. Stürmer and Snyder (2010, 41) carry this even further, arguing that

> First, one can expect that similar group membership between the helper and the person in need amplifies the impact of empathy in helping while, at the same time, it may attenuate the impact of potential individual costs for helping. Group-level similarity signals to the perceiver that the self and the other are "of the same kind" …. To the extent that people recognize aspects of themselves … in the other, the other's welfare becomes increasingly valued (not as a means toward some end, but, like one's own welfare, as an end in and of itself) …. Moreover, as people's focus of attention is on promoting or preserving the other's welfare (rather than their own welfare), they may pay less attention to the costs ensuing from this behavior for themselves.

This may be reinforced by the greater potential for knowledge-based empathy among people sharing identity. In contrast, the needs of impoverished people well outside of the ingroup simply may not be known by more prosperous individuals. A Malaysian Indian would probably be more likely to read a newspaper article about Malaysian Indians than an article about Malaysian Chinese. Second, whatever adverse experiences have been relatively common for the ingroup may be projected onto other members of the ingroup. Individuals are likely to be more aware and therefore sensitive to the insecurities shared by other ingroup members. Despite the deep polarization between the rich and poor in

The Underlying Psychology

Argentina, prosperous Argentines are more likely to believe that that other Argentines are more deserving of their assistance than, say, Bolivian immigrants.

These patterns often lead to the regrettable circumstance that the poorest people are the least likely to share elements of identity with the prosperous. However, prosperous individuals, who identify with a group on ascriptive grounds (ethnic, religious, linguistic, etc.) known to include a substantial portion of much poorer people, will view the poor more favorably and more deserving. One may also take solace in the possibility that the commitment to assist members of the ingroup can be reshaped by broadening the composition of what one regards as one's ingroup. This has been the hope of the national leaders of multiethnic countries such as India.

Thus, a critical question is whether broad pro-poor policies, that could provide assistance to many of the poor, can be attractive enough to prosperous members of mixed-income identity groups. A critical case in point is the Indonesian Chinese population, widely and inaccurately perceived as uniformly wealthy. Dahana (1997, 70) notes that Indonesian Chinese "are always identified with the rich"; the reality is that 70 percent of Indonesian Chinese are in modest occupations. Dawis (2009, 189) notes that "most [Indonesian Chinese] earn a living by becoming shop-keepers, handicraft and furniture sellers, and even road sweepers and trishaw pullers in the poorer areas of Indonesia." Prosperous Indonesian Chinese might support or acquiesce to broad pro-poor policies, yet the isolation of the Indonesian Chinese due to negative stereotypes against them increase the likelihood that the more prosperous would channel their altruistic impulse to support lower-income Indonesian Chinese.

Deservingness in the Context of Aggressive Poor

A particularly important scenario prevails when a segment of the poor takes aggressive actions to press for more resources. The prosperous may believe that these poor are undeserving because of the threat they pose. They may believe that the poor, instead of trying to improve their material situation through legitimate hard work, are trying in inappropriate ways to wrest assets from the more prosperous. The relationship between the poor and these others may be reframed as an instance of "realistic group conflict theory" (Sherif 1962). This could account for hostility toward the "threatening" group and the negative attributions toward that group as a way to rationalize the hostility.

Identity, Attributions, Deservingness Judgments, and Hostility   85

Alternatively, if the prosperous believe that these poor are legitimately aggrieved in how the economic structure or the social relations have kept the poor deprived, they are more likely to be sympathetic to the plight of the poor. If aggressive action results in physical violence or property destruction, the judgment by the prosperous needs to judge whether the poor had no choice but to be aggressive so that their demands could be taken into account.

Caveats Concerning Deservingness

It is important to note that not all prejudice leads to lower assessments of deservingness. A prejudiced assessment that people of a particular group are ignorant may predispose an individual to be willing to nurture members of that group. Nevertheless, many prejudicial attitudes feed into an assessment that a particular group is unworthy of assistance.

A norm of responsibility can overcome some negative stereotypes of the poor. Even if the poor are regarded as ignorant or feckless, the impulse of "care for the less fortunate" may be compelling. The case of the affirmative action provisions in India, explored in Chapter 7, initially benefited only the scheduled castes (Dalits) and scheduled tribes (Adivasi) – both widely regarded by other Indians as unsophisticated and of low capability. Similarly, conditional cash transfer (CCT) programs may be supported because of the belief that the conditions require poor families to overcome their presumed tendencies to ignore education and healthcare, and would deter a male head of household from squandering the cash on drink or gambling.

Even if some people meet one or more criteria of deservingness, a more prosperous individual may not be moved to help. A certain degree of pro-poor predisposition, typically reinforced by empathy, is necessary. Thus, an analysis of the multiple forms of empathy is in order.

Empathy
The fact that someone would believe that sacrifice is worth undertaking for other people requires recognizing – and caring about – the deprivations of the poor. Batson and Shaw (1991, 112) emphasize the role of empathy (essentially being able to imagine how others are thinking and feeling) as an important facilitator of appreciating need. The capacity for empathy promotes altruism, at least to some degree. Batson (2011, 7–8) distinguishes eight concepts of empathy: (1) knowing another person's internal state, including his or her thoughts and feelings; (2) adopting the

posture or matching the neural responses of an observed other; (3) coming to feel as another person feels; (4) intuiting or projecting oneself into another's situation; (5) current imagining how another is thinking and feeling; (6) imagining how one would think and feel in the other's place; (7) feeling distress at witnessing another person's suffering; (8) feeling for another person who is suffering.

Walter (2012, 9–10) argues that a reasonable simplification would be to distinguish between two constructs of empathy: "affective empathy and related affective phenomena on the one hand and cognitive empathy on the other hand." Thus, affective empathy entails sharing what the empathetic individual believes is the emotion felt by the target of empathy, or at least to have an emotional reaction consistent with the emotion of the target of empathy. Cognitive empathy entails understanding the situation of the target of empathy, possibly understanding the emotional state that this situation would cause in the target.

Limitations in knowledge about the poor can limit cognitive empathy, and hence affective empathy. For Bangladesh, Hossain and Moore (1999, 106) concluded that

The picture of elite understandings of poverty that we have constructed does not suggest heartlessness, the denial of affinity with the poor or responsibility for their welfare, contempt or, the kind of ignorant fear that can so easily turn into support for authoritarian political "solutions" to poverty. Instead, we find an elite group that (a) believe they have a real concern for the poor but actually know little about them; (b) would like to see more public action to tackle poverty but have little faith in the capacity of government to take effective action of any kind; (c) do not see poverty and the poor as a significant threat to their own lifestyle and welfare; and therefore (d) do not in practice see poverty as an urgent problem for any kind of action, public or private, and especially not for political action.

Despite the links between affective and cognitive empathy, the distinction is important. First, cognitive empathy, as the basis for recognizing that an individual or group is deprived, is a precondition of affective empathy. Second, even high levels of cognitive empathy may not elicit positive responses toward the poor. Even if prosperous people understand the situation of the poor, they may not find the plight of the poor to be compelling.

It is also important to recognize that both forms of empathy may involve some degree of inconsistency between the presumed and actual perspectives or emotions of the target of empathy. Shapiro and Gabbard (1994, 35) argue "empathy is not infallible – it can be accurate or inaccurate, depending on a multitude of factors, such as the quality and extent of the victim's expressiveness, the observer's perceptive ability, the observer's ability to identify with others, and the presence or absence of similar affective experiences in the observer's personal history."

Eisenberg and Miller (1987), based on an extensive meta-analysis of experimental findings, report mild to moderate positive correlations between empathy and altruism. However, in-depth cognitive empathy is not necessary for individuals to believe that others are in need. For example, an individual may presume that a situation that others experience would be a deprivation for that individual – "If *I* had such a low income, I would be miserable."

Several mechanisms can link empathy to altruism. Insofar as poor people share some aspects of identity, the perception of the similarities between the helper and the target will facilitate empathy (Batson et al. 1981, 2005). Empathy that arouses feelings of compassion for others who are perceived to be suffering may trigger altruistic behavior. Empathy in sharing the distress presumed to be felt by others may also trigger actions to help the others in order to reduce the individual's psychological distress (Batson, Fultz, and Schoenrade 1987; Stocks, Lishner, and Decker 2009). The distinction between the two emotional responses is important, because the reactions to distress caused by empathy might be reduced by turning away from the suffering people rather than taking actions to alleviate the suffering of targets of empathy.

PART III

LESSONS FROM PRO-POOR POLICY INSTRUMENTS

4

Conditional Cash Transfers

Conditional cash transfer (CCT) programs provide funds to low-income families if they maintain their eligibility by fulfilling conditions such as school attendance and regular healthcare for their children. Some programs require recipients to work or attend training programs.[1] By far the most common practice is to provide the money to the female head of household. This chapter focuses on the highly prominent Brazilian and Mexican CCT programs. These pioneering cases illustrate the psychology of esteem reinforcement for those who support these programs, reflected in the opportunity for noblesse oblige on the part of relatively prosperous people and to assert control over "less-accomplished" people. These cases also reflect the ambiguity of outgroup identification, as shown by the grave difficulties of establishing who is eligible for the benefits. Regarding the psychology of deservingness attribution, compliance with the conditions may be a crucial basis for deeming low-income people as worthy of benefits. The cases thus highlight the intersection of deservingness attributions, as outlined in Chapter 3, and the highly contentious issue of whether the poor are entitled to a "basic income" as a citizenship right (Murray and Pateman 2012). For countries with people clearly receiving less than what would be considered a "basic income," embracing the basic income as a right would mean a stain on the nation as a whole, challenging the self-esteem of the relatively prosperous. In contrast, the view that income requires responsible effort is consistent with the demand that cash transfers require compliance with conditions.

---

[1] An overview of CCTs within the broader context of social protection programs overall can be found in Grosh et al. (2008).

The implications for the identities of CCT participants are complicated. The identities of CCT participants – largely women – are shaped by the need to be compliant. In Mexico, for example, in addition to the childcare requirements, recipients have to participate in community activities (*faendas*) (Corona and Gammage 2017; González de la Rocha 2006). Although the rationale is empowerment, the control by administrators or by more prominent community members (*promotoras*) places most of the women in a subservient position. Cookson (2016) reports how in rural Peru, the women are subject to the directions, sometimes dictated in a heavy-handed way, by administrators of higher socioeconomic status.

On the other hand, compliant families can enhance their self-esteem and external reputation by demonstrating their responsibility. However, families that resort to deception to receive benefits despite lacking formal eligibility are exposed to ethical compromise. If excluded families reject the arbitrariness of eligibility and the legitimacy of demanding conditions, their identity may reflect an element of defiance vis-à-vis the state. Inclusion errors resulting from patronage add to the potential for cynicism on the part of the poor, whether participating in the program or not.

BACKGROUND

CCTs have been the most prominent poverty-alleviation initiative worldwide for the past two decades. Some programs were consolidations and expansions of preexisting programs, as in Mexico and Brazil. Some were introduced in economic-emergency situations, as in Argentina. Others were introduced to accompany and soften the impact of structural adjustment initiatives that otherwise would harm low-income families and possibly provoke disruptions, as in Indonesia and Turkey. CCTs are present in almost all Latin American countries and found in some countries in other developing regions (Molina Millán et al. 2018). Some programs are very modest, such as Cambodia's scholarships to female students at risk of dropping out of school (Molina Millán et al. 2018, 20). Some are quite significant in terms of the resources devoted to them, but only if the full set of expenditures associated with the program are taken into account.

This last point has important political significance. A potential selling point of CCTs is that the budget commitment, as a proportion of the GNP, is modest; the highest is 0.4 percent for the largest programs: Brazil and Mexico (Higgins and Pereira 2014). The likelihood that taxpayers would not recognize the associated budget commitments, especially to expand education and health services to accommodate the greater demand from families complying with the conditions, would keep the awareness of the full costs fairly low. Superficially, CCTs seem like a small price to pay for relatively prosperous people to indulge their noblesse oblige. This is reinforced by the claim that society as a whole benefits through the improvement of human capital, which would enhance the nation's long-term productivity. They can reduce conflict if implemented when expensive government subsidies are removed. In Indonesia, the 2005 cash transfer program introduced along with a dramatic reduction of budget-draining fuel subsidies in all likelihood helped to prevent the fuel riots that typically occur after subsidies are slashed (Widianto 2007).

Referring to the acceptance of CCTs in Latin America, Britto (2008, 186) argues

that there appears to be a broad consensus on the "public" nature of goods, such as education or health in the region . . .. In this sense, the fact that CCTs are related both to the present living conditions of poor children, and future human capital and (with presumably positive effects in competitiveness) make them acceptable to middle-class voters and elites. They are seen as a way of helping the "deserving poor" to escape poverty and, simultaneously, boosting the elusive phenomenon of sustained national economic growth.

CCTs are vulnerable to several operational and political obstacles. Obviously, a bureaucratic overhead is required to identify recipients and monitor compliance with the conditions, although NGOs may be able to assume much of this burden in order to safeguard the bulk of the transfer in order to assist the neediest families. Requiring school enrolment and children's healthcare could add so much to the demand on these social services that the quality of the services may decline. Some families may be too poor to keep children in school or obtain healthcare (Medrano 2013, 209). In addition, the funding may be precarious. As Graham (2002, 18) notes

Given the extent of need and limited public funds, some targeting will always be necessary. On the other hand, too much emphasis on targeting in the context of high numbers of eligible poor can result in the very poorest being left out. This is a particular concern if the program uses demand-based criteria in the allocation process, as the experience of the Trabajar program in Argentina suggests. A recent study of an effort to limit Trabajar funds found that it was the poorest recipients who ended up losing program support, as the more vocal demands of more organized, less poor groups were more successful at accessing increasingly limited funds . . .. In other words, effective targeting of the poorest in the context of high levels of eligible poor requires sufficient funds.

Contrary to Britto's assertion of broad consensus among elites and middle-class voters on the virtues of CCTs, considerable anti-CCT opposition exists, even in the countries where they are prominent. Therefore, Graham's concern of budget shortfalls must be taken seriously. Understanding the sources of opposition is complicated. One might expect that people who are poor but not so poor as to qualify for CCTs would oppose them out of envy, or on the grounds that they divert resources away from a broader range of the poor. However, in Latin America at least, anti-CCT attitudes can be inferred not only from agitation for the basic income approach but also from defections from voting for incumbents committed to CCT programs. This indicator reveals that the opposition comes from elites and well-to-do people in general. Corrêa and Cheibub (2016, 67), relying on surveys conducted by the Latin American Public Opinion Project, find that for governments prominently committed to CCT programs, "[r]icher, better-educated, liberal, and skeptical citizens who had voted for the incumbent in the past tend to abandon that electoral base and switch their loyalty to the opposition." They conclude that "it is fair to say that the Latin American upper classes are likely to react strongly and negatively to targeted cash transfers and tax increases" (Corrêa and Cheibub 2016, 52). A kinder diagnosis than elite indifference (López 2013) is that the wealthy may favor other means to improve the well-being of the poor (Reis 2005), such as greater expenditure in education. Perhaps an unstated concern of relatively prosperous people is that cash transfers, even if conditional, could open up the floodgates to more extreme demands for redistribution. It also may be that relatively poor people who are not currently eligible for transfers similarly may regard current programs as a step toward greater redistribution, and therefore would not want to undermine the establishment and potential expansion of CCTs.

Beyond the practical issues of CCTs are psychological aspects related to outlooks regarding deservingness. López (2013), focusing on Brazil and Uruguay, concludes that the elites lack a sense of responsibility to improving the lot of the poor. As outlined in Chapter 3, deservingness judgments become moot if a sense of responsibility is lacking. Any guilt associated with a self-serving rejection of such programs can be assuaged by condemning the inevitably somewhat poor targeting of the programs. For prosperous people who pride themselves on their hypervigilance, these possibilities may both reinforce their negative stereotypes of the poor and provide a rationalization for opposing transfers. In addition, the ambiguity as to who qualifies can lead to violence. Indonesia has had episodes of villagers attacking the village headman over decisions on CCT eligibility.

The primary focus of this chapter is on Brazil and Mexico, the two pioneers in establishing CCT programs. Not only are these programs bigger than any others, they were also established before the international financial institutions validated this approach through both research and funding. Therefore, the acceptance of CCT initiatives had to be earned without the imprimatur of these institutions.

BRAZIL

With the coverage of roughly 14 million families and 48 million beneficiaries, Brazil's *Bolsa Familia* is the world's largest cash transfer program. The program "alone explains between 10 percent and 15 percent of the reduction in income inequality observed in the 2000s" (World Bank 2016b, 106). Both this program and the Mexican counterpart discussed in the next section are credited with reducing the Gini coefficients, which had been at 60 for Brazil and 54 for Mexico, by 2.7 points in each case, after the effective implementation of the CCT programs. This may seem strange in light of the small fraction of GDP devoted to CCTs. However, a rigorous analysis by a team from the Instituto de Pesquisa Econômica Aplicada, the UNDP International Poverty Centre, and the Carnegie Endowment for International Peace established this reduction, controlling for changes in labor income, social security transfers, and other income sources (Soares et al. 2009).[2]

Bolsa Familia was formally enacted as a federal program in 2003, but it is useful to note that CCT programs in Brazil originated at the subnational level. As early as 1995, the Federal District and the city of Campinas instituted cash transfers conditioned on school attendance. Both school attendance and health care for the children were

---

[2] They explain

> The conditional cash transfers proved to be an important inequality-reducing factor in all three countries – in Mexico and Brazil they were surpassed only by labor income. But their contribution to the fall in inequality was disproportionately high given their small share in total income. With a share less than 1% of the total income in all three countries [Chile was included in their analysis], the CCTs were responsible for 15% of inequality reduction in Chile and 21% in Brazil and Mexico. Just to give an idea of the relative impact on inequality of the CCTs, in both Mexico and Brazil they were more than enough to counteract the increase in the concentration in social security incomes, although their share in total income amounts to a fraction of the latter.

96 Lessons from Pro-Poor Policy Instruments

conditionalities in Campinas. Soares (2011, 56) points out that these programs emerged in the context of intense discourse as to whether Brazil should adopt a guaranteed basic income as a right of citizenship. Thus, the premise that families must earn the transfer was controversial from the outset.

In 1997, the federal government offered a 50 percent education-conditioned cost-sharing arrangement to low-income municipalities, which attracted only a fraction of qualified cities. In 2001, the federal government established a countrywide education-conditioned transfer program, a health-care-conditioned program, and an unconditional cash transfer program to offset the higher cooking gas prices due to the reduction of subsidies. Other programs, covering child labor and food insecurity, added to the cluttered set of programs and bureaucracies. Like the affirmative action program that President Cardoso initiated in the same year, the cash transfer programs can be understood as an effort, ultimately unsuccessful, to weaken the appeal of the more leftist Workers Party.

In preparation to handover the government to the Workers Party in 2003, the Cardoso administration recommended the consolidation of these cash transfer programs, to overcome problems of coordination and duplication. A new Ministry for Social Development and Confronting Hunger was established to oversee the program.

According to Britto (2008), this Ministry's leaders, in keeping with the doctrine of the citizen's right to a guaranteed basic income, did not consider the conditionalities to be of high priority. The backlash against this position is illuminating in terms of attitudes toward deservingness:

The initial position adopted by the [Brazilian] government agency in charge was that monitoring whether beneficiaries were complying with the programme's conditionalities was not a priority: the cash transfer provided by *Bolsa Familia* was to be seen as a citizenship right, in the context of a basic income approach, and the conditionalities are simply a reinforcement of basic universal rights . . .. Nevertheless, the media and the general public do not appear to have accepted this perspective. With the news that the federal government did not in fact check whether beneficiary families were ensuring their children's attendance at school and/or visiting health centers reach the newspapers, opponents from both the left and the right united to accuse the government of transforming a genuinely innovative scheme into an old-fashioned and paternalistic handout. Urgent measures had to be taken by programme managers to create a system to monitor these conditionalities and, if they were not met, to put in place corresponding sanctions (eventually leading to the suspension of benefits).

(Britto 2008, 187)

Conditional Cash Transfers

Even at that, the transfers to the very poorest families were unconditional, reflecting the deservingness criterion of high need.

In principle, the explicit criteria of eligibility, and monitoring of compliance, would ensure that deserving families, and only deserving families, would receive *Bolsa Familia* benefits. However, unlike many other CCTs (including Mexico's *Prospera*) that use proxy means tests, eligibility for *Bolsa Familia* is based on self-reported income, only loosely cross-checked by federal indicators that cover only formal-sector wages. According to Soares, Ribas, and Osório (2010, 177), although fewer than 10 percent of non-poor Brazilians receive CCT benefits, nearly half of the Brazilian beneficiaries are not technically eligible (compared to just over a third of the Mexican beneficiaries).[3]

The decision to require conditions, a combination of fairly easily evadable income restrictions and lax monitoring, left Bolsa Familia in the ambiguous status of denying that benefits are a right, but making it more open than the formal targeting dictated. This openness has left Bolsa Familia vulnerable to accusations of patronage. Soares (2011, 55) concludes "That the programme is not embedded as a right has lent it the flexibility to adapt but also brought it under more scrutiny and accusations of being used for political purposes than any other social assistance or protection project in the country."

Mexico

Mexico's Prospera (formerly Oportunidades, established in 2002 but based on a more limited 1997 Progresa program) is one of the oldest and largest CCTs, providing benefits for a quarter of Mexican families. Although the 0.4 percent of GDP is modest compared to remittances

---

[3] For the 2000–2011 period, Stampini and Tornarolli (2012, 3) found that the exclusion rate was roughly 45 percent for all poor families; Soares, Ribas, and Osório (2010, 177) estimated 59 percent, based on 2004 poverty rates. From the perspective of covering poor families unconditionally, this would be regarded as a huge disappointment, but not necessarily from the perspective of rewarding the people qualified and willing to adhere to conditions. Regardless of whether the excluded have been noncompliant or simply have been neglected, the partial coverage could reinforce the perception that the program is reserved to the deserving. However, the leakage to beneficiaries who did not meet eligibility requirements was roughly 50 percent according to both the Stampini and Tornarolli and Soares, Ribas, and Osório estimates. To be sure, most of these technically unqualified recipients are rather poor themselves. Nevertheless, the combination of exclusion and leakage dilutes the targeting of the program, just as the Afro-Brazilian affirmative action program has as well.

98 *Lessons from Pro-Poor Policy Instruments*

constituting roughly 2.2 percent of GDP, remittances go to only 7 percent of households (Doyle 2015; World Bank 2016a). Moreover, like other CCTs, the Mexican program entails other costs and sacrifices by non-recipients. The need to meet the increased primary educational demand has required diversion of funds away from tertiary education. Lustig, López Calva, and Ortiz Juarez (2014, 137) report that

The relative ratio of spending per student in tertiary versus primary education declined from a historical maximum of 12 in 1983–88, to less than 6 in 1994–2000 …. More resources on the supply-side and the implementation of demand-side subsidies for education through Progresa/Oportunidades changed the incidence of public spending on education from being slightly regressive in 1992 to being progressive in 2006.

In parallel, the greater demand on the health system increased public spending as a proportion of GDP by 23 percent.[4] The 2016 OECD assessment of the Mexican health system concluded that "The most important health system reform of recent years was the introduction of *Seguro Popular* (SP) in 2004, which extended publicly-funded health insurance to 50 million Mexicans who were previously uninsured."

The case provides three insights. One is that sustainable cash transfer programs can emerge from short-term considerations; in this case the concern over social dislocation and political uproar when Mexico entered the NAFTA free-trade agreement with Canada and the United States. Second, in the Mexican context of a long but checkered history of social welfare programs, the highly rule-based program serves to legitimize social spending that previously had been accused of unfair patronage – even if patronage still exists. Finally, each iteration has given successive governments the opportunity to relabel, restructure, and expand the program.

Mexico, like other Latin American countries, has long had social welfare systems, largely built up piecemeal through programs with restricted sets of beneficiaries for restricted reasons. The exception was the PRONASOL Program (1989–1994), so ambitious that Diaz Cayeros and Magaloni (2003, 2–3) estimate that *if* it had been precisely targeted to the poorest Mexicans, it would have alleviated a third of Mexico's poverty. The dominant PRI Party, for the first time challenged by parties on the Right and the Left, needed to address the growing perception of

---

[4] From 2.6 percent in 2000 to 3.2 percent in 2013, in constant dollars (OECD 2016, 119; Sáenz de Miera Juárez 2017, 26).

corruption, electoral fraud, and patronage. The PRI therefore, presented PRONOSAL as a decentralized approach that would avoid the pattern of presidential patronage. President Salinas de Gortari, with the strong PRI congressional majority, was able to quadruple the PRONASOL budget over the course of his presidential term (Diaz Cayeros and Magaloni 2003, 3). However, Diaz Cayeros and Magaloni (2003, 2) point out that despite the regionally decentralized structure, it was centralized in terms of how the Salinas administration directed the resources to politically key areas (Diaz Cayeros and Magaloni 2003; Kaufman and Trejo 1996; Niño-Zarazúa 2016).

The Salinas administration also launched the 1994 PROCAMPO Program, which provided cash transfers to farmers to compensate for the reduction in price supports that the highly controversial NAFTA Agreement required. Just as cash transfers were implemented in Indonesia to compensate low-income families when fuel-price subsidies were cut in 2005, PROCAMPO had the dual purpose of social protection and the political motive of blunting the potential for disruption.[5]

In 1997, *Progresa* consolidated the cash transfer mechanisms and, for the first time, instituted an elaborate system of eligibility and monitoring for low-income rural families to qualify for CCTs. The program eclipsed a food subsidy program that was draining the national budget largely for the sake of the urban sector, even though poverty was concentrated in rural areas (Niño-Zarazúa 2016, 4). *Progresa* remained restricted to the rural sector until 2000, when it was extended to the urban poor as well. This was assisted by the largest loan ever made by the Inter-American Development Bank (IADB). The IADB and the World Bank have lent more than US$6 billion, allowing the Mexican government to stretch out taxpayers' financial obligation.

Following the unprecedented defeat of the PRI in 2000, Vicente Fox of the Partido de Acción Nacional did not attempt to dismantle the program. Under yet another label *Prospera* (relabeled in 2014, under another PRI administration), has maintained essentially the same structure.

This program illustrates how a patronage-based, undisciplined approach to poverty alleviation could be transformed into a highly explicit, systematic approach. Ironically, it has been criticized as a "complex mechanism of social engineering" (Standing 2008, 14). Standing adds

---

[5] The demonstration of the seriousness of this potential was the "Zapatista revolt" in southern Mexico that occurred despite PROCAMPO.

The cash transfer consists of three components – a household nutrition allowance, a schooling subsidy for each school-age child that rises in amount by grade and that is higher for girls of secondary-school age, and an annual payment to cover the cost of books and uniforms. To complete the social engineering function, the amount of cash transfer that any household can receive is capped, one intention being to avoid giving families an incentive to have more children, another being to reduce what the policymakers think might be benefit dependence. To receive the transfers, children must maintain a school attendance record of 85 percent, while mothers and children must have regular medical checks and parents must attend parenting classes.

(Standing 2008, 14)

However, the critique by Standing and others of the Program's paternalism needs to be assessed as a reaction to the prior criticisms of the pre-*Progresa* favoritism that did a far poorer job of concentrating on the neediest families. An assessment of *Oportunidades-Prospera* also needs to recognize the importance of conveying the commitment to assist only the deserving. Of course, some formally ineligible families have received benefits, just as some potentially eligible families have not. Even so, the doctrine of *aiming* for a CCT that would serve only the deserving is certainly compelling to some of the prosperous population.

Brazil, Mexico, and Deservingness

Brazil and Mexico have somewhat different profiles in the contexts and rationales for pro-poverty programs. The Mexican governments have been able to justify the expansions of social welfare programs on both long-term considerations – human resource improvement to enhance the productive workforce (Reid 2016) and bringing them into the market economy – and the short-term deservingness criterion of need, as Mexico was beset by economic transitions and crises that clearly increased the vulnerability of low-income families. The Mexican CCT expansions were crisis responses. The Brazilian governments, generally riding high on the economic growth during most of the 2000s, were more directly addressing the preexisting and more pervasive poverty. Brazil's tax effort has been more successful than Mexico's as well, and, as mentioned in Chapter 7, Brazilians have had to face the stigma of having the world's most unequal income distribution.

The governments of the two countries share the concern that social welfare policies are vulnerable to accusations of patronage, and therefore vulnerable to rejection by prosperous people. The conditionality, although enforced inconsistently in both cases, has been, at a minimum, a commitment to develop a system targeting the deserving. This has been an increasing challenge, as the expansion of coverage has meant the expansion of leakage to ineligible families (Stampini and Tornarolli 2012, 15).

However, some degree of leakage can be an advantage in securing adequate support from people who might otherwise believe that they or other members of their ingroups would benefit. Pritchett (2005, 5) notes that "while 'leakage' is often discussed as if one wanted to eliminate it altogether, it is easy to construct models that explicitly bring in considerations of political economy in which *even from the point of view of the poor* more leakage is better." This logic holds as well for other limited benefits, such as the subsidies for goods and services and inclusion in CCT programs.

In general, then, CCT designs strive to overcome two, often difficult, challenges to overcome the temptation of prosperous people to reject the deservingness of the poor. First, CCTs are intended to indulge the self-esteem of prosperous people who might otherwise begrudge sacrificing their taxes for the poor. Second, CCTs can mitigate the problem of perceptions of unworthiness. Adhering to program rules demonstrates the worthiness of the families. Both should be understood in terms of the importance of perceptions of deservingness, which in turn depend on the stereotypes of the characteristics of the poor. Standing (2008, 9–10) asserts that "policymakers and their advisers use conditionality as a political device to legitimize the transfer with middle-class voters and financial agencies." In this sense, critiques of CCTs – that they are paternalistic instruments of social engineering – miss the point that paternalistic social engineering enhances the attractiveness of the CCT model. Prosperous people might oppose transfers to the poor who are not held to some requirements. The support for CCTs demonstrates that regardless of whether surveys indicate an overall perception that poor people are lazy or irresponsible, prosperous people can distinguish among the poor through programs that reward responsibility.

CCTs have additional attractions from the perspective of esteem-seeking prosperous people. In supporting CCTs that require the norms of attending to child welfare, they are affirming their own commitment to these values. They are also in the estimable position of dictating, if only indirectly, the behavior of others in a paternalistic fashion. While this last point can attract prosperous people gratified to support a program that formally assists only those who meet the program criteria, other people, whether wealthy or poor, dispute the appropriateness of conditions.

102 Lessons from Pro-Poor Policy Instruments

The perspective that poverty is a condition brought on by an unfair economic structure denies the fairness of imposing conditionalities. Standing (2008, 10) argues that "the growing interest in conditional cash transfers as an aid and development tool will lead to a realization that most forms of selectivity and conditionality are conveniences at best while being costly, inequitable, inefficient and offensive to basic egalitarian principles."

5

Social-Sector Spending Targeting the Poor

The magnitude of government-provided pro-poor social services is the product of the overall budget allocation for social services and the degree to which this budget is concentrated to the poor. Enormous variation exists in how governments finance and deliver social services, and how these services can be targeted especially to the poor. This chapter highlights the psychological bases for supporting or opposing additional government spending that directly targets the poor by focusing on two cases of wide swings in such funding: Argentina and Brazil. The psychological dynamics include the presumption of malice toward outgroup leaders involved in policy disagreements. The ebullient moods during economic booms, as shown in the Brazilian case, can overcome the polarization that attributions of malice can create. Thus, the Brazilian case demonstrates the possibility of inducing noblesse oblige sentiment to counter the shame that would erode the self-esteem of the relatively prosperous, for whom the national identification has been highly salient. Yet, the swings in mood can reverse this sentiment dramatically. Argentina, in particular, lacking the sustained booms that have created optimism during periods in Brazil, demonstrates the powerful impact of extreme stereotyping, stark polarization, fraternal deprivation, and the dynamics of mutual disdain.

GENERAL BACKGROUND

Bias in Existing Social-Service Spending

Three factors limit the degree to which social spending benefits the poor in education, healthcare, and protection from employment disruption. First, the social-service budget may be allocated to services relatively inaccessible for the poor. Second, deficits in a particular social service may reduce the effectiveness of other services (e.g., poor health limiting educational attainment). Third, social service quality may be low because of the preference of service providers for employment in more prosperous settings.

Education

Despite the progress made since 2000 in primary-education enrollment rates in both middle- and low-income countries, it is important to take the quality of education into account as the basis for higher productivity. It is concerning that the quality of primary education in low-income countries is undermined not only by limited funding, but also by the increased pressure on the education system due to the widespread reforms of extending mandatory years of attendance. These reforms, which often enhance the reputation of the government insofar it appears to represent a greater commitment to education, is a case of restriction by partial incorporation if the education budget is not increased to accommodate the greater number of students. The World Bank's most recent comparable (2013) estimates of the proportion of gross national product devoted to primary education by the lowest-income countries (those eligible for World Bank Group concessional loans or grants) is only 10 percent. This compares to 14.4 percent for countries eligible for standard World Bank loans and 19.3 percent for the OECD countries. The most recent (2011) comparable estimates for the proportion of gross national product devoted to secondary education is 16.8 percent for "low-income countries," compared to 25.1 percent for OECD countries.[1]

The expenditures on higher education reveal a bias in favor of wealthier people in allocating lower expenditures on primary and secondary education and higher expenditures on tertiary education compared to developed countries. The World Bank estimates the proportion of gross domestic product devoted to tertiary education for developed countries to be between 12 and 13 percent, whereas for developing countries the range is between 16 and 17 percent.[2] Considering that smaller proportions of students in developing countries attend tertiary education, this comparison is strong evidence of overinvestment in tertiary education in such countries. Supporting this assessment are evaluations in particular

---

[1] These data from World Bank indicators do not report the same years or categories for the primary and secondary education expenditures (World Bank 2019).

[2] World Bank (2019).

Social-Sector Spending Targeting the Poor

regions. A 2008 World Bank assessment of education in the Middle East and North Africa asserted that "the pattern of public expenditure is biased in favor of students at higher levels of education compared with other regions, which reflects a bias in favor of the socially privileged class" (World Bank 2008, 33). Torche (2014, 18), comparing Latin American countries to developed countries, concludes that "Latin American public spending is less progressive, favoring higher education, which favors the middle class." Thyne and Moreno (2008, 926) add that the disruptive potential of middle-class students has played a major role: "The root of the unequal distribution of educational funding favoring university education stems from student protests during the 1960s, which prompted governments to grant either free or heavily subsidized university education." For Brazil, featured so prominently in this book, Wjuniski (2013, 162) notes "the misallocation of public resources between the levels, favoring higher education in the long-run and leaving secondary education behind." For India, an equally prominent case, Balatchandirane (2000, 194) concludes that at the start of this century, "[t]he Indian State acquiesced with the attempts of the socially dominant classes to increase their stranglehold on the resources of the State and perpetuate the skewed distribution of the educational sector favoring higher education."

In addition, the rural–urban education gaps remain very high, particularly in South Asia and sub-Saharan Africa (United Nations Development Programme 2013, 121, 136, 140). The typically greater poverty in the rural sector is both a result of poorer economic status and a cause for inferior education, as more qualified teachers often prefer to teach in urban areas.

The difficulty of financing education in developing countries is illustrated by the perverse consequences of eliminating tuition fees.[3] This widespread reform does relieve low-income families from one fee. However, Mugo, Moyi, and Kiminza (2016) argue that eliminating tuition fees often reduces teacher-student ratios and erodes the quality of teaching. In addition, other fees for uniforms, transportation, and school supplies typically remain impediments to school attendance.

---

[3] Koski et al. (2018, 4) provide a partial list of nations that eliminated tuition fees: Cameroon, Ethiopia, Ghana, Kenya, Malawi, Rwanda, Uganda, Zambia, Benin, Burkina Faso, Burundi, Lesotho, Mozambique, Namibia, Tanzania. Zimbabwe is noted as not having eliminated the tuition fees.

106   *Lessons from Pro-Poor Policy Instruments*

Healthcare

Insofar as rural people are predominantly poor, their lack of access to quality health services means that this typically large segment of the poor population is disadvantaged. Rural health clinics have greater difficulty in attracting highly qualified healthcare professionals unless they are paid premia to live outside of the cities. Moreover, the economic rationales for placing sophisticated medical equipment in rural clinics are lacking. Second, in many countries the greatest risk for the poor is exposure to communicable diseases, requiring both major investment in sanitation and medical services geared to treat these diseases. In contrast, for more prosperous people, the balance between risks of communicable and non-communicable diseases tilts further toward the noncommunicable diseases. Third, the enhancement of national prestige favors spending on tertiary-care hospitals.[4]

Protection from Employment Disruptions

Government support for low-income people facing employment disruptions has been an enormous challenge, taking different forms depending on whether the disruptions are widespread and acute, or chronic vulnerability that affects more limited numbers of people. Widespread, acute disruptions caused by economic recessions or natural disasters occur precisely when governments are stressed by the disruptions themselves. Governments may respond with emergency cash transfers, but long-term assistance for protection during long recoveries is often lacking.

Equally important, the coverage of conventional unemployment insurance programs is typically restricted by the limited scope of the formal sector, which in turn severely limits the collection of

---

[4] Castro-Leal et al. (2000, 68) reported that for Côte d'Ivoire, Ghana, Guinea, Madagascar, South Africa, and Tanzania:

> These countries have three-tiered public health systems, with basic clinics and dispensaries at the first level, district level hospitals at the secondary level, and referral and speciality hospitals at the tertiary level. Resources (and hence services) are generally concentrated at the tertiary level. Typically, less than 25% of recurrent expenditures accrue to the primary level .... In almost all countries, health care personnel (particularly physicians) are concentrated in urban areas, where they provide tertiary level care, and are comparatively scarce in rural areas' Although resources and services are heavily focused on specialized health care, the main causes of illness and death in all seven countries are preventable and easily treated diseases, such as acute respiratory illness, diarrhea, and malaria. In Madagascar it is estimated that 90% of illnesses could be prevented or treated at the primary level, provided the services are of good quality and accessible to the majority of the population.

contributions by either employers or employees (Perry et al. 2007). The recent innovation of individual savings accounts to cover employment disruptions requires administrative capacity that many developing countries lack (Vodopivec 2013).

Budget and Administrative Dynamics

The capacity to increase social services to low-income people requires a breadth of changes, not only in budget allocations but also in administrative effort. Often, laws and regulations, and new institutions, are required as well. Such changes involve greater risk and uncertainty, typically leaving open heuristic dynamics that could set relatively prosperous people at odds with these initiatives if previous experiences are believed to have had adverse consequences for them. When the explicit commitment to expand social services for low-income families goes unfulfilled because of administrative bottlenecks, the poor are more likely to resent what they are apt to see as false promises.

ARGENTINA: POPULISM AND POLARIZATION

For decades, Argentina has choked itself on polarization and cynicism. The Argentine paradox is that despite strong economic potential, and widespread pro-poor and redistributive sentiment, middle-income Argentines have resisted initiatives claiming to be pro-poor and lower-income Argentines have opposed sound productivity-enhancing initiatives. From 2003 to 2015, a populist leadership that knew that it could never win over the Center or Right, and requiring continued support from the embittered and vulnerable Left, engaged in profligate spending that antagonized the Center and Right even more, and led to economic collapse.

On the one hand, prosperous Argentines, even more than those of many of other Latin American countries, believe in the importance of sound government programs for social protection as well as economic growth. Surveys indicate that Argentines of all income levels have been sympathetic to the plight of the poor. Among respondents surveyed in seventeen Latin American nations, Argentines were the most dismissive of the premise that equal economic opportunity exists for all (Graham 2002, 21). More recent surveys confirm the prevalence of the Argentine interpretation that poverty is not the fault of the poor. Camacho Solis (2012, 40–42) summarizes the contemporaneous surveys in Argentina

108   *Lessons from Pro-Poor Policy Instruments*

and Peru: nearly three-quarters of surveyed Argentines believe that those in need are poor because society treats them unfairly, compared to 62 percent among Peruvians. Moreover, only 16 percent of the Argentine respondents who believe that the poor are unfairly treated believe that there is a chance for the poor to succeed, compared to 39 percent among Peruvians. Therefore it is not surprising that the 2010 survey of the Latin American Public Opinion Project found that 82 percent of Argentine respondents agreed with the statement that "The Argentine state must implement firm policies to reduce inequality" (Lodola and Seligson 2011, 282).

Yet the combination of policy impasses, economic crises, and ineffective protection of the poor from economic downturns has yielded both overall economic stagnation and even less growth for the poor. From 1980 to 2017, per capita income increased by only 29 percent. The income share of the bottom quintile of the population in 1980 was 5.3 percent; their share in 2016[5] was 5.0 percent. In short, the average annual income gain of the bottom quintile of the population over this period is less than 0.6 percent. The poverty headcount, though extremely low in 1980 in terms of both the percentage of population living on less than US2011\$1.90 per day (0.2 percent) and US2011\$3.20 (0.4 percent), was even worse in 2016 (0.6 percent and 2.4 percent, respectively) (World Bank 2018c). During the Kirchner years, the income share of the bottom quintile had recovered from its lowest points around the year 2000. Yet with the prospect of austerity required to recover from the economic imbalances of the 2003–2017 period, it is unclear whether the very poor will be neglected even further. Ravallion (2002) reported on the vulnerability of the poor during periods of government cutbacks; during the 1980–1997 period, when the Argentine government had to cut overall spending, the cutbacks on pro-poor spending were greater.

Background

With class and ethnic antagonism going at least as far back as the 1940s, the destructiveness of Argentine conflict had gone through insurrection, severe repression, and thousands of deaths. Yet for the past three decades the conflict shifted to policy impasses and social polarization that have strangled the economy of a country with perhaps the greatest potential in

---

[5] The most recent estimate found in the World Bank database (World Bank 2018a).

Social-Sector Spending Targeting the Poor

Latin America. Except for the 1991–2001 peso-dollar Convertibility Plan[6] that ultimately led to Argentina's greatest financial crisis from the mid-1990s through 2002, any government policy, whether Peronist or anti-Peronist, has been taken by the opposition as intolerable.

The exception was the Convertibility Plan, a draconian measure to stem the hyperinflation of the late 1980s through 1990. Although the scheme was unraveling by the mid-1990s, the successive regimes lacked enough political capital to wean the country from its impact. Making pesos convertible into dollars when Argentina's balance of trade deteriorated led to increasingly distorted exchange rates, decline of hard currency reserves, massive debt, bank failures, and a highly unwelcome investment climate. This plunged Argentina into a depression entailing a nearly 20 percent GDP decline from 1999 to 2002 and over 20 percent unemployment by 2002.

During the crisis, the Argentine government was incapable of marshaling sufficient support for a sustainable recovery approach. Benton (2009, 656) notes that President Fernando de la Rúa (who resigned in December 2001) "was unable to rule over provincial leaders and therefore faced nearly constant congressional stalemate from provincial delegations opposing measures contrary to local interests." When, finally, the dollar-peso parity had to be abandoned in 2002, the government had to suspend international debt payments, with at least 15 years of economic problems as a consequence.

The lack of support for government initiatives is not surprising in light of the widespread cynicism toward both the executive and the Congress. The 2016 Latinobarómetro survey of some 1,200 Argentines found that 62 percent of the representative sample have little or no confidence in government and 64 percent express little or no confidence in Congress. In some respects, lack of faith in government is amply justified, not only in terms of the perceived selfish motivations, but also in terms of the politicization of state institutions that are supposed to be apolitical. This is the case of blatant manipulation of policy-relevant statistics by the national statistics agency Indec.[7]

---

[6] The February 1991 Convertibility Law that put the peso in parity with the US dollar permitted Argentines to obtain dollars by submitting pesos to the central bank.

[7] Instituto Nacional de Estadística y Censos. Boräng et al. (2014, 10) relate that:
In the years preceding the 2007 onset of politicization, Indec's official statistics, including the consumer price index (CPI) and gross domestic product (GDP), followed standard international practices in their calculations and methodology; they were thus largely considered credible. Starting in January 2007, the accuracy and coverage of statistics

In the wake of the 2001–2002 economic meltdown, Nestor Kirchner, a Peronist[8] populist, was elected president in 2003, and was succeeded by his wife, Cristina Fernández de Kirchner (2007–2015). They expanded benefits for the poor, but huge budget overruns, renationalizations, debt defaults, and a host of other investment-discouraging policies reduced the credibility of and confidence in economic policies. The Peronists' effort to reverse the economic decline prior to the 2015 election exacerbated the unsustainable government spending. Rosenblatt (2016, 21) summarized

> In 2015, with presidential elections approaching, the economy stagnated, inflation remained high, and foreign exchange pressures continued. Fiscal policy remained without a clear medium-term framework and without quantitative fiscal rules at the federal level. Political budget cycles re-emerged. Monetary policy had multiple and expansive objectives and central bank financing of the government was institutionalized. The broader framework, or direction, for macroeconomic policy making was unclear, other than general political statements on "not repeating the mistakes of the 1990s." Even understanding the size of fiscal and monetary problems was difficult, given doubts about macro statistics, and increasing use of off-budget fiscal mechanisms. In terms of the definition of credibility, and the characteristics of credible policy, outlined in the introduction, the path forward on credible macroeconomic policy could be challenging, to say the least.

The economic disaster, in requiring drastic economic retrenchment, had severely hobbled the new administration, to the point that the Center-Right government of Mauricio Macri lost the 2019 presidential election, placing the Peronists back in power, without evidence that their policy approaches will have moderated. In short, Argentina is a clear example of the deleterious impact of destructive conflict other than open, intergroup violence. The level of open intergroup violence has been low since the mid-1980s, although more than thirty deaths occurred in 2001 food riots and rampant looting, which the Center-Right blamed on

---

began to decline dramatically. As *The Economist* ... put it, "Since the government seized control of the statistics institute in 2007 the discrepancy between the official inflation number and that reported by independent economists has been up to 15 percentage points." "Blatantly inaccurate inflation statistics" were complemented by the distortion of other figures linked to inflation, including a possible overestimation of GDP growth by two percentage points per year .... In 2014, the country, moreover, stopped publishing poverty rates altogether .... The manipulation of statistics led to formal IMF warnings to take "remedial measures" to report statistics according to IMF's rules or else risk not being able to secure additional loans, or, at the extreme, being expelled from the IMF.

[8] "Peronists" are members of the movement, currently primarily represented by the Justicialista Party. Perón labeled his political-economic ideology "justicialismo," a hybrid corporatist-populism that has been appropriated by both left and right movements over the more than 70 years of its existence.

Peronist provocateurs goading the rioters to more aggressive confrontation. Although Argentina's robbery rate is the highest in Latin America, the murder rate is very low by Latin American standards (Cutrona 2018, 5). The crushing conflict has been the distrust-based reactions of the Right and the Left against the initiatives of the other.

The populist measures, if they had not been extreme, could have led to sustainable improvements for the poor. Prior to the economic implosion and the clear defeat of the populists in 2015, several pro-poor policies were enacted. Social protection had long existed for workers in the formal sector, but only under the Kirchners was it extended to the informal sector. Spending on the social insurance system strongly favored middle-income beneficiaries, reflecting the powerful role of organized labor (Graham 2002, 20), and the zero-sum mentality of union leaders in the contest for budget resources. The Kirchners, with the support of the Peronist trade union leaders, largely overcame the resistance of organized labor. In addition, some progressive reforms occurred in education. Potenza Dal Masetto and Repetto (2012, 42) reported that "The distribution of spending on education is highly progressive in all levels of compulsory education ..." However, higher education remained largely the province of the prosperous: "spending on tertiary education has a much lower index of progressivity ... since it benefits mostly middle and high-income groups" (Potenza Dal Masetto and Repetto 2012, 42).

The Transformation of Key Identities

Argentines' most salient identities and stereotypes have changed substantially over the decades. Waves of European migration to Buenos Aires resulted in social segregation along Euro-ethnic dimensions, as reflected in the middle- to upper-class Club Italiano, Club Alemán [German Club], Club Centro Galicia, Club Social Israelita Sefardi, Club Japones de Burzaco, the Burlingham Country Club, and others. Low-income urban workers, largely from Italy and Spain, were politically marginalized until the mid-1940s, when they were mobilized by Juan Perón. This defined the most prominent distributive battle as pitting workers versus owners along classic class lines.

However, over the years many of the newer European immigrants rose economically, some of the rural European immigrants had mixed-race offspring, some indigenous and mixed-race people came to the cities and occupied the lowest economic roles. The middle- and upper-class people of European heritage diminished their ethnic distinctiveness. In 2005, the president of the Club Alemán [German Club] in Buenos Aires declared, on the Club's 150th anniversary:

Our purpose, in effect for a long time, is to continue with actions that dispel the public opinion that the [Club Aleman] is a very closed institution, an impression that held when this was [common] societal behavior, typical of a community that held its European history very close. But then came an Argentinization in several senses, and we aspire to demonstrate this goal of openness.

For prosperous Argentines, the importance of national identity, and particularly an identity as a nation of European heritage and culture, placed in a region with predominantly indigenous and African populations, cannot be overestimated. Bass (2006, 434), based on two years of anthropological research, argues, "Although I found that there is a strong positive nationalism in Argentina, these middle-class 'porteño' [Buenos Aires residents] descendants of European immigrants often still closely identify with their parents' and grandparents' countries of origin. It could be said that many of these middle-class porteños see themselves as Europeans lost on a Latin American continent." The self-image of the prosperous Argentine emphasizes sophistication, particularly the porteños. This identity requires them to distinguish themselves from the traditional, rural people other than the large land owners.

Urban and Rural Marginality

The Peronist success in gaining income shares for organized labor, both during Perón's rule (1945–1955) and even during anti-Peronist military and governments, came at the expense of the rural poor. This came especially from the north, where the bulk of the indigenous Argentines originate. The urban poverty resulting from rural-to-urban migration that has not been absorbed into the organized, formal workforce exists alongside the rural poverty.

The racial polarization, with a very long history that includes the "Desert Campaign" (1833–1834) and the "Conquest of the Desert" (1872–1884) that decimated indigenous populations, has evolved away from explicit prejudice of European-heritage Argentines toward Indians and Afro-Argentines. The highly romanticized image of gauchos highlights their behavioral characteristics – loyal, wild, unschooled, and ferocious – rather than the fact of their mixed, indigenous, or African heritage. The identifications are relatedly complicated by the historical overlay of regional conflict and ethnic differences. The struggle between

Social-Sector Spending Targeting the Poor

Buenos Aires and the "provinces" has existed since independence, pitting unitarian (centralized, Buenos Aires-centered) governance against federalist (provincial autonomy) governance. The bulk of the indigenous Argentines originate in the northern provinces, where many remain despite internal migration to Buenos Aires and other cities. Many indigenous immigrants from bordering Bolivia and Paraguay still reside in these areas, though some of them also have migrated to the cities. Intermarriage has resulted in a mixed-race population that may be as high as 20 percent.

The number of Argentines who are not of full European blood belies the common view of a white nation. Verkholantseva (2016, 18 [translated from Spanish]) notes that mestizos are much more numerous than the conventional wisdom in Argentina holds; the mestizos suffer from discrimination. Verkholantseva offers – somewhat at odds with the first two points – an "out of sight, out of mind" explanation:

The amount of immigration of white people to the country made it seem that the vast majority of modern citizens have only European features. The total absence of mestizos in Argentina is largely a myth, in fact the predominantly Amerindian population is the one that predominates. However, those minorities have almost no access to urban areas and are seldom integrated into the society of large cities. Unfortunately, the pejorative qualification for someone who manifests indigenous or un-European traits is still common. For these reasons most of the Argentine cities consist of a white population, and the Amerindian element does not manifest itself phenotypically.

This is complicated by the difficulty of distinguishing indigenous or mixed-race immigrants from neighboring countries and the Argentine migrants from the north. Argentines of European extraction often believe that indigenous-looking individuals are not Argentine at all, but rather are immigrants. Courtis et al. (2007/2009, 29) emphasize the ease of maintaining the identity of Argentines as Europeans by presuming that mixed-race people are not Argentine:

From the point of view of a hegemonic Eurocentric perception, clear distinctions between a "provincial person" and an immigrant from a bordering country are, *at first sight*, blurred. Given that the population of the city of Buenos Aires is widely immigrant, it is difficult to tell *at first sight* the difference between its inhabitants and the inhabitants of the rest of the country who, in turn, are hard to distinguish from the inhabitants of bordering countries. The focus of contempt is the culturally constructed social biotype of the Latin American mestizo [italics in the original].

The middle- and upper-income Argentines' contemporary image of low-income people, whether believed to be immigrants or native-born, is a more politically and economically anchored stereotype. Regardless of their racial background, low-income people are viewed by more prosperous people as ignorant and naïve. The perception is that low-income people are gullible to the contemporary Peronist populism, duped by the feckless policies of leaders like the Kirchners. A crucial point is that class and ethnicity have become so intertwined that persisting racist views can be indulged with less taint of overt bigotry. Despite the ethnic gulf obvious to external observers, Argentine polarization reflects stereotypes defined along class lines. Courtis et al. (2007/2009, 29) offer an insightful interpretation:

The analysis of the discourses that racialize the worker who moves from a province to the capital city leads us to consider the numerous debates that have revolved around the relation between the categories of race and of social class in Latin America. On one hand, there were those who understood issues linked to racism to be subsidiary to class issues. On the other, there were those who proposed a high degree of independence between both issues. Finally, there were intermediate positions that, while insisting upon ethnic questions, encouraged a prolific overlapping of both issues, considering them not to be equivalent although strongly interwoven. This last stance, which, we believe, best illustrates the case of Argentina, is perhaps backed up by a "factual" resolution of this debate ... the local social structure displays a varied "coloring" in such a way that inferior positions tend to be allocated to the more bronze-skinned people, who are the result of various forms of mestizaje that involve a great degree of native and African heredities, whereas more powerful people tend to occupy the most "whitened" strata.

This runs parallel to the construct of "symbolic racism" (McConahay and Hough 1976), developed to explain the resistance of white Americans to pro-black policies despite the strong decline in explicit racist attitudes. "Symbolic racism" attributes negative characteristics to members of an ethnic group not explicitly because of an acknowledged bias against the group, but rather because members of the group lack particular positive attributes. Political sophistication clearly is one such perceived attribute, but so too is lack of industriousness. In terms of attitudes toward the deservingness of the poor to receive benefits that would require further sacrifices by the prosperous, the minority who would oppose making the sacrifices question the work ethic of the poor. One middle-class respondent to Giurata's (2018) interviews maintained that poverty is due to "a loss of the culture of work" (Giurata's 2018, 57 [translated from the Giurata Spanish text]).

The Argentine case illuminates the Gestalt theory insights outlined in the prior exposition of attribution dynamics, namely that the attributions

Social-Sector Spending Targeting the Poor 115

of motives are linked to the positive or negative attributions of initiators, and hence to the positive or negative evaluations of the initiatives. In the Argentine case, the Center and Right, having disdain for the Kirchners, expressed blanket condemnation for the initiatives during the Kirchner period. Leftists, seeing (or admitting to) no commonality with the recent Center-Right government, presumed Macri's policies were intentionally malevolent. The stereotype of ignorance and naïveté attributed to lower-income Kirchneristas exists in sharp contrast with the stereotype attributed to more prosperous anti-Kirchneristas as uncaring, without the full humanity of concern for the less fortunate. Some 2017–2018 interviews with Kirchner supporters in Buenos Aires reveal a perception of new President Macri officials and supporters as heartless and selfish.

A Kirchnerista 2018 survey respondent said, "The person who does not recognize that others are vulnerable … to me personally that seems like a bad person …. People who say 'mine, mine, mine' are not human, they do not have humanity, they cannot see the other" (Giurata 2018, 60 [translated from the Giurata Spanish text; condensed]). Another January 2018 Kirchnerista interviewee revealed the depth of despair and animosity upon the victory of the anti-Kirchnerista president:

My mother died on August 3, 2016. Macri won the elections in November 2015. He was sworn in as president on December 10, 2015. In March of 2016, my mother … told me that since Macri won had she felt very bad, and that she knew that she would die very soon … because she already knew that the worst Argentine tragedy was coming and did not want to be here to see it because she had seen many. So, among other things, I hold the Macri government responsible for the fact that I do not have my mother
(Giurata 2018, 1 [translated from the Giurata Spanish text]).

This also fits the classic dynamic of infrahumanization[9] (Haslam and Loughnan 2014) held by the poor toward the middle-income people and leaders associated with them exacerbate the polarization.

The stereotypes serve ingroup identity, though the dimensions are fundamentally different. In the case of anti-Kirchneristas – largely middle- and upper-income Argentines – their self-ascribed sophistication is reinforced by their contrast with the image of Kirchneristas as naïve. For Kirchner supporters, their self-ascribed moral righteousness and solidarity are buttressed by the perception of anti-Kirchneristas as selfish and uncaring. Peronist identity is much more than a political affiliation; it is a

---

[9] "Infrahumanization" refers to the assessment that particular people lack the ethical standards that ought to be expected of fully human individuals.

116   *Lessons from Pro-Poor Policy Instruments*

highly self-aware, self-attribution of deprived social status. Ostiguy (2007, 2) argues that behind the political divide of Argentina's Left versus Right is a sociocultural divide of "Low" versus "High," for which Low "is defined as the use and/or manifestation of culturally- *popular* traits, manners, modes of speech, tropes, and particularly of the local or national – i.e. bounded and locally-specific – form of this popular culture, in the political arena. In terms of traits *realmente existentes*, it denotes 'cruder' tastes, demeanor in behavior, and expressions and ways of speaking of political representatives in the public arena." This self-image was deliberately established by Juan Perón himself. James (1993, 23) recounts:

> [Peron's] constant use of couplets from Martin Fierro [José Hernández' 1872 epic poem about a fictional gaucho, written in the vernacular], or his conscious use of terms taken from lunfardo argot [the slang of the dockworkers] grates on modern sensibilities. However, we should be careful to appreciate the impact of his ability to speak in an idiom which reflected popular sensibilities of the time. In accounts by observers and journalism of the crucial formative years of Peronism we frequently find the adjectives *chabacano* and *burdo* used to describe both Peron himself and his supporters. Both words have the sense of crude, cheap, coarse and they also implied a lack of sophistication, and awkwardness, almost a country pumpkin quality. While they were generally meant as epithets they were not descriptions Peronists would necessarily have denied.

Evidence of the sociocultural foundation of Peronism is further illustrated by the fact that the movement remained strong even after policy shifts to the Right. As Levitsky (2003, 107) points out, Peronist President Carlos Menem (1989–1999) severely weakened the union movement, thus eroding the class commitment of Peronism, although class identity was reasserted following Menem's administration.

Peronist identity has strong parallels to the mindset of the Isaanese in Thailand (Chapter 8) in self-attributions that acknowledge some aspects of inferiority: less educated, less polished, and so on. Yet, in contrast to the Isaanese, who are more likely to attribute their status to their noble occupations as farmers, Peronists are more likely to attribute their lower status to the dominance of non-Peronists. Loxton and Levitsky (2018, 132–133) note how much of Peronist identity has been molded by the long history of repression against the movement. Peronist identity also has some parallels to the identities of poorer neighborhoods in Colombian cities in accepting the socioeconomic designation defined by the neighborhood and embracing the attribute of crudeness in speech and other forms (Chapter 6).

Social-Sector Spending Targeting the Poor

Another factor that may account for the highly polarizing stereotypes is the huge cognitive load (Biernat, Kobrynowicz, and Weber 2003) brought on by the confusion, uncertainty, and unsettled nature of politics and policy, exacerbated by extreme rhetoric. It is important to note that neither side of the divide has a cognitive frame to know or understand the stereotype of themselves held by the other. Kirchneristas are so convinced that their diagnosis of the malice and ill intent of the opposition is obvious, that the idea that their opponents would regard Kirchneristas as naïve seems implausible. The anti-Kirchneristas, insofar as they are in principle predisposed to sound pro-poor policies, would reject as absurd that they are uncaring.

The attribution bias[10] (Heider 1958; Pettigrew 1979) of regarding temporary and situationally driven behavior of others as manifesting their intrinsic attributes exacerbates this polarization. The opposition to the Kirchners' pro-poor measures, which indeed proved to be unsustainable, has been taken as proof of the intrinsic heartlessness of the anti-Kirchneristas.

BRAZIL

The Brazilian case has received largely favorable attention, in terms of both the tax system and the explicit budgetary commitment to social services. Abad and Lindert (2017, 255) judge Brazil's spending programs on education (nursery school, primary, and secondary), health, family aid, and cash transfers as progressive. Among Latin American countries, Brazil ranks only behind Chile and Uruguay in state spending on "social security and welfare" (Huber, Mustillo, and Stephens 2008, 428). While the subsidies to cover contributory pensions (typically available to the relatively more prosperous workers in the formal sector) constitute 9.1 percent of GDP, total social spending amounts to 25.2 percent of GDP (Higgins and Pereira 2014). Despite heated debates on the fairness and inefficiency of the tax system, both the proportion of tax collection and the tax effort are undeniably impressive compared to most other Latin American countries and developing countries in general.

It is illuminating that the pushback against the high tax effort has not focused primarily on the targets of spending. Rather, one focus is on inefficiencies of both the tax collection and social-service spending.

---

[10] Which Heider famously labeled the "fundamental attribution error."

Lessons from Pro-Poor Policy Instruments

Another is the supposed unfairness of the tax system, and the argument that reducing the tax burden on the "new middle class" (a peculiar label discussed below). Silveira et al. (2013, 6) report that:

> In discussions on taxes and social spending, two issues (or problems) are voiced by most politicians, journalists, opinion leaders, researchers and academics. On the one hand, it is believed that the tax burden in Brazil is too high and that the return, via public policy, falls far too short of what taxpayers contribute. This burden, the argument holds, is unfair; poor people pay much more, as a proportion of their income, than rich people. As a corollary to this consensus, there is a demand for lower taxes so that there may be more income and consumption. This cause is strongly backed by the middle class and, according to certain analysts, is shared by the new middle class, a stratum of the population that has reached a new income level and has increased and improved consumption patterns in the durable goods market.

In the 1990s the Brazilian government invested heavily in health care and education programming, setting up the unified health system (Sistema Único de Saúde) and establishing national education curriculum guidelines while expanding access to education for poor children. Brazil is also quite distinctive in having the budgetary commitment to education enshrined in the constitution, with an explicit earmark:

> Article 212. The Union shall apply, annually, never less than eighteen percent, and the states, the Federal District, and the municipalities, at least twenty-five percent of the tax revenues, including those resulting from transfers, in the maintenance and development of education.[11]

The improvements in labor productivity helped Brazil to take advantage of the capital brought in through the commodity boom, leading not only to rapid economic growth but also to incorporating more of the poor into the formal economy and overall increases in the wages of unskilled workers. The income distribution improved markedly (World Bank 2016b, 103–107).

It is worth noting that although the concept of "racial democracy" has been roundly denounced as a myth that permitted neglect of the problem of race-based discrimination, this conception for many decades reduces the sharp racial and class distinctions so common in many countries. Ingroup and outgroup distinctions are much more difficult to make given the fuzziness of the boundaries. Kühn (2014, 161) first depicts the rosy interpretation of a unified and proud Brazil:

---

[11] Constitution of Brazil. www.v-brazil.com/government/laws/titleVIII.html.

Social-Sector Spending Targeting the Poor

Being proud to be Brazilian was characteristic of all social classes .... The narrative of being Brazilian is related to the Brazilian history of migration, including Indian, European and African roots, and particular way in which slavery was practiced and overcome in Brazil. The power of amalgamation and ethnic blending is highlighted in the Brazilian narrative ...: Brazil unifies the strengths of these different origins and combines them into a unique power – all this in a country that is very rich in natural resources .... The special and unique power of Brazilians is linked to such collective symbols as Carnaval or Samba, which reinforce the imagined capacity of Brazilians to mixup a different range of elements in a consistent and enchanting unity.

Yet, Kühn (2014, 161) adds that it has been "shown that this narrative has been strongly and systematically pushed by Brazilian governments in the first half of the 20th century in order to strengthen national identity and prevent potential tensions and conflicts between social groups."

This reflects the widespread Brazilian identity as participants in the unifying project of national maturation. Brazilian urban planner Vicente del Rio (2010, 71) reflects the common sentiment that Brazil is "a new country in the making with undeniable advances in political representation, governance, social programs and income distribution." This is in striking contrast with the Argentine polarization and the common middle-class identification with their family's country of origin. Bass (2006, 434–435) writes that "It could be said that some of these middle-class porteños [residents of Buenos Aires] see themselves as Europeans lost on a Latin American continent. This identity crisis has been aggravated economic and political decline, which began during the 1930s and was accompanied by a growing sense of national failure."

The Brazilian "project" took on a far more leftist turn following the economic and political instability under centrist or right-wing governments succeeding military rule, including the impeachment of one of the presidents. In 2002, the labor union leader Luiz Inácio "Lula" da Silva of the Workers Party was elected and fulfilled two terms, followed by his protégé, the former guerrilla Dilma Rousseff (deposed through impeachment in 2016). Though both adopted the rhetoric of populism, their political and economic approaches, dubbed by some observers as the "pink tide" (Bull 2013) (in contrast with the "red tide" of highly authoritarian communism or extreme socialism), were more inclusive to all sectors. The da Silva and Rousseff governments undertook broad multisector consultation, and more business-friendly policies than the business sector could have imagined before Lula took office. However, it is worth noting that both Brazil's conditional cash transfer program Bolsa Familia and the Afro-Brazilian affirmative action program were established under

120 *Lessons from Pro-Poor Policy Instruments*

President Fernando Henrique Cardoso (1995–2002), a centrist who was trying to fend off the Workers Party electoral challenge. The fact that the enactment of Cardoso's programs was regarded as having the potential to fend off a populist challenge is likely to have reduced resistance to Cardoso's pro-poor policies.

Under Rouseff, a curious effort to change the societal conceptions of social class identities was underway through the President's endorsement of a redefinition of economic classes proposed by the Brazilian economist, Marcelo Neri (2008, 2011). Neri proposed that the majority of the Brazilian population had joined the "Classe C" (with two classes above and two below), constituting (at the time of his writing) 53 percent of the population with monthly incomes ranging from US$500 to US$2,000. Neri labeled this cohort as the "new middle class." The plausibility of labeling these people as "middle class" is challenged by the fact that some members of this "new middle class" depend on public housing. Elevated to Minister of the Secretary of Strategic Affairs under Rouseff, Neri then oversaw a new classification: the poor (zero to US$62 monthly); the vulnerable (US$62 to US$112); the low-middle class (US$112 to US$170); the middle-middle class (US$170 to US$247); the upper-middle class (US$247 to US$392); and the upper-class (US$392 upwards) (Kopper 2015).

Critics, especially sociologists, unsurprisingly object to the defining of class by income levels alone (Pochmann 2014). Yet the Rouseff administration embraced the approach as conveying that Brazil had succeeded in poverty alleviation. Kopper (2015, 23) concludes that

Neri's research bestowed a scientific endorsement upon the government's heralding the end of endemic poverty. In 2012, during a celebration speech of Project "Brazil without Misery," President Dilma Rousseff vividly recommended Neri's book to everyone "interested in understanding the country's recent changes." Adding on what seemed to be the beginning of a fruitful partnership, she said, "It is because of his studies and analyses that we improve our social policies. He is a great collaborator of the federal government."

This congratulatory effort to declare success must have been reassuring to prosperous Brazilians, with the economic growth shared among income levels. Costa (2018, 66) adds to the congratulations:

After the Workers' Party (PT) came to power in 2003, remarkable economic and social improvements have been reached in Brazil. Thus, in line with developments observed in several Latin American countries, inequalities in Brazil have declined in this period. During the two administrations of former President Lula da Silva

Social-Sector Spending Targeting the Poor

(2003–2006 and 2007–2010) and the first administration of President Dilma Rousseff (2010–2014), economic growth, improvements in the labour market, progress in deprived regions, and pro-poor policies interacted positively as drivers of inequality reduction.

Mood Shifts in Brazil

Yet, with the recession starting in 2015 – the World Bank declared in 2017 that Brazil, after disastrous Venezuela, had the worst economy in Latin America (Rapoza 2017) – it is unclear whether attitudes toward poverty alleviation have changed. But it is quite clear that the climate and mood have changed, reflecting the long-standing ambivalence in the Brazilian self-image. Brazilians' recognition of widespread *jeitinho* (cutting corners to take advantage), the long-standing joke that "Brazil is the country of the future, and always will be," and the corruption heavily publicized in 2017–2018 are even more painful, given the ebullience prior to the downturn. The reaction has been greater polarization, vindictiveness, and extreme reactions, including ousting Rousseff on controversial grounds and the resumption of the army's invasion of low-income Rio de Janeiro neighborhoods to root out criminals.

Of course, the ambivalence of Brazilians toward income distribution and self-esteem has a much longer history. The self-respect of prosperous Brazilians had been challenged, at least since the military gave up power in mid-1980s, by arguably the most unequal income distribution in the world, with grinding poverty centered in the Northeast region with the highest Afro-Brazilian population (Hernández 2005). Cristovam Buarque, a Brazilian senator as of 2006, as well as former Minister of Education, Governor of the Federal District of Brasília, and Rector of the University of Brasília, asserted that "Many Brazilians are ashamed of the country's poor rate of basic education, ashamed that it ranks first in the world regarding inequality, ashamed that half of the population lives in poverty" (Buarque, Špolar, and Zhang 2006, 219). Nordhaus and Shellenberger (2007, 60) posited, "As a country of great artists, architects, diplomats, designers, and engineers, and as a people who speak Portuguese in a region where Spanish dominated, Brazilians justifiably see themselves as special and unique. At the same time, many Brazilians are ashamed of the persistence of widespread poverty, violence, and lawlessness." The responses of the 2016 Latinobarómetro (2018) survey registered 84.3 percent of the public believing that the distribution of income is unfair or very unfair, the third highest proportion in Latin America, after Chile and Colombia. In addition, the legacy of having operated with the race-blind conception for many decades contributed to the reduction of sharp racial and class distinctions that are so common in many other countries. Ingroup and outgroup distinctions are much more difficult to make, given the fuzziness of the boundaries.

6

Pro-Poor Subsidies and the Problem of Leakage

The challenge of providing the poor with lower prices for goods and services without having the subsidies captured by wealthier people can illustrate the psychology of prosperous people desisting from taking advantage of subsidies intended for the poor. India and Colombia, the two countries featured in this chapter, demonstrate the compatibility of relatively prosperous people's self-esteem and their resisting the capture of subsidy benefits. Both cases illustrate how official recognition of the willingness to pass up subsidized goods or services can contribute to this self-esteem, reinforced by the opportunity to engage in noblesse oblige. The Colombian case of neighborhood designations dictating qualification for subsidized utility pricing also exemplifies changes in the salience of self-attributes, and even greater esteem for the wealthy by the designation associated with subsidizing poorer people. For all of the income groups, the designation per se becomes a surprisingly salient self-identification, even for residents of poor neighborhoods in accepting an inferior status. Social identities become more rigid as a consequence. In the Colombian case a trade-off exists between economic gain and social stigma for residents of the poorer neighborhoods – an unusual example of a subsidy that cannot be accessed without a visible signal of status, with the potential to contribute to polarization. The Indian cases – relatively prosperous people formally relinquishing subsidies for liquefied petroleum gas (LPG), and some simply passing up the opportunity to buy subsidized grains – comprise personal choices. These demonstrate a combination of noblesse oblige and consumer taste that belie the widespread pessimism toward subsidized pricing. These cases also demonstrate that generosity can exist within the same cultural context as the

124   *Lessons from Pro-Poor Policy Instruments*

self-serving behavior displayed by some Indian groups as described in Chapter 7 on affirmative action.

The Thai case is distinctive in taking advantage of the logic of inferior service rather than product. The universally low fee for service at public hospitals (like the LPG case involving the option for prosperous families to relinquish an economic advantage), eliminated the public stigma of treating low-income families as welfare recipients.

GENERAL BACKGROUND ON SUBSIDIES AND LEAKAGE

Five approaches have emerged to enhance the purchasing power of low-income people as alternatives to increasing their earned incomes or transfers. One approach is to limit the prices that any purchaser would have to pay. Yet, such price controls run the risk of reducing supply or creating a black market that hurts the poor who cannot pay the even higher black-market prices. The other approaches strive to avoid these problems by providing adequate resources.

Thus, a second approach is to reduce prices for everyone, while maintaining supply through direct government provision or by compensating state or private providers that otherwise would suffer deficits and possibly cease operations. The downside is the large budget obligation and the "leakage" of benefits to more prosperous people, while the drain on the budget diverts funds that could be used for the poor. In addition, the wealthier purchasers are often the largest users of the subsidized goods or services, such as gasoline and water. If budget deficits become unsustainable, the withdrawal of the subsidy runs the risk of disruption. However, even the poor often resist the reduction of subsidies, even if they lose in the long run. Both pure impatience (the preference for earlier rather than later benefits) and strategic impatience (preference for earlier benefits because of uncertainty as to whether later benefits would materialize) are typically at play.

To reduce the budget obligation, a third approach is to limit the government's costs by restricting eligibility to the poor, through direct or indirect means testing. The disadvantage is another form of leakage: wealthier people purchase the underpriced goods or services fraudulently, or eligible recipients sell their vouchers or purchases to wealthier people. This reduces the benefits for the poor, insofar as they have to sell for less than the market price.

A fourth approach is to limit subsidies to goods or services that wealthier people would disdain (i.e., "inferior goods" or "inferior services"). The range of inferior goods and services includes foodstuffs, fuels, transportation, health care, and education. A classic example is the low-cost rice and grain mixture offered under the Marcos administration to low-income Filipino families. Wealthier Filipinos had been very unhappy when at times rice shortages compelled the government to order grain distributors to mix corn with rice.[1] It is evident that prosperous Filipinos are reluctant to consume such mixtures (Balisacan 1994, 154; Minguez 1978).

A fifth approach can avoid governmental budget obligations completely through price regulations that place a greater burden on the wealthier so that poorer people would have to pay less. This entails cross-subsidies involving the wealthier paying more than the poorer. One variant is to charge different rates in different areas, presuming that sufficient income differences exist across these areas. Another variant, "tiered" or "bloc" pricing, is to charge the same rates for all, not necessarily with overall subsidized rates, but imposing greater costs through higher rates for consumption above specified levels.

REDUCING SUBSIDY LEAKAGE

Subsidized LPG in India

The home use of LPG is extremely important for reducing indoor air pollution, which is the leading cause of death worldwide of children under five years of age (Gould and Urpelainen 2018, 396). The Government of India has long subsidized LPG purchases for any household, regardless of income, in order to promote the substitution of LPG for solid fuels. Because urban residents use most of it, the subsidy largely goes to the cities. The subsidy was very costly to the government, and most of the rural poor could not benefit from the health improvements because they could not afford the installation of LPG hookups. In 2014, the Government of India launched an ambitious initiative (PaHaL) to reform

---

[1] Minguez (1978, 24/28) recounts:

> The Masagana 99 Program was launched the light of the worst rice situation the production levels were greatly reduced by crop years 1970-71, 1971-72 and 1972-73 as a "program for survival" in Philippines has suffered when typhoons, floods and tungro. Rice was imported at very high prices. For the first time in the Philippine history, rice was allocated and distributed and people had to consume rice and corn mixture. To the Filipinos, rice is the "staff of life" and rebellion may possibly arise from this kind of crisis.

126 *Lessons from Pro-Poor Policy Instruments*

the LPG subsidy (Sharma and Sharma 2016), with impressive success in reducing leakage.

In addition, a remarkably clear-cut example of material sacrifice by more prosperous people has occurred related to this initiative. Mittal, Mukherjee, and Gelb (2017, 3) note, "India's cooking gas subsidy is the largest direct benefit transfer program in the world"; as of 2018, it had 177 million subscribers. They judge the program as successful because "[it] is a rare case of success in achieving reform in the difficult area of energy subsidy reform. PaHaL has increased efficiency and reduced leakages compared to the previous in-kind subsidy regime, resulting in significant fiscal savings for the government at [a] fraction of the cost of the program" (Mittal, Mukherjee, and Gelb 2017, 3). Most remarkable from the perspective of more prosperous people making sacrifices for the poor, a subsidiary "Give It Up" initiative has induced more than 10 million families to relinquish their subsidies.[2]

Because LPG is very much in demand by industry, selling LPG cylinders purchased at subsidized prices would be a way for low-income families to receive cash while still using solid fuels for home use. This was a very serious leakage problem prior to the PaHaL program.

Instead of the usual subsidy that directly reduces the retail price of a good, the PaHaL program maintains the unsubsidized retail price, but transfers the subsidy equivalent to the bank accounts of all subscribers, unless they opt out of the subsidy. The government capped the number of LPG cylinders for each household, culled out duplicate and "ghost" accounts to reduce the number of cylinders that could be resold, and provided the subsidy transfer only for the limited number of cylinders (twelve per household). The annual value of the subsidy is just under US$20 per household.[3] With median household income of less than a tenth of US median income, the subsidy could be considered as equivalent to US$200 – a substantial amount.[4]

Most relevant in terms of the focus on pro-poor predispositions, the willingness of more than 10.5 million households to relinquish their right to the subsidy has been promoted by a high-profile "Give It Up" campaign. The campaign involves statements by Prime Minister Modi, both

[2] Official website of the Give It Up program. www.givitup.in/, March 1, 2019.
[3] Pillarisetti, Jamison, and Smith (2017). Estimating nine cylinder refills per year per household, at a refill cost of US$8.70 per cylinder unsubsidized and US$6.60 per cylinder subsidized, yields an annual subsidy of US$18.90.
[4] Indian median income is US$6,000 at purchasing power parity, compared to US household median income of US$60,000.

Pro-Poor Subsidies and the Problem of Leakage   127

in India and abroad, boasting of the philanthropic spirit of those who relinquished their subsidies. The campaign also features slogans such as "Feel the Joy of Giving," and its framing as a social movement ("Give It Up Movement"). It is supplemented by appeals by prominent actors, testimonials by people who had relinquished their subsidies for the sake of the poor, and a "scroll of honor."

An important "philanthropic" enticement for those relinquishing their subsidies is the government's commitment to provide free installation for a poor household for each of the relinquished subsidies. At the same time, the government has committed to providing free connections to 80 million households. At least 20 million households have already received free connections (Gould and Urpelainen 2018, 398).

The gradualism of the reform, with one formal change and then a voluntary program, was effective in avoiding the disruption that very well could have occurred if the government had undertaken an abrupt, unilateral withdrawal of the subsidy. By 2017, limiting the number of cylinders that could be purchased at the subsidized rate, and the voluntary "Give It Up" program, had reduced the total subsidy by US$332 million annually (Mittal, Mukherjee, and Gelb 2017, 22), and relinquishments continue.

Subsidized Grains in India

Malnutrition among low-income people in India has prompted a huge grain subsidy program for rice and wheat, provided through the public distribution system (PDS) (Drèze and Khera 2015). This is India's largest social assistance program, and the world's largest food aid program, with the grains distributed to 800 million people. The program is a hybrid of an inferior goods approach and quotas on the volume of grain to which each household is entitled. The program has been quite controversial – not surprising, in light of the fact that its costs constitute nearly 1 percent of GDP. Despite variation across states, throughout India the grains are widely available at a heavily subsidized price; even families above the formal poverty line are entitled to PDS grains. The discounts are extremely steep (free in Tamil Nadu), and the coverage increasingly broad. Yu, Elleby, and Zobbe (2015, 408) describe the ballooning commitment of the program under the expansion mandated under the 2013 National Food Security Act:

[T]he fiscal cost of India's food subsidy has increased 25 fold over the past two decades; and its share in India's agricultural GDP has more than doubled from

128 *Lessons from Pro-Poor Policy Instruments*

2.2 % in the 1990s to around 5 % in the last decade .... These costs are set to rise further following the NFSA, as up to 75 % of the rural population and 50 % of the urban population will be able to purchase grains at prices at around one tenth of the current retail prices.

As a policy option, this subsidy program competes in the discourse with options such as cash transfers and straight vouchers. However, most recently Shrinivas et al. (2018, 6) conclude concerns over leakage of this grain subsidy program are not valid.[5]

Three facts help to understand why leakage of this program is limited. First, to a certain extent, the PDS rice and wheat are inferior goods (Shrinivas et al. 2018, 1), and accessing the outlet shops and waiting in line are inconvenient in many areas.

Second, some goodwill on the part of wealthier Indians has been evident. Dhanaraj and Gade (2013) report that a quarter of urban Tamils donated their subsidized grain to poorer families. Kozicka, Weber, and Kalkuhl (2016, 2) assert that "wealthier households restrain [*sic*] from consuming subsidized grains. This negative self-selection of wealthier households implies a high potential for cost savings that would be lost under a cash-transfer scheme."

Third, the degree of leakage varies dramatically across states, and over time. The Drèze and Khera (2015, 40) assessment examined estimated leakages for 2004–2005 and 2011–2012, a period of reforms undertaken by several states. Leakages of some states, such as Tamil Nadu (7.3 percent and 11.9 percent for the two periods), Jammu and Kashmir (23 percent and –3.7 percent), and Himachal Pradesh (27.0 percent and 27.1 percent), were quite low compared to the national average of 54.0 percent and 41.7 percent. Many states had consistently high leakage rates, as much as Rajasthan and Punjab at over 90 percent in 2004–2005. Yet remarkably, several states that undertook reforms dramatically reduced leakage: Bihar (91.0 percent to 24.4 percent), Chhattisgarh (51.7 percent to 9.3 percent), Odisha (76.3 percent to 25.0 percent), and Jharkhand (85.2 percent to 44.4 percent). It should be noted, as indicated in Table 6.1, that all five of these states are in the bottom half of Indian states in terms of per capita income, Bihar being the poorest.

---

[5] Srinivas et al. (2018) assert: "The PDS has been criticized on the grounds that the program is poorly targeted, does not reach the intended beneficiaries and hence may have little impact on nutrition. Furthermore, critics contend that PDS encourages only 'empty' staple cereal consumption, and thus may crowd-out more nutritious food items and not improve dietary diversity .... Our results suggest that these criticisms are not generally valid."

TABLE 6.1 *India: gross state domestic product (GSDP) ratio to the national average, 2017–2018*

South		West		North		East		Northeast	
Andhra Pradesh	1.26	Madhya Pradesh	0.71	Uttar Pradesh	0.49	Bihar**	0.34	Manipur**	0.52
Kerala**	1.45	Gujarat**	1.39	Jammu and Kashmir	0.76	Jharkhand*	0.56	Assam**	0.60
Tamil Nadu	1.48	Maharashtra	1.60	Rajasthan	0.89	Odisha**	0.72	Meghalaya**	0.60
Karnataka	1.55	Goa**	3.33	Punjab	1.27	Chhattisgarh	0.82	Tripura*	0.71
Telangana	1.60			Himachal Pradesh	1.42	West Bengal	0.85	Nagaland**	0.80
Pondicherry	1.76			Uttarakhand	1.57	*Andaman & Nicobar**	1.21	Arunachal Pradesh**	1.06
				Haryana	1.75	Sikkim	2.64	Mizoram	1.14
				Chandigarh	2.15				
				Delhi	2.92				

* 2015–2016.
** 2016–2017.
Italics: union territories.
Source: Government of India Ministry of Statistics and Programme Implementation, August 2018

The two states with perhaps the strongest reputations for progressive policies, Kerala and West Bengal, did poorly: West Bengal made only modest improvements (a leakage rate of 80.6 percent in 2004–2005 and 65.3 percent in 2011–2012); Kerala regressed to 37.1 percent from 25.6 percent.

The fact that reforms in registration, monitoring, and quotas could make such rapid and significant progress in states like Bihar, Chhattisgarh, Odisha, and Jharkhand promises that widespread reforms can rescue the PDS from the persistent opposition to the subsidies. More recent studies reinforce the growing success of efforts to reduce leakage. Shrinivas et al. (2018, 1) report that:

PDS beneficiaries consumed 83% of the subsidy's implicit income transfer in the form of food, suggesting that the subsidy did not cause them to substantially reduce their consumption of non-subsidized food. The effect of PDS subsidies on food consumption is highest in households where women have more control over the food budget, suggesting a role of intra-household bargaining. Overall, our results suggest that in-kind staple food subsidies can lead to large improvements in nutritional outcomes of poor households.

The point that Shrinivas et al. make about "intra-household bargaining" is also an important consideration in the debate between cash transfers and in-kind subsidies. Insofar as women control food expenditures, and the male could control cash payments even if they formally go to the female head of household, the family's welfare may be enhanced by food subsidies more than by cash transfers.

Colombia's Residency-Based Subsidies

For many years the utility rates[6] for the residents of Bogotá, Colombia, as well as other Colombian cities, have varied from one neighborhood to another, with poorer neighborhoods enjoying lower rates. This was done by designating neighborhoods from Stratum 1 (the poorest) to Stratum 6 (the wealthiest). The worst neighborhoods, typically occupied by very recent migrants, are "without stratum" (Uribe Mallarino 2008). The strata correspond largely along a north–south continuum, with the northern neighborhoods of Bogotá receiving higher designations.

Residents of Stratum 1 receive up to a 50 percent discount on the rates needed for cost recovery, although subsidies vary across services, while

---

[6] This covered rates for electricity, gas, water, telephone, sewer, and trash collection.

residents of stratum 6 neighborhoods pay a premium of up to 20 percent (Alzate 2006, 16–17). For residents of the higher-designated neighborhoods (5 and 6), the premium is equivalent to a property tax insofar as the revenues are dedicated to the provision of municipal services. One crucial difference, in terms of poverty alleviation, is that a property tax collected by a municipality might not be reallocated to subsidize or otherwise benefit the poor.

If this were a simple administrative device, it could be considered as just one of several possible mechanisms to charge the wealthy more than the poor for basic utilities, such as assigning higher rates for greater usage. The system also has parallels to the inferior goods approach. Although a very limited number of wealthier Bogotanos take advantage of the lower utility rates by living in low-stratum neighborhoods, the lower status of these neighborhoods make them inferior goods insofar as they lack the prestige of neighborhoods with higher designations.

The stratum system has a major impact on social identities. Some observers bemoan the stigma of identifying Bogotanos by their low-stratum residence. Critics point out that stratum designation has become an extremely important signifier of class (Alzate 2006; Bonilla, López, and Sepúlveda 2014; Jessel 2017; Uribe Mallarino 2008). Yet the more practical first-order consequence in terms of poverty reduction is the acquiescence by the most prosperous Bogotanos to the policy of directly subsidizing lower-income residents at all. Assuming that the wealthy have considerable power in shaping this system, why would prosperous Bogotanos tolerate this policy? In addition, the system has serious weaknesses: the correlation between income and stratum designation is not terribly strong (Alzate 2006), and political pressures have been applied to get neighborhoods lower designations so as to reduce costs.

A plausible explanation lies in the social distinctions that redound positively for the prosperous. The system adds to the prestige of those who can afford to live in higher stratum neighborhoods; Stratum 6 neighborhoods are equivalent to a Beverly Hills address. The system also reinforces the segregation of the rich and poor. Bogotanos of modest means are deterred from moving into neighborhoods of higher designations, unlike the urban patterns in many other Latin American cities where low-income housing encroaches into wealthy neighborhoods. In short, this approach entails a trade-off between the virtues of a relatively low-leakage pro-poor subsidy and the problems of social polarization.

The social cost of this policy is prejudice against people labeled by the residents in lower strata. Bogliacino, Jiménez Lozano, and Reyes (2018), based on "lab and field" experiments with over 1,000 respondents across the strata, find that lower-strata residents are perceived as less trustworthy. Presumably this could result in hiring discrimination against people living in lower-stratum neighborhoods.

Some evidence also points to the possibility that stratum labeling undermines the aspirations of lower-stratum residents. Uribe Mallarino (2008, 143) argues that the stratum designation traps low-status people in identifying with their stratum, citing findings that these people do not wish to rise above their stratum. The stratum designation is an important signifier of their identity, practices, and modes of speech.

School Vouchers

Whereas the utility subsidies are a direct cross subsidy from wealthier homeowners, another Colombian approach (the PACES Program) involved direct governmental payments to families in the two lowest strata. To maintain high school attendance by low-income students, the government provided vouchers to cover school fees (Barrera-Osorio et al. 2008; Epple, Romano, and Uruiola 2017; King et al. 1997; King, Orazem, and Wolgemuth 1999). The Program was initiated in 1991, in order to make private high schools affordable to ease the pressure on heavily impacted public high schools. The grants, covering annual registration and tuition fees up to a maximum of roughly US$180, were funded by a formula of 80 percent from the national government and 20 percent from the municipality. Municipalities participated voluntarily – which ultimately led to the demise of the program. At its height in 1995, 90,000 students were attending private schools with the vouchers (King, Orazem, and Wolgemuth 1999).

Yet, only a quarter of Colombia's municipalities agreed to participate, depending on the financial capacity of the municipality and the presence of private schools willing to take voucher students. King, Orazem, and Wolgemuth (1999, 489) attribute the termination of the program in 1997 to rising costs of monitoring to discover counterfeit vouchers or ineligible people using them, and the development of other forms of private school subsidies. Of course, direct subsidies to private schools would not be as insulated from leakage to students of more prosperous families, unless the schools would take on the obligation to confine fee waivers to low-income families.

It is worth noting that private high school administrators had the option to refuse to accept voucher students. In addition, the most expensive private high schools were out of reach to low-income families. The students of these high schools had higher national test scores, perhaps reflecting higher quality of the education (King, Orazem, and Wolgemuth 1999, 485), given their lower student-teacher ratios, but also may have resulted from better-prepared students entering the schools. Both of these factors meant that the private schools available to students using vouchers were, to a certain extent, inferior service goods.

One of the key differences in the sustainability of the utility subsidies and the school voucher subsidies is the absence of the need for government funding for the utility subsidies, by relying on private residents rather than on vulnerable public funds. The lack of paralyzing outcry against the private cross-subsidization of utilities must be considered a victory for the appeal to noblesse oblige and the noneconomic compensation of status.

Thai Health Care

A highly successful example of an "inferior service" is the "30-Baht Health-care Scheme" enacted under Thai Prime Minister Thaksin Shinawatra in 2001. By limiting the fee for a public hospital visit to 30 baht, equivalent at that time to roughly US$0.75, the affordability of hospital visits to the poor improved markedly over the prior more expensive and incompletely implemented programs. Everyone was assigned to a designated hospital, but wealthier people could choose to pay more at other hospitals, including private ones. Seeking medical service at a public hospital is widely regarded as less appealing for those who could afford private hospital fees.

A 2006 assessment by the Thailand Development Research Institute, an organization generally critical of Thaksin's economic policies, nevertheless assessed the 30-Baht Health-care Scheme as effective in reducing poverty: "the households that were impoverished because of health-care burdens decreased by two-thirds as a result of the expansion of coverage toward universal coverage. The above finding is similar for all regions, but is more pronounced in rural areas" (NaRanong and NaRanong 2006, 6). Focus group results indicated that the program did not increase unnecessary visits: "Almost every patient indicated that, when possible, they would stay away from hospitals as much as they could. Many were amazed at the notion that someone would be willing to seek more, or unnecessary, care just because the 30-Baht Scheme had been put in place" (NaRanong and NaRanong 2006, 5).

Phongpaichit and Baker (2016, 68) point out that this universally available subsidy eliminated the stigma that had been associated with the need for low-income families to show welfare cards indicating their poverty, just as the voucher system Colombia did. They note that the public display of deep poverty of those who previously required cards to qualify for heavily subsidized service entailed both embarrassment and poor treatment. The basic point is that compared to means-tested subsidies, universal subsidies disguise the impoverishment of the lowest-income families and make health care a right.

7

Affirmative Action

Affirmative action (or "reservation") programs provide perhaps the most insightful window on the relationships among identifications, perceptions, and pro-poor policy. Affirmative action programs that designate particular sets of people as deserving favorable treatment both reflect and reinforce identifications and attributions. Affirmative action programs are distinguished from other benefit-targeting instruments by the ostensible goal of overcoming economic (and sometimes social) deprivations of variously defined groups. This is accomplished by providing privileged access to university admission, scholarships, university credits for community service work, bureaucratic jobs, and/or contracting with state institutions. Typically, part of the rationale is to redress past discrimination.

The four cases of affirmative action featured in this chapter, Brazil, India, Malaysia, and Sri Lanka, all exemplify the psychology of changing salience of self-attributes. They all reveal that poverty attributions and deservingness judgments can be highly questionable. The Brazilian and Indian cases clarify how formal designations can alter identifications and can change the scope of the ingroup. They demonstrate the ambiguity in assessing program eligibility because of the fuzzy boundaries of defining specific outgroups. They also illustrate how esteem can be sought through seeking more prestigious designations. The Indian case is distinctive in the efforts of some groups to self-categorize with higher-status groups, but without changing their core ingroup identification. It also reveals a paradoxical reversal of the meaning, for some groups, of the designation of "backwardness" from negative to positive attribution in terms of esteem.

Both of these cases demonstrate that ethnically dominant groups can be induced to support programs that privilege other groups suffering from deprivation. This belies the skepticism as to whether such explicit targeting can succeed, at least for a while, when ethnic and cultural identity overlaps with socioeconomic status. Over time, the Indian program has suffered serious targeting erosion, while the Brazilian program remains extremely vulnerable to reversal. Nevertheless, India's affirmative action program was largely well targeted for four decades, and the Brazilian program has elevated the need to address racial discrimination. The fact that the programs have targeted respect deprivations due to ascriptive identities (Dalits and Adivasi; Afro-Brazilians), accounts for why more straightforward means-tested benefit instruments would not have the same breadth of impact. Like all of the other instruments, affirmative action launched with laudable goals has both a distinctive rationale and serious pitfalls.

The Malaysian and Sri Lankan cases, highly distinctive from the bulk of affirmative action programs worldwide in benefiting the politically dominant groups, reflect complicated stereotyping patterns that serve to rationalize the programs. Malay leaders have exaggerated the wealth of other groups; Sri Lankan leaders had exaggerated the Tamil threat – until it became a self-fulfilling prophesy. In both cases, the dominant group has invoked its questionable historical victimization. The discrimination of the affirmative action programs in these two countries has national identifications, particularly among the minority groups. In Sri Lanka, rather than stereotyping all Tamils as the same, the government leaders have exaggerated the differences between the two Tamil groups. The tragic Sri Lankan case also demonstrates the complexity and ambiguity of judgments of deservingness.

GENERAL BACKGROUND

On the positive side, some affirmative action programs have been successful in improving the plight of long-deprived groups. This is certainly true for initial periods for two of the most prominent cases, India and Brazil. Yet, they may also exacerbate conflict and even perpetuate discrimination. For affirmative action programs based on ethnic (as opposed to gender) distinction, the programs increase the likelihood that ethnic distinctions will harden and that ethnicity will become a more important pivot of political and policy contention. Dupper (2014, 14–15), based primarily on his work on South Africa, argues that one of the central features of affirmative action is to redistribute social goods (such as jobs and places at university) along group lines. However, one of the dangers in this is that it may promote rather than undermine the differentiation of social groups. It may ... "freeze" individuals into the very status identity that a substantive equality aims to eliminate .... In addition, it may also perpetuate stereotypes .... Critics have alluded to the dangers inherent in replicating apartheid's racial grid in the pursuit of affirmative action. One of the consequences of making these racial categories salient is that it gives them ... an "illusion of ordinariness," which prevents a critical and reflective consideration of the social meaning of the existence of races.

Such "freezing" of inborn distinctions extends far beyond the South African context. Costa (2018, 60) argues:

In Latin American societies, the role of ascriptions in shaping social inequalities is especially relevant due to the fact that being identified with categories coined to describe subordinated groups during the colonial period such as "black", "mestiza/mestizo", and "india/indio" still determines, to a large extent, the position occupied by individuals in current socio-economic hierarchies. In most cases, these colonial categories have been removed from the legal or policy framework, and, in cases where they do still appear, they are used not for discriminating against groups but rather for naming target groups of affirmative action policies in favour of blacks, women, indigenous peoples, and so on.

Indeed, the prominence of the categories formally invoked in affirmative programs may even strengthen the perception of the targeted groups as deficient, undermining their economic, political, and social prospects beyond the confines of the affirmative action benefits. Thus Costa (2018, 60) argues that "these categories operate as ascriptive filters in everyday life, hindering the correspondent groups from accessing higher social positions, even in those cases for which formal equality of opportunities do exist." Entering an academic or bureaucratic institution as someone within an affirmative action category may be stigmatizing.

In addition, affirmative action benefits may come to be contested as any other economic assets. This explains, in part, why the targeting of affirmative action commonly becomes increasingly contentious, and the benefits for the neediest people are diluted. In some cases, the support of affirmative action programs by people who are themselves not covered can strengthen self-esteem of relatively prosperous identity groups, in demonstrating altruism. However, in some instances self-esteem may be seen as enhanced by demonstrating power; therefore, some groups may try to assert their power by pushing to qualify for affirmative action benefits themselves.

138 *Lessons from Pro-Poor Policy Instruments*

Despite these thorny issues, affirmative action programs are widespread. Jenkins and Moses (2014, 5) note the breadth of affirmative action programs in both developed and developing countries:

About one quarter of nations across the world use some form of affirmative action for student admissions into higher education. Although these policies go by many names – affirmative action, reservations, alternative access positive discrimination – all are efforts to increase the numbers of underrepresented students in higher education. Various institutions or governments on six continents ... have programs to expand admissions of nondominant groups on the basis of race, gender, ethnicity, class, geography, or type of high school. Several combine these categories. These combinations show that policies to offset racism or other forms of xenophobia can complement policies to fight economic disadvantages.

Most of the affirmative action programs for higher education were developed in the 1990s or 2000s, even while some of the most prominent, long-standing programs were coming under greater criticism, including in the United States and India. The impetus to address the disadvantages of groups suffering from past or present discrimination through affirmative action became an international focus through highly visible events such as the World Conference on Racism in Durban, South Africa, in 2001.

Two types of cases are worth exploring in depth: affirmative action programs initiated to benefit politically weak groups and programs imposed by politically powerful groups to benefit their own group. Thus, programs for Indian Dalits ("untouchables") and Adivasi ("tribals"), and the program for Afro-Brazilians, fall into the first category. The cases of Malaysia's affirmative action program favoring Malays, and the Sri Lankan affirmative action program favoring Sinhalese, fall into the second category. The rest of the chapter considers these cases because they most keenly epitomize the dynamics of identity and shifting bases of self-esteem.

In cases of affirmative action that privilege truly deprived groups, it may seem cruelly limiting that affirmative action programs often are confined to admission to universities and government positions, insofar as the bulk of low-income children cannot qualify. Yet, the successful cases of upward mobility through affirmative action may reduce the stereotypes of the groups as children become respected graduates or perform well in government positions. Certainly the fact that some of India's Dalits become professionals after graduating from university provides a rejection of the stereotype of Dalits as ignorant and incapable of upward economic mobility.

Affirmative Action

The granting of affirmative action eligibility has been employed in diverse ways, not always engaging self-esteem-enhancing sacrifice by more prosperous people. One crucial distinction among affirmative action programs is that while some programs are designed to benefit minorities (Uighurs, Ma, and others in China; Afro-Brazilians in Brazil), others benefit the majority (e.g., Blacks in South Africa, Malays in Malaysia, Sinhalese in Sri Lanka). In fact, there is a long history of majority groups granting favored status on themselves by limiting access and privileges to minorities, in many instances on the arguable grounds of past disadvantages facing the majority population.

As we shall see, like other instruments designed to reduce poverty, affirmative action programs need to be safeguarded from erosion, as wealthier people gain eligibility, thereby draining off the resources dedicated to the programs. Yet, affirmative action programs also face the complex dilemma as to whether the programs should recognize identities as defined by the individuals claiming eligibility, or by how the society in general perceives them.

India's Reservation System

India's affirmative action "reservation system" provides profound insights into the promise of channeling self-esteem-enhancing predispositions to a pro-poor program, but also the program's deterioration when sociopolitical standing was caught up with esteem based on strength. This system, greatly expanded beyond the limited programs under the British Raj and enshrined in the Indian constitution, was focused on the clearly most deprived Indians, the Dalits, and the Adivasis.[1]

Embracing the limited precedents set under British rule that reserved positions in universities and public administration only for the Dalits and Adivasis, the Indian leadership expanded the system throughout the country. Social as well as economic discrimination were cited as the justification for affirmative action, as part of the grand project to transform India into a democratic, egalitarian society that would eliminate the socioeconomic impact of the caste system. Indeed, affirmative action in higher education and bureaucratic jobs has resulted in some elevating

---

[1] To be sure, prominent Dalits were instrumental in enacting the affirmative action; most notably the jurist and highly prominent social reformer Bhimrao Ramji Ambedkar, yet the support of upper-caste Indian leaders was essential.

some of the original two eligible categories (Deshpande and Ramachandran 2016, 27).

The provision of benefits to virtually powerless groups raises the question of why higher-status Indians, in an extremely impoverished country overall, would countenance yielding job and university opportunities. Certainly, the egalitarian spirit of the independence movement played a role, yet the social psychology of ingroup status enhancement is also enlightening. Indian leadership was dominated by Brahmins, such as Jawaharlal Nehru, and other high-caste people, such as Mohandas Gandhi, of a prominent merchant Vaishya[2] subcaste. The affirmative action programs afforded the upper-caste leaders the opportunity to express their paternalistic superiority. Gandhi's term for the Dalits, "harijan" – "Children of God" – was widely viewed as paternalistic by the Dalits themselves (Muralidharan 2006, 34). This was a striking example of negative stereotyping reinforcing a strongly pro-poor accomplishment. Much effort on the part of leaders of the Congress party went into programs of "uplift" for Dalits. Both the action and the rhetoric afforded the opportunities to indulge both altruism and superiority. Lest there be any doubt of the paternalistic posture vis-à-vis the poor, Gandhi himself wrote in 1936 that the Dalits "have certainly not the intelligence to distinguish between Jesus and Muhammad and Nanak," and that some Dalits "are worse than cows in understanding" (Gandhi 1936, 360; cited in Nesiah 1999, 43). Despite these elements of prejudice – or perhaps because of them – the reservation system was progressive at the outset in focusing on the most marginal populations.

The "Creamy Layer": Relatively Prosperous Indian Jatis As "Other Backward Classes"

Nowhere is the leakage of benefits that otherwise would go to poorer groups more obvious than in India with respect to the expansion of affirmative action reservations for university admission and government jobs. Beginning in the late 1970s, other Hindu groups claimed that their low standing within the Hindu varna (caste) system entitled them to the status of "Other Backward Classes." This has given them separate quotas than those of the Dalits and Adivasis, to qualify for national or state

---

[2] In the Hindu caste system (*varna*), the Vaishya, though below the Brahmans and the Kshatriyas, are "twice born," the second "birth" being spiritual, and therefore among the "upper castes."

Affirmative Action 141

reservations for university admission and government jobs. Although economic deprivation has been a prominent criterion in granting OBC status, many wealthier subcastes (*jatis*), through political alliances, disruption, and intimidation, have qualified as OBCs. Most of these subcastes are of the Shudra caste (the fourth classification of the varna system, beneath Brahmins, Kshatriyas (warriors), and Vaishyas (merchants)), but some Vaishya *jatis* have received OBC status as well.

Empirical evidence reveals that some *jatis* have qualified without the socioeconomic deprivation that ought to justify qualification. Based on data from the 2011 to 2012 India Human Development Survey (IHDS), Deshpande and Ramachandran (2016, 1) examine

claims of three communities, viz., Jats in Haryana, Patels in Gujarat and Marathas in Maharashtra, to be classified as Other Backward Classes (OBC) in order to gain access to affirmative action. Comparing these three groups to the other major caste groups – Brahmins, Other Forward Castes, existing OBCs and Scheduled Castes and Tribes (SC and STs) in their respective states – on socio-economic indicators such as household consumption expenditure, poverty, access to infrastructure, self-declared practice of untouchability, education and occupational status, we find that these three communities are closer to the dominant groups – Brahmins and Other Forward Castes – than to the existing disadvantaged groups – OBCs and SC-STs. Thus, their claim to backwardness is not justified by empirical data.

Today, more than 40 percent of the Indian population qualifies for OBC status, along with the 28 percent of the population who are Dalits or Adivasi. With roughly 70 percent of the population in these three categories, the targeting of affirmative action is obviously problematic, which has given rise to bitter contention over whether the more prosperous *jatis* (the "creamy layer") should be disqualified from reservations.

From a poverty alleviation perspective, the problem of the great expansion of OBC status has been regressive. Although OBCs have a separate reservation category, insulating Dalits and Adivasi from OBC competition from wealthier, better-prepared applicants puts poorer OBCs at a severe disadvantage. Wealthier OBC families can afford to send their children to private schools, giving them an advantage over poorer OBCs. Heyer and Jayal (2012, 67) highlight the divisiveness within the set of OBCs: "Intra-group differences have also surfaced amongst OBCs, provoked by the fear that the quotas would be monopolised by higher-caste OBCs, such as the Yadavs, for example ... Upper-caste resentment against the policy reservations has also triggered a new awareness and entrenchment of caste identities."

Exception to Social Identity Theory?

In light of the prominent tenet of social identity theory that people desire to enhance the self-esteem of their ingroups, it is perplexing that certain prosperous *jatis* would try to gain the apparently demeaning official status of "backward." Although the Indian Constitution explicitly reserves the term Other Backward Classes for "socially and educationally backward classes," leaders of some of the most prosperous and prominent *jatis* have fought tooth and nail to obtain and retain OBC status and privileges. Their caste associations, pressuring political parties to grant or preserve OBC status, are powerful in no small part because they provide the benefits of affirmative action to their group members. "Backwardness" has lost much of its significance as an attribute of true backwardness.

The most plausible explanation for this apparent paradox is that the self-esteem and standing of some *jatis* are tied to demonstrations of power. This no better demonstrated than the confusing identifications of the northern Indian Yadav *jatis*, originally peasant-pastoral groups that have seen high levels of economic advancement. They boast of their business and political accomplishments, while vigorously defending their OBC status.

As the claim of backwardness for achieving and maintaining OBC status has lost its significance as a negative attribute, it has gained esteem in signifying the power to claim advantages in university admission and government positions. In short, OBC status enhances ingroup self-esteem insofar as that self-esteem is based on power. Going beyond the educational benefit of attending university, the goal articulated by Yadav in the above quotes is to use the higher status imparted by university education to supplant the dominance of Brahmins. Thus, the contestation over OBC status is a distributional struggle across political, social, and economic status.

In addition, the struggle over qualifying as an OBC has been responsible for considerable violence. Jaffrelot (2006, 184–185) reports that in fairly early years of the expansion of OBC status:

In 1990, the upper caste students, reacting against Mandal [the commission report opening the way for expansion], protested against both their loss of job opportunities and the challenging of a sociopolitical order they had always dominated (quotas in favor of the Untouchables [Dalits] having hardly affected them). Street demonstrations multiplied, students set themselves on fire (there were 63 such self-immolation cases), and the Supreme Court finally ordered the announced measures to be suspended.

Affirmative Action 143

However, the expansion proceeded despite court decisions.

One of the most prominent current cases involves the agitation by the Jats[3] of Haryana. In early 2016, the Jats engaged in protests against denial of OBC status, which escalated to burning vehicles, houses, and public buildings, sabotage of physical infrastructure, and robbery of an arsenal. Fifteen deaths were reported (Chatterji 2016).[4]

Ambiguity of Deservingness Criteria

The very painful confrontations unleashed by expanding affirmative action rest, in part, on the lack of a bright-line division between who do and do not deserve to qualify (Bayly 1999). The national and state governments' efforts to "graduate" (i.e., disqualify) wealthier *jatis* from OBC status, or to place them in a higher-income OBC category to receive smaller quotas, have aroused unyielding opposition (Jaffrelot 2006; *Rediff News* 2017).

It is important to note that the efforts of groups to enhance their status does not come from a rejection of the caste system. Obviously, claiming that one's *jati* deserves OBC status is an implicit acceptance of the caste system. In fact, some *jatis*, rather than rejecting the caste system because of their low standing within it, try to elevate their status within it, a pattern labeled as Sanskritization (in recognition that the Sanskrit scriptures defining the system). Some Yadav activists claim higher-caste Kshatriya (warrior) status, based on their highly arguable descent from a King Yadu and even of a putative warrior deified as Lord Krishna (Gooptu 1997, 891–893). The claim of Kshatriya status is just one example of how some OBC groups have reinforced their claim of higher status within the caste system by adopting practices associated with the higher castes. Yet, this clearly would be a disappointment to India's founders, who were committed to equality.

This "Sanskritization," though not a new phenomenon,[5] is particularly illuminating in light of the agenda of many originally lower-caste *jati*

---

[3] "Jats," a highly prominent group in many northern Indian states, are not to be confused with "jatis," the term for subcastes.

[4] I am grateful to Shambhavi Sahai for bringing this case, and the general practice of "Sanskritization," to my attention.

[5] Rudolph (1965) cites several cases of low-caste subcastes in the mid-nineteenth century adopting upper-caste clothing, abandoning "polluting" occupations, agitating to be permitted to enter temples previously off-limits, and asserting Kshatriyah status on the basis of claiming ruling status in the distant past.

144 *Lessons from Pro-Poor Policy Instruments*

associations to claim higher-caste status, even while trying to undermine the political and administrative status of Brahmins. Yadav (2009) argues:

> We often hear that reservation is a means to uplift the targeted community, to give opportunities to the deprived sections so that they may move upwards in education and jobs. Some persons even equate the reservation policy with poverty alleviation, job creating and education spreading programmes. These are vulgar understandings of reservation and create confusions and lead to wrong conclusions. One of these wrong conclusions is to keep the so called creamy layer among the backward out from reservation ambit. Even many backward caste people welcome the exclusion of the creamy layer from reservation ambit as a result of wrongful understanding of reservation.
>
> Reservation is nothing but a means to break the monopoly of handful of castes called upper castes …. Bureaucracy, police, judiciary, army, academics etc. are components of Indian state, or for that matter of any state, which are characterized by its monopolization by the brahmin and other upper caste people. Out and out undemocratic character of Indian state is not only due to its excessive centralized structure but also due to its social structure and character which is indicated by the dominance of its top, middle and low posts by the brahmin and other upper caste people.

Yadav (2015) further maintains the perplexing view that poverty alleviation is not at issue with affirmative action: "Reservations cannot uproot poverty. It requires other remedies. In fact, poverty has no connection with reservations. Reservations are meant to provide representation in power to all sections. It is meant to ensure that the deprived castes become partners in the governmental, administrative and democratic institutions so that the roots of the Indian nation state are strengthened." According to this logic, replacing caste status with economic status misses the importance of the political battle: "In India, there can be only one basis for reservations and that is caste. Reservations on any other grounds will not only be against the basic principles of social justice but will have disastrous long-term sociopolitical implications" (Yadav 2015).

These conflicts have led to enormous cynicism among Indians aware of the ways that prosperous *jatis* have attained OBC status. Despite efforts to restore the importance of addressing socioeconomic deprivation through the reservation program (Deshpande and Yadav 2006), the contribution of self-esteem-seeking in inducing pro-poor predispositions has been severely diminished. Perhaps this seeming disregard for ingroup self-esteem can be explained by the *jati* leaders' view that they are in a purely a distributional struggle. "Backward" has been shorn of its meaning, and original affirmative action goals may be irrelevant to *jati* leaders serving their people. The Indian case exemplifies the subversion of a

Affirmative Action

formerly pro-poor program because the group's standing – its political prowess – is enhanced by demonstrating its success in qualifying for affirmative action without a genuine economic deprivation rationale.

Finally, because contention over affirmative action maintains the importance of *jati* identity, whether or not a particular *jati* is accorded higher status, individuals remain tied to this identity and to the people within it. Although over the centuries many Hindus embraced Islam to escape low-caste status, self-categorization is not an option for Indians who remain Hindus. Individual status depends on the advancement of the *jati*, which helps to explain the importance of efforts to have affirmative action status, and the Sanskritization initiatives, despite what many observers would consider the implausibility of both.

Reform Efforts

As with the other affirmative action cases examined in this book (with the exception of Sri Lanka), initiatives have been launched to reform the program in India. The initiatives and reactions to them are highly enlightening in reflecting what affirmative action eligibility symbolizes and how identities are modified over time. The contention over the "creamy layer," and affirmative action overall, has given rise to a proliferation of reform efforts, for both government positions and university seats.

Regarding government positions, through guidelines developed by a "National Commission for Backward Classes" founded in 1993, and parallel commissions at the state level, some wealthier *jatis* were excluded from government positions (Deshpande and Yadav 2006, 2420). Yet, in 2015, in the face of agitation, the Commission backed off of establishing an average annual family income threshold equivalent to roughly US$15,000, elevating it to US$21,000 (Ghildiyal 2015); when the median family of six was earning less than US$4,000.

Regarding university admission, the reformers in opposition to eligibility for wealthier *jatis* hoped that officially established standards could be established and enforced. In 2006, Deshpande and Yadav (2006, 2420) asserted:

The exclusion of the "creamy layer," as per the definition evolved by the National Commission for Backward Classes (NCBC), is already in operation for job reservations. This could be applied to professional education …. This would guard against the bulk of the benefits being cornered by a handful of landed OBC communities that are much better placed than the rest to take advantage of caste-bloc based benefits. This would also ensure that the lower OBC

146 *Lessons from Pro-Poor Policy Instruments*

communities, mainly artisan and service communities whose educational condition is often worse than the upper crust of the SCs, will gain something from the new scheme.

No uniform standards emerged. The university reservation practices have been altered – some would say undermined – in a more disaggregated way, not only reflecting the flexibility that a federal system provides for state-level discretion, but also the discretion that universities have exercised in interpreting the regulations. For example, the highly prestigious Presidency University in Kolkata has been criticized for "de-reserving" seats that would go the OBCs, Dalits, and Adivasis (Sharma 2018). A controversial provision of the Reservation Act in Higher Education Institutions[6] provides the opportunity for universities to fill seats otherwise reserved for affirmative action applicants by setting standards high enough to exclude these applicants. The treatment of any category, Dalit, Adivasi, or OBC – creamy or not – ends up in the hands of bureaucrats and university administrators. In cases like this, the disdain for the entire system undermines the prospects of the neediest and most deserving as well as the others.

Still Neglected

In addition to the erosion of OBC targeting, the effectiveness of affirmative action for those who have not been squeezed out by the "creamy layer" has also been disappointing with respect to the Adivasi. Although "Adivasi universities" exist in Madhya Pradesh, Chhattisgarh, and Jharkhand, the geographic isolation of most Adivasi, combined with the likelihood that university attendance is virtually unthinkable, severely limit Adivasi potential to take advantage of affirmative action. Without university education – and low high school completion rates – the government employment reservations also often go begging. Back in 1999, Nesiah (1999, 51–52) reported that "[t]ribals who have sought reserved

---

[6] Where reservation of seats for one or many courses or streams in a particular academic session becomes unavoidable, the following procedure of de-reservation shall be followed:

> (a) If, after duly entertaining all applications to fill up reserved seats, it is found that some seats reserved for the Scheduled Castes, Scheduled Tribes, Other Backward Classes, Category-A and Other Backward Classes, Category-B remain unfilled during the academic session for want of suitable number of candidates from the respective categories, those seats may be de-reserved and filled up by general candidates where it is specified that due process for filling up of the seats by the candidates of the specific categories have been followed by the institutions concerned and no suitable candidate for the reserved categories is available to fill up those seats. No vacant reserved seat shall be carried forward to the next academic year, under any circumstances.

Affirmative Action

employment or reserved admission to educational institutions have often failed to meet minimum requirements, so that the bulk of their quotas have remained unfulfilled or, in some cases been filled by Dalits." Thorat and Desai (2012) demonstrate that this problem remains because of the weakness of preuniversity education among Adivasi.

Indeed, the plight of some Adivasi pose the fundamental challenge of enhancing the well-being of populations that are geographically isolated, largely beyond the reach of state services, outside of the money economy, and often leery about contact with others. The task is further complicated by the fact that although Adivasi constitute a formal designation, significant variation exists within this category. Generically, the term refers to peoples ostensibly of longest residence within particular areas ("first settlers"), who are neither Hindu nor Muslim.

Although the national government has launched many programs targeting the Adivasis,[7] the varied status of Adivasi is a serious challenge for a singular policy category. Nesiah (1999, 49) distinguishes among three distinct statuses for Adivasi:

The first group comprises the minority of tribals who have successfully adapted to modern circumstances, in a very much part of the mainstream, and enjoy a relatively high status in Hindu society. An example would be the Raj Gonds. In the second category are the many more tribals who have been partially "Hindu-ized" but have been less successful than those in the first group and have been assigned a lower status in the social hierarchy. Thirdly, there are the tribals in the hills and in the remote forests who have resisted assimilation, rejected alien cultural influences, and remain cut off from mainstream Indian society.

Nesiah's recommendation was that pro-poor programs based on reserving advantages beyond the reach of the Adivasi ought to be replaced with regional development programs that would put resources directly into Adivasi areas:

Unlike the Scheduled Castes, most Indian tribals live in concentrated settlements and can be reached by development programmes which are area-specific but not based on group affiliation. Tribals receive constitutional safeguards extending beyond those accorded to scheduled castes, e.g. reservation of tribal lands. Tribals also do not lose their tribal status and religious conversion, whereas an individual's Scheduled Caste status is lost if he or she converts [to] any religion other than Hinduism or Sikhism.

(Nesiah 1999, 51)

---

[7] Upadhyay and Pandey (2003, 193) reported that more than thirty-five national programs had targeted the Adivasi by 1990.

148   *Lessons from Pro-Poor Policy Instruments*

Nesiah probably could not anticipate a major consequence of regional development strategies applied in Adivasi areas. The 2004–2005 resurgence of the so-called Naxalite insurgency was a reaction to the threats to property rights and other problems arising from the influx of migrants and corporations into development-targeted areas. Regional development will be examined in the next chapter.

BRAZIL'S AFRO-BRAZILIAN AFFIRMATIVE ACTION

Without an appreciation for how group identity changes over time, sometimes quite abruptly, one cannot understand the stunning changes in Brazilian attitudes toward Afro-Brazilian affirmative action (Schwartzman 2009). As mentioned earlier, explicit racial awareness prior to the 2000s was submerged by the comforting myth of "racial democracy" denying the relevance of race *per se*. Poverty was largely viewed as a regional "Northeast" and occupational "subsistence farming" phenomenon. The 2001 Brazilian policy of formal recognition of the discrimination against people of obvious African ancestry (as well as the very small indigenous population) was a remarkable departure. Htun (2004, 61) notes that Brazil "has prided itself on being a multi-hued 'racial democracy.' The culture celebrates mixity, and racial categories are fluid and ambiguous. Yet Brazil is profoundly stratified by color, and for decades, the state did nothing to alter the situation. In fact, it suppressed efforts to challenge the racial democracy myth and sought to whiten the population by encouraging European immigration."

The change was initiated by President Fernando Henrique Cardoso (1995–2002), a very Caucasian-appearing former sociologist, who nevertheless claimed that his own great-great-grandmother was black and great-grandmother was mulatto. With roughly half of the population classifiable as "black or brown" (*preto* or *pardo*), and clearly much higher poverty among phenotypically Afro-Brazilians, it is striking that intensive deliberations within the Brazilian government occurred no earlier than the mid-1990s. Htun (2004, 61) argues:

It is difficult to overstate the significance of these particular changes in government policy at the turn of the century. For decades, talking about race in Brazil was heretical. People were hostile to challenges to the racial democracy thesis and reluctant to admit to racism. Moreover, recent policies are premised on novel understandings of identity: targeting "blacks" requires a recognition of racial distinctions among the population as well as a dichotomous definition of race (wherein "blacks" and "browns" become "blacks"). Yet Brazilians have thought

Affirmative Action

of themselves not as a people composed of distinct "races" but as a multi-colored national race. This helps explain the horror felt by many people toward the idea of quotas and the emotional nature of the controversy generated by affirmative action. It is not just social policy that is at stake, but the country's understanding and portrayal of itself.

The public universities, which are prestigious and, because of the constitutional prohibition against charging tuition, depend predominantly on government funding, instituted various levels of quotas for Afro-Brazilians and indigenous people. They also established quotas for graduates of public high schools, which are shunned by prosperous Brazilians. Graduates of public high schools, if they "identify" as Afro-Brazilian, could apply for quotas under either or both criteria.

Two aspects of the adoption and implementation of the affirmative action program are quite surprising from the perspective of interest-group politics. First, despite how radical this departure seemed to be, in terms of both myth and concrete policy, the program was put in place in the federal universities with surprisingly little organized opposition in at least some of the key locations. Schwartzman (2009, 228) reports that the law passed in 2001 by the Rio de Janeiro state legislature "was conceived and approved without much debate ..." and was strengthened thereafter.

Second, the adoption of Afro-Brazilian affirmative action runs counter to the conventional political premise that benefits go to groups that can exert sufficient influence over the policy process through political strength or the threat of disruption. An Afro-Brazilian advocacy movement did exist, but it had very few resources and little political influence. Skidmore (1992, 12) noted "[t]he relative lack of militant Afro-Brazilian protest in twentieth-century Brazil." Hernandez (2005, 684–686) argues that the lack of overt, official discrimination, such as the "Jim Crow" laws in the U.S. South, provided less impetus for the mobilization of Afro-Brazilians, as did the hope that intermarriage or career success would permit social advancement absent explicit barriers. Htun (2004, 62) points out that:

No pro-affirmative action constituency was powerful enough to mobilize a threat, rich enough to offer rewards, or connected enough to promise votes on election day. Armed only with arguments, critics of Brazil's racial order appealed to reason and a sense of justice to advance their cause. In a country struggling to prove its liberal credentials to the world, arguments about the connections between race, equality, and democracy found receptive ears.

Other authors (e.g., Schwartzman 2009) give more credit to social movements pressing for measures to reduce race-based poverty and

150 *Lessons from Pro-Poor Policy Instruments*

discrimination. She notes: "The slow transition from the military dictatorship to democracy during the late 1970s and 1980s allowed for a revival of the Black Movement, influenced by the civil rights and 'Black Power' movement in the United States. The new Movimento Negro Unificado (founded in 1978) gave rise to a series of grassroots black movement organisations" (Schwartzman 2009, 226). All of these observers emphasize the role of academics in empirically demonstrating the pervasiveness of discrimination against darker Brazilians and the dim prospects of existing mechanisms to bring about socioeconomic convergence. Afro-Brazilian activists, along with intellectuals restored to government and university posts following military rule, embraced a new "racial project": "simultaneous an explanation of racial dynamics and an effort to reorganise the social structure along particular racial lines" (Winant 1992, 183–184).

Prosperous Brazilians initially did not contest affirmative action as vehemently as did prosperous Indians when the OBC initiative was launched in India. In light of the magnitude of the quota system, which has supplanted many non-Afro-Brazilians' entrance into their preferred university, the mildness of reactions by the prosperous is illuminating. The embrace of the new "racial project" across many (but certainly not all) quarters among prosperous Brazilians is consistent with the reevaluation of Brazilian identity introduced in Chapter 5 of this book.

One possibility is that faced with the specter of more radical policies from the Left, prosperous Brazilians concerned were willing to yield some access to university or bureaucratic positions to preempt mobilizing *pretos* and *pardos* who would likely support the leftist Workers Party. Another, quite prominent interpretation is that compared to more threatening potentials of race-based inequality, the affirmative action program is an example of "restriction by partial incorporation": enacting policies and programs that appear to meet demands, but limiting their impact (Lasswell and Kaplan 1950, 282–283). It is significant that the prominence of the initiative, rather than being a tactical problem, is a political advantage in terms of responding to pro-poor pressure without provoking a destructive backlash.

A decade later, the Workers Party President Dilma Rouseff greatly strengthened the affirmative action policy by enshrining it in the 2012 "Law of Social Quotas," establishing how eligibility as an Afro-Brazilian should be determined for consideration by federal universities:

Affirmative Action

Article 1: Federal institutions of higher education linked to the Ministry of Education will reserve in each selective class for undergraduate admissions at least 50% of its seats for students who have completed high school in public schools.

Article 3: In each federal institution of higher education, those vacancies referenced in Article 1 of this Law shall be filled by self-declared pretos, pardos, and indígenas and persons with disabilities.

The key term is "self-declared." Legally, anyone who declared identification as Afro-Brazilian was to be considered as such.

Previously, the states had been mandated to pursue affirmative action in universities and public sector employment, but the decisions were to be made by the states and, in practice, by the universities themselves. Under the 2012 law, each university still established its own procedural protocol; for example, requiring a letter explaining why the individual would identify as Afro-Brazilian (Bevilaqua 2015). However, the 2012 law went further in terms of the magnitude of the commitment required of the federal universities. Its ambition is indicated by the expectation that the number of students admitted to the fifty-nine federal universities under the program would rise to 56,000 from 8,700 within four years (Romero 2012).

Despite the criterion of self-declaration, some applicants have been deemed to be too light-skinned to be admitted through the affirmative action quota. High-profile court cases resulted, with mixed consequences. The universities have experienced conflict between darker students and lighter students claiming Afro-Brazilian identity, with hundreds of light-skinned students expelled – accused of fraud – after being denounced by groups comprised of darker students (de Oliveira 2017; TeleSur 2016). The successor government, following Rousseff's highly controversial ouster, has seized on the problem of ambiguity by creating a commission to exclude individuals who do not appear to be Afro-Brazilian from qualifying for the quotas for civil-service jobs or state university admission, regardless of whether they express their identification as Afro-Brazilian. In short, the phenotype has won over expressed identity.

This is not simply a technical question, nor just a manifestation of the widespread challenges of ambiguity of what laws and regulations should be invoked when these rules are subject to different interpretations. It is, fundamentally, the ambiguity about what race means as a social construct. From the perspective of the individual, his or her identification as Afro-Brazilian – or any other racial category – entails an emotional attachment. In some cases, this may have been an attachment of convenience, but, at least for now, identity is disqualified as a criterion.

Conclusion: Racism Repressed

The deepest insights from Brazil's affirmative action experience revolve around the dilemma of honoring identities while trying to offset the stigma and the poverty of those who fit the stereotype of dark skin, uneducated, unsophisticated Afro-Brazilians. The affirmative action program has made Afro-Brazilian identification more salient, for both practical reasons and the very fact that high-profile policies and debates have focused on it. Yet the objective of enhancing the channels through which phenotypically Afro-Brazilians can advance economically and socially has weakened the relevance of identifications.

The irony is that the effort to reduce discrimination against obviously Afro-Brazilian individuals now relies on the stereotype, an external assessment, rather than the internal belief of how individuals define themselves. In effect, the denunciations of lighter-skinned claimants by activist groups of darker students strengthen the relevance of the stereotype, even as the activists try to strengthen Afro-Brazilian identity.

How do we understand a country whose light-complected citizens pride themselves on not being racist, and yet regularly discriminate against darker Brazilians? The jokes against Northeasterners (Fontes 2016, 39–40) emphasize their poverty and their primitive, violent, slovenly nature, but not their blackness. Layton and Smith (2017, 54) report that "controlling for various objective measures of economic status, dark skin tone is a strong determinant of perceiving class and gender discrimination, as well as racial discrimination. In other words, race underlies discrimination even when respondents fail to perceive it as race-based." Yet Layton and Smith (2017, 52) also noted:

Consistent with Brazilian national myths, respondents [from the Northeast] were much more likely to report discrimination due to their class than to their race. Nonetheless, the respondent's skin color, as coded by the interviewer, was a strong determinant of reporting class as well as race and gender discrimination. Race is more strongly associated with perceived "class" discrimination than is household wealth, education, or region of residence; female gender intensifies the association between color and discrimination.

The Brazilian case is puzzling in that prior to the launch of the affirmative action program, the Brazilian discourse certainly had a significant focus on poverty and the skewed income distribution, but the discourse was eerily neglectful of the racial aspect. Little explicit indication existed that Brazilians felt guilty about the extremely strong correlation between African phenotype and poverty. Perhaps this reflects the fact that roughly half the population has some degree of African blood. Focusing on race as a problematic attribute might be taken as an aspersion on anyone with African ancestry, even if only partial. In addition, an emphasis on race could have brought up painful ambivalence. On the one hand, sharing African heritage may lead individuals to believe that they were exempt from responsibility and guilt for discrimination against Afro-Brazilians. On the other hand, if race had been prominent in public discourse, Brazilians with some degree of African heritage might have felt guilty for not addressing the fraternal deprivation of darker Brazilians.

After Cardoso initiated the quota policy, racial identification became more salient, and more Brazilians self-identified as Afro-Brazilian in the census (Htun 2004). Later, as opposition arose to privileging university or job applicants whose phenotype does not reflect African ancestry, the phenotype criterion replaced the self-identification criterion (Bevilaqua 2015; TeleSur 2016). This may shrink the proportion of Brazilians who regard themselves as Afro-Brazilian. This might have the positive effect of focusing benefits more sharply on individuals who are more deserving of support to overcome discrimination, but it may also increase tensions between light- and dark-skinned Brazilians.

The future of Brazil's affirmative action, as with other pro-poor programs such as the Bolsa Familia conditional cash transfer program, hinges on whether the newly emergent polarization and the deteriorating psychological climate continue, despite a perfect storm of crises. Lasswell (1935/1965, 60–65) introduced several categories of such crises; originally applied to international relations, they hold just as well for domestic crises. An "insecurity crisis" has arisen due to the economic and political crises. The economic crisis is obvious, in light of the collapse of the commodity boom and the high spending of the Workers Party. The politically based insecurity crisis, as Lasswell (1935/1965, 61) notes, is particularly acute when the rivals (in the Brazilian case, mobilized Right and Left) are roughly equal in strength. Such crises harden positions and narrow identifications.

The other crises – exasperation and indignation – are more emotional. An "exasperation crisis," provoked by the frustration that the powerful cannot effect changes among the less powerful, is manifested in Brazil because of the inability to stem the rising crime rates, despite pro-poor policies, as well as inability to reconcile the contending criteria for affirmative action. It is reinforced further by the disappointment over Brazil's failure to maintain its progress to catch up economically with Chile and Argentina. The climate of exasperation is likely to reduce the patience that the prosperous have toward needy Afro-Brazilians and the

154 *Lessons from Pro-Poor Policy Instruments*

poor in general. An "indignation crisis" has been triggered by the Odebrecht bribery scandal that now has Lula da Silva incarcerated. All of the Workers Party policies are vulnerable to the outrage stemming from the scandal, reinforced by exasperation. This perfect storm has already undermined Afro-Brazilian unity, and, in all likelihood, will lead to the reduction of pro-poor programs.

MALAYSIA

Malaysia's affirmative action program, greatly expanded beyond the modest pro-Malay program established under British rule, illuminates how majoritarian favoritism improved the standing of Malays, but at the cost of impeding ethnic reconciliation, undermining long-term economic development, and exacerbating destructive conflict manifested by outmigration and disinvestment.

Background

After expelling heavily ethnically Chinese Singapore in 1965, Malaysia's ethnic composition was two-thirds Malay, one-quarter ethnically Chinese, and 7 percent Indian. Malays were predominantly agricultural; Chinese engaged in commerce; Indians, originally brought in to work in the plantations, had diversified occupationally. This starting point had the usual implications for relative income levels. Hassan, Asan, and Muszafarshah (2011, 113) summarize that:

most of the Malays, who lived in low-income states, were involved in the traditional agriculture sector and were less productive, while non-Malays (most of them migrated to Malaya in the early 1900s) lived in high-income states (colonial concentration states), and were involved in the non-agriculture sector or modern agriculture sector with high productivity …. Most of the indigenous Malay population which remained in the agriculture sector, mainly in rural areas, or in the less-developed regions of the East Coast of peninsular Malaysia, was largely bypassed by the new development.

The defining moment of Malaysia's escalation of affirmation action was the 1969 anti-Chinese riots, precipitated by election results resulting in opposition parties encroaching on the Malay-dominated ruling coalition. The diagnosis by leaders of all groups was that Malay resentment, reinforced by the belief that the British had favored the Chinese, was the root cause. Leaders representing the Chinese and Indian Malaysians acceded – presumably reluctantly – to a sweeping reservation system

Affirmative Action 155

under the 1971 "New Economic Policy" (NEP). Although the Malaysian Constitution did not specify the special privileges of affirmative action, the measures have encompassed land reservations, public-service quotas, license and permit quotas, scholarships, and reservations in higher education (Yusof 2012, 131). Even now, developers are required to give Malays discounts when they buy new houses (*The Economist* 2017).

The NEP was explicitly cast as a means "to eradicate poverty among all Malaysians and to restructure Malaysian society so that identification of race with economic function and geographical location is reduced and eventually eliminated, both objectives being realized through rapid expansion of the economy over time."[8] Thus it is striking that Malaysia's affirmative action, as in India, was to be temporary. Yet it prevails more than four and a half decades later.

The chastening came after dramatic UMNO legislative losses in 2009, when a new Prime Minister promised to reform the economic model as well as to relax some of the authoritarian security measures (although the latter were actually strengthened). The economic-policy liberalization initiative of the "New Economic Model" (NEM) was presented as eliminating much of the preferential treatments as well as drastic cuts in fuel and food subsidies. Momentum had been building to reform the system that had been in force for nearly three decades, despite the early promises of its temporary nature and amid growing concern that the social integration was eroding rather than improving. Yusof (2012, 178) argues that the debate over whether the Malaysian model has deterred conflict "would not have stimulated such a widespread and deep interest if not for an already smoldering climate of civic disgruntlement." The resentment, disillusionment with hypocrisy, and feelings of being trapped as a permanently maligned minority fueled the desire of many Malaysian Chinese and Indians to isolate themselves and, in the extreme, to emigrate. As Al Ramiah and Ramaswamy (2013, 203) note, "non-Malay Malaysians (especially those who are more educated) express a desire to disengage with Malays and to migrate from the country if the opportunity should arise."

The impetus, then, was to embed the affirmative action reforms within a broader package to respond to the vulnerability that the Malaysian economy demonstrated during the East Asian financial crisis of 1997. The tensions that increased during and in the aftermath of the crisis made it seem ripe to tackle the affirmative action problems: "New concerns in the

---

[8] Cited in Sabbagh (2004, 6).

reclamation of equal citizenship rights by non-Bumiputera, the need for interethnic 'liberal' solidarity to counter contending Islamic systems ... and the strengthening of the new politics of civil society goes beyond ethnic gains ... constituted the compelling reform agendas in the fashioning of the more inclusive plural Malaysia" (Yusof 2012, 178).

Thus the "New Economic Model" initiative began with a first ambitious postelection reform document. Jan and Saiful (2011) report that the initial proposal "called for a radical shift from focusing on helping the Malays to helping the bottom 40% income groups regardless of ethnicities. This is a noble attempt. The document argues that 'past affirmative action programmes have also inevitably propagated and embedded a distributive and entitlement culture and rentier behavior.'"

However, despite the dissatisfaction with the existing policies by all groups, the backlash by Malay groups against abandoning affirmative action was strong and effective, emboldened by their awareness that the government would be vulnerable if these groups were to back other political contenders. Haryono and Khalil (2018, 5) note that:

Any policy change that touches on Malay privileges is risky. The launch of the NEM Part 1 in March 2010 led to an outcry from Malay nationalists, particularly about the lack of a "Malay agenda" . . .. This eventually led to the pro-Malay agenda being reborn in the Concluding Part document. Complaints from ethnic Malay pressure groups are taken very seriously by the government. The Prime Minister's party, UMNO, is an ethnic-based Malay party. Thus, UMNO leaders, and especially the Prime Minister who is also UMNO President, cannot ignore the demands and threats made by Malay nationalist campaigners . . .. [T]he influence of Malay nationalists, through UMNO, in Malaysian national politics cannot be ignored.

The result was a significant reversal of the reform proposal. Jan and Saiful (2011, 2) report that "government wavering became apparent . . .. [S]ome suggestions were quietly killed off . . .. [T]he tone changed almost completely, suggesting 'targeted special programmes for certain groups outside of the bottom 40% (. . .) should continue.'"

The persistence of Malaysian affirmative action reflects at least four factors. First, overall, Malays are still poorer, although the gap has narrowed (*The Economist* 2017) and the incomes of the bulk of Malays have risen above the conventionally defined poverty lines.[9] Rural Malays

---

[9] Nixon, Asada, and Koen (2017, 3) summarize:

Malaysia's sustained rapid real GDP growth of 6.4% per annum from 1970 to 2015 reduced the incidence of absolute poverty from 49.3U% to 0.6% . . .. Some challenges remain, with higher rates of absolute poverty in rural areas (1.6%), for children under

Affirmative Action

and the urban poor may still blame the Chinese, but the advantages have largely accrued to much wealthier Malays who could avail themselves of the business opportunities often in collaboration with Malaysian Chinese. A recent assessment by *The Economist* (2017) reflects the widely accepted conclusion that Malaysian affirmative action "allows a disproportionate amount of the benefits of affirmative action to accrue to well-off Malays, who can afford to buy the shares set aside for them at IPOs, for example, or to bid for the government contracts." When state lands were privatized, the main beneficiaries from land reservations were wealthy Bumiputera (Malay and other indigenous) landowners and moneylenders (Nesiah 1999, 201). Therefore, the statistics demonstrating convergence are heavily weighted by the incomes of the privileged, while the majority of Malays see Chinese and Indian Malaysians as still wealthier.

The second factor is the fact that the affirmative action, though enacted as an emergency expedient, legitimized ethnic favoritism in the eyes of the Malays. Jomo and Hui (2003, 444) maintain that "while the NEP probably eliminated some ethnic Malay resentment of Chinese economic success by accelerating the advance of Malay middle class and business interests, it may well also have generated even greater Malay expectations of their rights, entitlements and privileges under the Malaysian sun."

The third factor is that the economic costs of foregone opportunities of the program can be gauged only through sophisticated analysis. Such analysis is always contestable in political discourse, in contrast to the concrete figures of enrollments, contracts, and other accomplishments that program defenders can demonstrate. Arguments based on the counterfactual analysis asserting long-term failures to take advantage of industrialization opportunities are difficult to convey. In addition, on the subjective level, the magnitude of dissatisfaction could not be assessed fully because of the harsh prohibition against questioning the affirmative action policies. In 1971, an amendment to the Malaysian Constitution forbade, among other policies, questioning Article 153 of the Malaysian Constitution, that grants the special affirmative action status of the

---

15 (1.7%) and for particular ethnic groups (Orang Asli 34%; Bumiputera Sabah 20.2% and Bumiputera Sarawak 7.3%) still a focus of poverty reduction efforts, with programmes providing food, financial aid and skills training. Income inequality has gradually reduced from very high levels, with low income households and previously disadvantaged ethnic groups benefiting more than proportionately. The income share of the top 20% of households compared to the B40 [bottom 40 percent] has declined substantially over this period, at a faster rate than Malaysia's overall Gini coefficient for household income.

Bumiputras (Means 1991, 7; Nesiah 1999, 202). Even proposing changes, therefore, would constitute sedition. This also permitted the government to claim that affirmative action was successful in furthering integration. Guan (2005, 215) noted that: "The government has frequently argued that the preferential policy of raising Malay participation in the economy and higher education would help to ensure stability and foster national integration."

The fourth factor is the risk aversion of the leaders of the long-ruling Malay party, UMNO. Not only were they chastened by the 2010 backlash against the initiative to transition to a poverty-based rather than ethically based approach, but also they knew that Malay favoritism virtually guaranteed continued UMNO dominance. It has been the party of preserving Malay privileges.

Consequences

Economic Trajectory

The consequences of Malay affirmative action are perplexing. There is no doubt that poverty reduction among Malaysians has been remarkable. Yet, recalling that the incomes of the poor typically rise in concert with the overall economy, much of this reduction is the result of overall economic growth common throughout Southeast Asia, as is the reduction of income inequality. Yet because of the strong correlation between overall economic growth and the income growth of the poor, the longer-term prospects for poverty alleviation have been jeopardized because favoring Malay-owned businesses has undermined industrialization and has diverted investment into low-productivity sectors. Tan (2013, 23) concludes that:

Deindustrialisation and the shift towards resource-based manufacturing and unproductive sectors were reinforced by changes in the direction of FDI [foreign direct investment] flows and emergence of PI [portfolio investment] as a result of financialisation. These processes were part of broader accumulation strategies driven by domestic class formations, in particular the need to balance growth with political pressure for redistribution to accommodate a new Malay middle and business class.

However, the favoritism accorded Malay-headed firms, while making some Malays very wealthy, has not maximized the size of the prosperous middle class. As in the case of India, and to a lesser extent Brazil, the leakage of benefits to the non-poor is distressingly high. This is true despite government efforts to limit the "Ali Baba syndrome" of non-Malay firms

Affirmative Action 159

buying up Malay shares, or Malay firms fronting for Chinese entrepreneurs (Navaratnam 2002, 18).

The lack of enthusiasm for the affirmative action program lies in the absence of any element of individual or group self-esteem in supporting the program. Chinese and Indian Malaysians cannot feel magnanimous about a program forced upon them. Malays demanding the continuation of favoritism in effect acknowledge their collective failure to reach the levels of prosperity or occupational standing of the Chinese or Indian Malaysians. Parallel to the case of India's wealthier OBCs, Malays demonstrate naked political power based on numbers rather than merit. In Malaysia, as in India, people of all three major ethnicities are cynical about the operation of the affirmative action programs.

The development of a Malay middle class is also limited by Malays' difficulties to succeed in the face of the typical bias against people believed to be in their positions or credentialed only because of affirmative action. The literature on affirmative action is replete with arguments that students admitted through affirmative action not only labor under their own doubts about their capacity, but also under suspicion by others. The same holds for Malay business people who have contracts because of affirmative action preference, and of Malay business people who are incorrectly believed to have the contracts because of favoritism. The business opportunities are hollowed further by the fact that shrewd businesspeople would opt for working with Chinese-owned firms or majority-Chinese-owned firms with Malay fronts (Whah and Guan 2017). Yet, economic opportunities have also been lost because of non-Malay alienation and apprehension, reducing skilled human capital across all sectors: "As schools, universities and the bureaucracy have become less meritocratic, Chinese and Indians have abandoned them, studying in private institutions and working in the private sector instead. Many have left the country altogether, in a brain drain that saps economic growth" (*The Economist* 2017, 18).

This apprehension also contributes to the volume of illicit capital flight. The estimate of illicit financial outflows from Malaysia over the 2005–2014 period ranges from 8 to 12 percent, compared to the Philippines at 7 to 8 percent, Thailand at 2 to 4 percent, and Vietnam at 4 to 5 percent (Global Financial Integrity 2017).

One obvious question is whether Malay gains justify the economic losses. *The Economist* (2017, 18) offers an insightful comparison: "Malays in neighbouring Singapore, which abjures racial preferences, have seen their incomes grow just as fast as those of Malays in Malaysia.

160   *Lessons from Pro-Poor Policy Instruments*

That is largely because the Singaporean economy has grown faster than Malaysia's, which may in turn be a product of its more efficient and less meddling bureaucracy. Singapore, too, has been free from race riots since 1969."

Sociopolitical Relations

The impact of Malaysia's affirmative action has been starkly mixed in terms of intergroup relations. Norhashim and Aziz (2005, 36) judged that "Prejudices about the capabilities and traits of the various races began to fall slowly." In terms of political stability, Yusof (2012, 159) notes:

Malays are the most politically dominant group, while the Chinese ... are economically powerful. Because of this configuration, there seem to be compensatory mechanisms on both sides, and potential for envy and resentment which could lead to violence is stultified. Given the not-so-large size of Malays (53 percent of population) and the not-so-small size of Chinese (26 percent), neither group alone influences political outcomes, particularly in electoral politics. Hence, it is the forging of cross-cutting alliances and compromises between these major groups with other groups that kept the alliance formula alive.

In contrast, Lee (2017, 1), certainly reflecting the Chinese Malaysian perspective, expresses the darkest interpretation, that:

the debate over affirmative action in Malaysia is wrapped up in larger debates over citizenship and democracy. A policy designed to remedy inequalities among groups is now seen as a tool for marking who belongs (Muslim Malays) and who does not, raising minority fears that the refusal to rethink affirmative action reflects a broader trend to redefine Malaysia either as a state that belongs to the ethnic Malays, in which Indians and Chinese are at best subordinate guests, or as a Muslim state, in which Hindus, Christians and others are subordinated.

The Economist (2017, 18, 19) assessment concurs:

If the benefits of cosseting bumiputeras are not as clear as they first appear, the costs, alas, are all too obvious. Malays have stopped thinking of affirmative action as a temporary device to diminish inequality. As descendants of Malaysia's first settlers, they now consider it a right.

The result is that a system intended to quell ethnic tensions has entrenched them. Many poorer Malays vote reflexively for UMNO, the Malay party that introduced affirmative action in the 1970s and has dominated government since then, for fear that another party might take away their privileges. With these votes in the bag, UMNO's leaders can get away with jaw-dropping abuses, such as the continuing scandal at 1MDB, a development agency that mislaid several billion dollars, much of which ended up in officials' pockets, according to American investigators. Minorities, in turn, overwhelmingly support parties that advocate less discrimination against them.

The dramatic scandal that brought down Prime Minister Najib Razak in 2018 has not loosened the rigid party structure, nor increased the potential to reform the affirmative action that none of the elite favor. *The Economist* (2017, 19) argues that "defining [affirmative action beneficiaries] by race is a mistake .... It would be much more efficient, and less poisonous to race relations, to provide benefits based on income. Most recipients would still be Malays. And defusing the issue should pave the way for more nuanced and constructive politics. Perhaps that is why UMNO has resisted the idea for so long."

The Malaysian experience raises the prospect of other countries settling on a long-term redistributive arrangement to increase the incomes of the poor progressively in exchange for a commitment, explicit or tacit, that a sufficiently large contingent of the poor will desist from destabilizing violence. This is not to say that the Malaysian solution of affirmative action for the numerically and politically dominant group is an optimal approach. One premise of such an approach is that concern for the disruptive potential of the poor is great enough to induce the relevant non-poor to accede to the bargain. In India, the truly poorer groups have not evidenced enough dissatisfaction or capacity to pose a threat to demand more than the diluted affirmative action program. In Brazil, the threats of violence in the post-guerrilla and repression era of the 1960s and 1970s have been turned inward toward street crime and drugs.

SRI LANKA

Affirmative Action at Its Most Destructive

The affirmative action program in Sri Lanka demonstrates how definitions of group identities shape the claims of discrimination, and, in this case, have led to egregious discrimination through an affirmative action program that contributed to enormously destructive conflict. The 25-year insurrection of Tamil separatists (1983–2009), with over 80,000 deaths and over 2,500,000 Tamils seeking refuge in India alone (Dasgupta 2003), was strongly shaped by the direct affirmative action in university admission and indirect affirmative action through language policy. The case also illuminates the ways that the identity as citizens can be contested. The Sinhalese-dominated government has instituted favorable treatment for the Sinhalese majority for more than six decades, combining a pro-Sinhalese affirmative action program with language policies and other measures that provoked the Tamil separatist movement. This is a

162 *Lessons from Pro-Poor Policy Instruments*

TABLE 7.1 *Poverty headcount by province, Sri Lanka, 1990/1991–2016*

	1990/91	1995/96	2002	2006/07	2009/10	2012/13	2016
Sri Lanka	26.1	28.8	22.7	15.2	8.9	6.7	4.1
Western	19.1	16.3	10.8	8.2	4.2	2.0	1.7
Central	30.7	36.2	25.1	22.3	9.7	6.6	5.4
Southern	30.2	32.6	27.8	13.8	9.8	7.7	3.0
Northern	–	–	–	–	12.8	10.9	7.7
Eastern	–	–	–	10.8	14.8	11.0	7.3
North Western	25.8	27.7	27.3	14.6	11.3	6.0	2.7
North Central	24.5	24.7	21.5	14.2	5.7	7.3	3.3
Uva	31.9	46.7	37.2	27	13.7	15.4	6.5
Sabaragamuwa	31	41.7	33.6	24.2	10.6	8.8	6.7

Source: Government of Sri Lanka Department of Census and Statistics www.statistics.gov
.lk/EconomicStat/EconomicStat2017.pdf

more extreme case of majority-serving affirmative action than the
Malaysian case, with a more specious claim of past discrimination. The
impact of discrimination against Tamils, as indicated in Table 7.1, is
clearly demonstrated by the greater poverty headcount in the Northern
Province, in which Tamils comprise 93 percent of the population. The
Eastern Province, with the second-highest incidents of poverty, as a Tamil
plurality of 39 percent, with Sinhalese constituting only 23 percent and
Muslims ("Moors") making up the rest (Newhouse and Silwal 2018, 3).

Background

The ancestors of both the Sinhalese and the so-called Sri Lankan Tamils
migrated from India beginning more than a thousand years ago. The "Sri
Lankan Tamils" could claim ancestry in particular Sri Lankan districts
(Peebles 1990, 31). The so-called Estate Tamils (or "Indian Tamils") had
been brought in to work the coffee and tea plantations beginning in the
1840s. At the time that the British willingly granted independence in
1948, having just lost India, the Sinhalese constituted roughly 70 percent
of the population. The "Sri Lankan Tamils" were 11 percent of the total
population; the "Estate Tamils" were 12 percent. That proportion
declined over the years as many Estate Tamils were expelled and Sri
Lankan Tamils emigrated to avoid violence.

The first postindependence government was under the Sinhalese–Tamil
coalition United National Party (UNP), though representing the far more
numerous Sinhalese, the Sinhalese leaders were more powerful within

Affirmative Action 163

the UNP. The government moved to deny citizenship to the Estate Tamils. This was taken as a threat to the Sri Lankan Tamils as well as the Estate Tamils. Singer (1996, 1147) points out that the treatment of the Estate Tamils was very much of concern to the Sri Lankan Tamils:

Once independence was granted, one of the first things the Sinhalese-dominated government did was to disenfranchise the Estate Tamils – who made up almost half of the Tamil population on the island at the time and who had lived there for generations – on the grounds that they were "Indians" and not really Ceylonese. Many Tamils date the beginning of the current ethnic conflict to that event. Obviously, India did not want to take back over a million poor Tamil estate workers, who would certainly be unemployed. However, through negotiations lasting many years, large numbers of the Estate Tamils did return to India while others managed to gain Sri Lankan citizenship. The disenfranchisement of the Estate Tamils in 1948-49 was certainly unnerving for the Ceylon Tamil population. Almost immediately the Federal Party came into existence among Tamils, demanding a federal system for Ceylon.

Ultimately, many Estate Tamils were forced to move to India, through agreements between the Sri Lankan and Indian governments. Although many of the families of Estate Tamils had come to Sri Lanka more than a century ago, citizenship rights degenerated into bargaining between the Sri Lankan and Indian governments. Some Estate Tamils were granted Sri Lankan citizenship, particularly if they were property owners and educated; eventually most who were not sent to India became Sri Lankan citizens. Despite the harsh treatment by the Sinhalese-dominated government, Estate Tamils stayed out of the civil war, if only because the separatist movement was sited in the North, far from the Estate Tamils' residence in the tea-producing Kandyan Hills in central Sri Lanka.

Growing Ethnic Polarization

As disputes arose over the proportionality of legislative representation, the federalist initiative, and the fate of the Estate Tamils threatened with expulsion, a small Tamil party and a growing Sinhalese Sri Lanka Freedom Party (SLFP) emerged. Horowitz (1989) points out that because the political party structure separated into Sinhalese and Tamil parties, the two Sinhalese parties, the UNP and the SLFP, have had to cater to Sinhalese interests in their seesaw competition for power, the SLFP more extremely.

By 1956, the uneasy coexistence between Sinhalese and Tamils crumbled with the electoral victory of the far more polarizing SLFP. The government almost immediately initiated the "1956 Official Language Act" to restrict the language of government to Sinhalese, to be phased in gradually because of the dominance of English among government officials and various concessions to Tamils (Oberst 1988, 182). Ultimately – though it took several decades – Tamil became an "official language." Yet, the initial exclusion and long-term discouragement of non-Sinhalese-speaking individuals from the bureaucracy has lasting effects, given the fact that once entrenched, it is difficult to redress ethnic imbalances in the bureaucracy. In addition, university instruction in Sinhalese discouraged Tamils from enrolling (Singer 1996, 1148).

As the SLFP and the UNP vied for power over the years, they both became largely Sinhalese parties. Whenever the SLFP controlled the government, the conditions for the Tamils became more discriminatory. Pro-Sinhalese affirmative action for university admission was instituted in 1973 through assigning different entrance-examination scoring criteria (Tamil students suffered a 20-point disadvantage) and by district quotas (Gunawardena 1979; Roberts 1978, 368). Roberts (1978, 368) reported that by 1978 the policies had reduced Tamil enrollment in the "prestigious science-oriented courses" from 40 to 25 percent. The voting district rules gave the Sinhalese even greater legislative representation than their share of the population.

The Sri Lankan Tamils had many grievances, not the least of which were the periodic anti-Tamil riots by Sinhalese. Yet dissatisfaction with the language policy, the bias in government employment, and the imbalanced parliamentary representation added greatly to the agitation for a federal system to provide the Sri Lankan Tamil areas with more autonomy and protect Tamils from attacks. Some Tamil groups began sporadic attacks on state targets in 1972. Rebuffed in the demand for a federal system, armed groups explicitly committed to secession began in 1977. In 1983, attacks on Sri Lankan soldiers led to brutal retaliation by both the army and Sinhalese rioters in a form of collective retaliation that forced roughly 150,000 Tamils to flee the country (Fearon and Laitin 2011, 202). This escalated to brutal civil war. The most aggressive Tamil group, the Liberation Tigers of Tamil Eelam (LTTE) terrorized both Tamils and Sinhalese. With the crushing of the LTTE in 1997, the civil war came to an end.

The first key contextual fact is that language – Sinhalese and Tamil – not only has been the first-order definition of ethnicity, but also largely overlaps with religion (Buddhist Sinhalese and Hindu Tamils). The relevance of these obviously highly salient overlapping cleavages undermined a biethnic coalition party that could have addressed the Sinhalese–Tamil benefits balance much more constructively.

Second, the category of "Tamil" is extremely complicated and of highly contested nature. The uncontested aspect is the consensus that two Tamil communities exist in Sri Lanka, separated geographically within Sri Lanka and by the history of their arrival in the country. The total number of Tamils at the time of Sri Lanka's independence in 1948 was nearly 23 percent of the population. The latest (1946) census before effective independence in 1948 counted "Ceylon Tamils" (later "Sri Lankan Tamils") as 11 percent of the population. They began migrating to Sri Lanka at least a thousand years ago, and the so-called Indian Tamils or Estate Tamils, constituting 12 percent of the total population, Yet, prior to Sri Lanka's independence, they were British subjects, thus of equal status as the Sinhalese and the Ceylon Tamils, along with a variety of smaller minorities (Shastri 1999: 68–69). However, being subjects of an empire does not ensure citizenship following independence, especially since independence is typically accompanied by disavowal of colonial structures.

Problematic Deservingness

How could the Sinhalese rationalize such blatant self-favoritism over such a long period? It loses its legitimacy in light of the legacy of periodic violent attacks on Tamils prior to the civil war, and the declining relevance of the argument that Sinhalese economic disadvantages were due to alleged British "divide-and-conquer" tactics that ended in the 1940s. The rationales that could be invoked by a politically and demographically dominant group to justify its own favoritism might include greater need, rights, past discrimination warranting reparations, and greater rectitude than other potential beneficiaries. In the case of the Sinhalese, none of these rationales would be convincing to outside observers.

Need
Part of the Sinhalese stereotype of Tamils is that Tamils are crafty in business, leaving Sinhalese economically vulnerable (Roberts 1978, 367). Government leaders also turned the Sinhalese against the Tamils by invoking the existential threat that Sri Lanka would be engulfed by India. Phadnis (1972, 1495) noted "the Ceylonese fear of the 'complete political and economic extermination of the Ceylonese, primarily the Sinhalese' and the harm caused to the 'sons of the soil' by Tamil dominance over the economic life of the country. Such fears have been raised, not only the

166   *Lessons from Pro-Poor Policy Instruments*

1930s and 1940s, but also in the 1960s by prominent political leaders of the island."

It is striking that the Sinhalese claim of disadvantages in bureaucratic employment and university enrollment was based on a self-serving treatment of the two Tamil communities as totally unconnected. This is remarkable to an outsider, inasmuch as ethnicity is the crux of the conflict. Focusing exclusively on the Sri Lankan Tamils and their moderately greater bureaucratic representation (11 percent of the population holding 19 percent of government positions), the ruling party claimed this Tamil "overrepresentation" justified the Sinhala-only government-language policy. Yet, at the time of independence, "Tamils" of both communities constituted 23 percent of Sri Lanka's population – greater than the 19 percent of bureaucratic positions.[10] The claim of "overrepresentation" of Tamils in government can be sustained only by regarding the two Tamil populations as distinct even though they are ethnically and linguistically extremely close. Kearney (1978, 527) judges that the ethnic imbalance in government employment was "often grossly exaggerated."

Rights

Sinhalese leaders have long maintained that Sinhalese have "sons of the soil" rights. Jayawardene (1983, 14–15) characterizes the "Sinhala-Buddhist" ideology:

[I]f the Sinhala people could put forward claims to being the first civilized inhabitants and therefore the legitimate "owners of the country," all other migrants who had come at a later date were regarded as "foreigners." The concept thus grew that Sri Lanka was the land of the Sinhalese and that non-Sinhalese who resided there were allowed to do so by grace and favour of the "master race" who had prior rights of possession and were the exclusive "sons of the soil."

However, the Sinhalese "sons of the soil" claim rests on very shaky grounds. The Sri Lankan Tamils also claim "sons of the soil" status. Fearon and Laitin (2011, 202) note that the Sri Lankan Tamils regard themselves as indigenous. Horowitz (1989, 202) points out that the Sri Lankan Tamils immigrated "on average" a thousand years ago. Daniel (1989, 22) notes the lack of clarity as to "who came first, the Sinhalese or the Tamils."

---

[10] See also Wickramasinghe (2012).

Reparations

The reparations argument rests on the assertion that under British "divide-and-conquer" rule (Eelapalan 2013), the Sinhalese suffered discrimination (particularly in government jobs). For this argument to be plausible, it would have to be established that the British favored the Tamils by elevating them in government positions. In fact, the greater facility in English that gave the Tamils advantages in education and applying for government jobs was due to the work of American missionaries rather than British instruction (Eelapalan 2013; Hashim 2013, 67). And, whatever Sinhalese may have thought that the British had done, the Tamils could not be blamed for British colonial tactics. Unsurprisingly, the Sinhalese rhetoric, with roots going back to the racial theories of the nineteenth century, posits Sinhalese heritage as North Indian "Aryan," and the superiority of Buddhism, as affirming their racial and moral superiority (Jayawardene 1983, 14–15).

Superior Rectitude

Phadnis (1972, 1493) noted that "[s]tudies on the Sinhalese-Tamil stereotypes reveal a mutual distrust often bordering on contempt and fear." Tamil "craftiness" connotes unscrupulousness, the Sinhalese Tamils have been stereotyped as usurious, miserly, and clannish (as in caste-conscious) (Daniel 1989, 23). In contrast, the Sinhalese stereotype of the Estate Tamils had been that they are "wretchedly poor, live in filth, are uneducated, wear rags, are good coolies and breed children who are docile domestic servants" (Daniel 1989, 23). In short, the Sinhalese view of Tamils is bifurcated along Sinhalese Tamil-Estate Tamil lines, both negative, though in quite different ways. The Sinhalese Tamils are to be feared; the Estate Tamils to be expelled or dominated.

Psychology of Mobilization

The Sinhalese SLFP provocateurs also took advantage of the victimization dynamic. In 1952 Prime Minister Dudley Senanayake warned that unless immigration from India were reduced, there would be "no question of war [with India] as Ceylon in that case automatically become part of India."[11] In fact, Tamil immigration soon declined dramatically. However, the specter of a flood of some of the more than 70 million Tamils

---

[11] Cited in Phadnis (1972, 1495).

168 *Lessons from Pro-Poor Policy Instruments*

across the Gulf of Mannar, swamping Sinhalese political control and culture, was a perennial trope by Sinhalese leaders.

Affirmative Action Insights Regarding Social Identity and Self-Categorization

An important insight into the dynamics of individual versus group mobility is the importance of the degree of rigidity of identifications. Sindic and Condor (2014, 41) argue that social identity theory

> provides a model of the ideological context in which the identity management strategies that people adopt to deal with an unsatisfactory social identity may be expected to lead to collective action .... The most important of these conditions is arguably the perceived permeability of group boundaries, that is, the extent to which people believe that it is possible for individuals to move between social groups. In so far as members of socially devalued groups perceive *individual mobility* to be possible, they may respond to their inferior status by attempting to 'move up' the social hierarchy and by psychologically dis-identifying with the group to which they currently belong. However, when such mobility is perceived to be impossible or undesirable, people may engage in various forms of collective activity aimed at changing the comparative value associated with their group as a whole.

Thus, in India, rigid subcaste identifications, precluding the possibility of reidentifying with other *jatis*, compel Hindus seeking upward social mobility to enhance the standing of the *jati* collectively. In contrast, dark-skinned Afro-Brazilians strive to protect the boundaries of this identity from phenotypically white Brazilians in order to reduce the competition for affirmative action benefits. Ethnic Chinese and Indians in Malaysia and Tamils in Sri Lanka, formerly and perhaps still among the more prosperous groups in the country, also cannot escape the ethnic identities rigidified by affirmative action programs. Representatives of these groups, attempting to fulfill their role in defending the interests of their respective groups, are less likely to support pro-poor policies insofar as the beneficiaries are likely to be of other groups.

Of course, ethnicity does not have to be the basis for affirmative action. It is possible to base eligibility for special benefits more directly on economic need. Two such approaches have been employed. First, reservations for admission to higher education can be based on the distinction between public schools (i.e., government-funded)[12] and

---

[12] Not to be confused with the British use of "public schools" to denote independent, and hence, private ones.

private schools, in those countries where public schools are perceived as being so inferior (or signaling low status) that more prosperous families would opt for private high schools. In Brazil, in addition to the problematic affirmative action program for Afro-Brazilians, a quota exists for public school graduates. This designation entails less contentious ambiguity than Afro-Brazilian identity, although some ambiguity is in the requirement that half of the public school quota is reserved for low-income families (Davis 2014, 76). Providing scholarships for low-income students who demonstrate academic accomplishment, supplemented by enrichment programs outside of the public school day, also can avoid the challenge of defining "sufficient degree of blackness."

8

Regional Development Targeting the Poorest Areas

The final broad approach to addressing poverty alleviation is to target investment to the poor regions of the country (Richardson 1982). It may not be the case that the very poorest people reside in that region, but a low regional per capita income is typically a good indication of the existence of many poor people. Equally important, insofar as people perceive that they are living in one of the poorest regions, they may very well press for investment to redress the disparity between their region and wealthier regions.

The case of Thailand's poorest region, the Northeast, Isaan, is noteworthy primarily because of how it exemplifies the dynamics of resentment leading to destructive conflict. Unlike the other cases, the focus is predominantly on the psychology of the poor. Their resentment, and presumption of outgroup malice, accounts for a breakdown of the equilibrium based on mutual intergroup respect – which nevertheless eventually alters the status of the poor as participants rather than passive subjects in policymaking. It is a striking case of toxic intergroup interactions based on distorted meta-stereotypes of outgroups' attributions of the ingroup, exaggerated evocation of victimization, and redefinition of desired self-attributes as negative if held by others. Despite the negative attributes projected onto most of the wealthy, many of Isaan's poor exhibit vicarious aspirational identification with wealthy and corrupt populists. The identities of Isaanese are marked with deep ambiguity, leading to acceptance of inferiority for some, self-attributes of superiority for others.

General Background of the Logic of Pro-Poor Regional Development

A common element of economic growth theory is that the levels of prosperity of initially poorer and richer regions within a country will converge. Poorer regions become more attractive as the high-return investment opportunities in the richer regions have already been taken (Barro and Sala-i-Martin 1992; Martin 1998). In addition, when governments proclaim plans to develop backward regions, expectations of convergence are likely to be even higher.

The reality, however, is that convergence is often illusory, as illustrated by the cases of India (Lolayekar and Mukhopadhyay 2017) and Turkey (Gezici and Hewing 2004). New opportunities may arise in the wealthier regions, adverse conditions (including political instability) may hold in the poorer regions, and national government spending simply may favor the wealthier regions. In addition, national government spending that may have reduced the disparities previously may have a smaller effect because of a fiscal decentralization trend. Lessmann (2012) examines the trends in inequality in fifty-six developing and developed countries from 1980 to 2009. He concludes that decentralization is associated with greater regional equality in developed countries, but greater inequality in developing countries. It is possible that economic growth gains can be redistributed more easily in developed countries. For developing countries, perhaps interregional redistribution is less likely, and economically backward regions remain unattractive for investment.

In many ways it is challenging to persuade even prosocial people in wealthier regions that the government should prioritize poorer regions. Favoring poor regions may not favor the poorest within those regions, and, in fact, regional development featuring natural resource extraction may lead to the displacement or other deprivations of poor people within the targeted region. In addition, knowledge of the conditions of poorer regions may be quite limited, and people of the wealthier regions may stereotype the residents of poor regions as content in living "simpler lives." Finally, people in wealthier regions can always point to poor people within their own regions. The reasons for people from wealthier regions to acquiesce to prioritizing other regions typically include self-interested concerns over unwanted migration into the wealthier regions, or the risks of destructive conflict. Thus, regional development as a poverty-alleviation approach may be more about the risks of ignoring the poorer regions. People of those regions may flood into wealthier regions, with high potential for destructive conflict.

172 *Lessons from Pro-Poor Policy Instruments*

When regional development does target poor regions, the related challenge is the potentially disruptive impact of development in areas that typically are poor because they are more traditional economically and culturally.

THAILAND

The regional development patterns of Thailand, and the surprising reactions to them, are highly revealing of the psychology of resentment and conflict, as well as the limitations of relying on overall income-distribution trends. The case has fascinating contradictions: people in the poorest region of Thailand have "come of age" in terms of political activism, although this has come at the cost of some violence and a military government. Political mobilization, and identities as politically engaged, have, for the time being, led to a stronger political exclusion than before the mobilization. The country's poorest region has benefited from regional development initiatives of the central government before, during, and after populist governments, confirming the convergence model, yet the populist leaders were driven from government and into exile. The psychology of political mobilization, interregional resentment, and evolving identities make this case highly illuminating. It is important to recognize how deference deprivations have fueled both the polarization of regional identities and the escalation of interregional hostility.

Thailand's challenges of poverty alleviation, contested identities, and conflict are felt most keenly in Isaan, the country's Northeast region. As the country's poorest region, many Isaanese harbor deep resentment against the Thai state and the more prosperous central (Bangkok) region. It may seem surprising that the main paradox of the psychology of conflict in Thailand is not sited in the South, with the high-profile Muslim–Buddhist confrontation. While the South has had a prominent international dimension over the secessionist movement to wrest parts of the South to join Malaysia, Isaan is irrevocably part of Thailand, despite its Laotian roots. Isaan shares Buddhism with most of the rest of Thailand, and a huge number of Isaanese get their livelihoods working in the Bangkok area, and send remittances back home. It is also puzzling that many Isaanese came to be anti-monarchist, even though the Thai Buddhist reverence for the late King Bhumibol Adulyadej[1] would be expected to be high in the deeply conservative region.

---

[1] The King died in 2016, succeeded by his son, Maha Vajiralongkorn. Attitudes toward the new King, who lives in Germany rather than Thailand, remain to be seen.

Regional Development Targeting the Poorest Areas   173

The depth of resentment and mobilization in Isaan has surprised observers with knowledge of the long-term trends in the relationship between the region and the central government. Charles Keyes (2014, vii), a longtime observer of Isaan, having written a book about the region in 1967, wrote in 2014 that

It seemed puzzling to me that there should still be a northeastern problem despite the fact that today Thailand enjoys friendly relations with Laos even though it has a communist-led government; despite the fact that rural northeastern earners clearly gain from the dramatic growth in the Thai economy over the past half-century even if not nearly as much as has the elite in the urban middle-class; and despite the fact that people with roots in the Northeast today have long since come to accept and understand that they are Thai even if they also retain strong attachment to their rural hallowed traditions.

The other surprising pattern is that although national income inequality has been declining[2] and Isaan's growth rate conforms to the convergence model, regional disparities in absolute terms have increased.[3] Equally important from a political perspective, awareness of overall improvements in income distribution have not reduced the anger concerning regional disparities. A World Bank (2018b) assessment concludes that "[a]lthough inequality has declined over the past 30 years, significant and growing disparities in household income and consumption can be seen across and within regions of Thailand, with pockets of poverty remaining in the Northeast, North, and Deep South." This brings into question the relevance of the overall income distribution as a driver of attitudes toward income discrepancies.

---

[2] The Gini index for Thailand over the two decades ending in 2009 went down by nearly four points, the greatest reduction in inequality in East and South Asia (Balakrishnan, Steinberg, and Syed 2013, 5). A 2017 World Bank assessment noted that the incomes of the poorest 40 percent of Thailand's population grew at nearly 5 percent annually from 2009 to 2013, compared to the growth rate of 3.5 percent of the economy as a whole (World Bank 2017a). This was not a quirk of the "Great Recession"; The World Bank (2017b) also noted that "Poverty declined substantially over the last 30 years from 67% in 1986 to 7.2% in 2015 during periods of high growth and rising agricultural prices." In 1981 the bottom 40 percent of income earners had 26 percent of total income; by 2013 it was 29 percent. The bottom 20 percent earned only 5.4 of the national income in 1981; this increased to 6.9 percent in 2014.

[3] This is because a wealthier region may be growing more slowly, but even a lower growth rate on a higher base may increase the absolute disparity. For example, a 4 percent annual growth for 5 years of a per capita income of US$20,000 would increase the income to $24,334. A 6 percent annual growth for 5 years would increase an initial income of $5,000–$6,691. Thus the initial absolute discrepancy of $15,000 increases to $17,643. This is why a focus on the absolute discrepancies can yield the conclusion that convergence does not hold for Thailand (Limpanonda 2015).

Background

With roughly 70 percent of the Isaanese population engaged in largely low-productivity agriculture, it is hardly surprising that Isaan has long been the poorest region, as shown in Table 8.1. Although Isaan is the most populous Thai region, the poverty is not attributable to relative overcrowding – the population density is lower than that of the South, and not much greater than the population density of the North; the density of the Central region, not surprisingly given the Bangkok area, is much greater.[4] Hundreds of thousands of Isaanese find work, usually in low-paid occupations, in the Bangkok area.

Before the 2000s, Isaan had not been a highly mobilized region politically aside from voting. However, in 2001 the business magnate Thaksin Shinawatra was elected with strong backing from Isaan as well as the relatively low-income Northern region where his family was based. In establishing his party and in campaigning for the 2001 election, Thaksin did not adopt the classic antiestablishment populist rhetoric. In fact, his coalition featured businesspeople, elements of the security forces, and established provincial politicians.[5] Yet eventually, he consolidated his support from the poor regions by enacting strongly pro-poor programs where greater proportions of the poor lived – and was rewarded with political support as a consequence. Phongpaichit and Baker (2016, 11) note:

The Thaksin government of 2001-05 [*sic*] introduced a universal healthcare scheme, several windows of microcredit, and additional farm price subsidies. The healthcare scheme is credited with moving several hundred thousand households above the poverty line by reducing household expenditure on health, and safeguarding poor households against the financial disaster of health crisis in the family …. The impact of the other measures are more difficult to gauge, but Thaksin was rewarded with high popularity, and people told surveys and interviewers that they gave him loyal support because of the impact of these measures ….

---

[4] In 2010, Isaan's population density was 112.3 persons per square kilometer; in the South, 125.4; in the North 68.7; the central region 1095.8. City Population: Thailand 2018.

[5] Pathmanand (2016, 136–137) points out that Thaksin's "first network" "included big business groups, provincial politicians, and elements from the Army and the police. Apart from the front-line prominence of big business figures, who normally preferred a more veiled political role, this network was only marginally different from others seen in the recent past." Similarly, Phongpaichit and Baker (2008, 63–64) note that "When Thaksin formed the Thai Rak Thai (TRT) party in July 1998, there was little sign of his later populism. Thaksin was a spectacularly successful businessman from prominent business family in Chiang Mai. On founding the party, he explained that its principal mission was to rescue Thai businessmen from the 1997 financial crisis and to restore economic growth."

Regional Development Targeting the Poorest Areas

TABLE 8.1 *Regional per capita income ratios to Bangkok and vicinity levels, Thailand, 1995–2016*

	1995	2000	2005	2010	2015	2016
Northeast	0.08	0.09	0.11	0.17	0.18	0.18
North	0.12	0.13	0.17	0.23	0.23	0.23
South	0.23	0.23	0.28	0.37	0.32	0.34
East	0.58	0.67	0.92	1.16	1.04	1.08
West	0.21	0.23	0.28	0.34	0.33	0.34
Central	0.36	0.42	0.50	0.68	0.63	0.61
Bangkok and vicinities	1.00	1.00	1.00	1.00	1.00	1.00

Source: Calculated from Government of Thailand, National Economic and Social Development Council. www.nesdb.go.th/nesdb_en/main.php?filename=national_account

Some of Thaksin's development policies had an even greater impact on Isaan because of the greater potential to replace low-productivity activity. Several policies promoted alternative economic activities with higher earning potential. For example, Kaboski and Townsend (2009, 30) note that: "The Million Baht Village Fund injection of microcredit in villages has had the desired effect of increasing overall credit in the economy. Households have responded by borrowing more, consuming more, and investing in agriculture more often than before. The village fund credit has had the effect of decreasing future assets, increasing future incomes, and making business and market labor more important sources of income." Policies of this nature were important in the partial transition of Isaan from traditional farming to more diversified economic activity.[6] Yet, more prosperous rural people – the emerging entrepreneurs – benefited from the development projects that the Thaksin government brought in Haughton (2009, 61).

Politically, upon discovering the pent-up demand for an antiestablishment populist, Thaksin supplemented the high-profile programs with highly publicized and personalized "performances" that skeptics regarded

---

[6] Ouyyanont (2017, 344–345) notes that:

> Rapid changes in agriculture had a profound effect on the Northeastern way of life. Capitalist production had expanded and replaced subsistence production . . .. After the green revolution in the 1960s, the proportion of rice grown for household consumption began to decrease, and many households started to grow rice commercially. Nevertheless, such decrease was less than in other regions partly because the expansion of market economy in the NE took place much later than in other regions. Many villages cannot sell their products due to limited transportation stemming from seasonal road conditions.

176 *Lessons from Pro-Poor Policy Instruments*

as crass. He broke precedent through highly staged televised encounters in which low-income individuals recounted egregious deprivations and then received cash directly from him.[7] The self-esteem of rural people rose as he cultivated the image of listening and responding, rather than isolating himself in Bangkok. His Thai Rak Thai Party also held mass rallies in many more rural locales than the centrist parties had, emphasizing the new image of the villager as a politically empowered participant in Thaksin's movement.

Low-income rural Thais took on a new image of engaged citizens, enhancing their self-esteem without having to give up their identities as farmers. Yet they were engaged only through the connection with the party leader. Such acts are quintessentially populist and symbolize a direct connection between the top leaders and citizens, bypassing the governmental apparatus. In the Thai case this also meant competing for loyalty with the monarchy, which previously had nearly monopolized such symbolic acts targeting social welfare.

Thaksin's promises on both poverty alleviation and economic growth were extravagant (Warr 2005, 392), far exceeding even the impressive progress on poverty alleviation that was accomplished. Phongpaichit and Baker (2008, 67) report Thaksin's promise of:

extension of the village funds, land deeds for every landholder, a government pond dug for anyone prepared to pay a small fuel cost, four new cheap loan schemes, free distribution of cows, training schemes for the poor, cheaper school fees, special payments for children forced to drop out of school because of poverty, an educational gift bag for every new mother, care centres for the elderly, more sports facilities in urban areas, cheaper phone calls, an end to eviction from slums, more cheap housing, lower taxes, more investment in the universal health scheme, a nationwide scheme of irrigation, and a deadline for the end to poverty.

While this led to cynicism the part of economically sophisticated observers, the ebullient reaction of his supporters, cast as being on the

---

[7] Phongpaichit and Baker (2008, 65) elaborate:

First, he manufactured a public presence significantly greater than that attempted by any previous Thai prime minister, primarily by using state-owned media now under his control. He launched a weekly radio show in which he talked to the nation for an hour about his activities and his thoughts on issues of the day. He dominated the daily television news and also appeared in several special programmes, including an evening chat show in which he lamented his predecessors' handling of the economy. In the final climactic sessions of the assets case, he walked the final stretch to the court through an avenue of supporters, pressing the flesh like an American electoral candidate. In an extraordinary innovation, the final summaries by plaintiff and defence in the assets case were run live as a television special.

Regional Development Targeting the Poorest Areas 177

verge of great economic advance and coupled with the new respect signaled by his attentiveness, was unprecedented in Thai history. Pitch (2004) noted the empowerment emerging from the impact of the programs, his responsiveness to their demands, and because citizens seemed to gain equal and direct footing in relation to the state.

It is worth noting that Thaksin is the antithesis of the poor Isaanese farmer; not just in terms of his wealth, but also in his pride in his Chinese heritage, as evidenced by his highly publicized visit to his grandfather's village in Guangdong during an official visit to China in 2005. It is rather common for low-income individuals to be attracted to extremely wealthy populist leaders, possibly reflecting the phenomenon of aspirational identification (Weinreich 2005, 9). The wealth implies success; having these successful people on one's side might lead to one's own success. Yet Thaksin was not "just wealthy"; he had also been a police officer, foreign minister, vice premier, and had earned a US doctorate in criminal justice. In short, aspirational identification had many bases in the adulation for Thaksin.

Thus, when the military deposed Thaksin in 2006 on charges of corruption, resentment crystallized in a series of often-violent confrontations involving the Isaan-based, so-called "red shirt" movement. Thaksin's party was then banned, resulting in a centrist civilian government that the red shirts considered illegitimate. The confrontations reached their most destructive point in the spring of 2010, when the red shirts burned Bangkok sites, including the huge Central shopping complex, the stock exchange, banks, the headquarters of the state electricity corporation, and other government offices. They also burned the municipal building[8] of the major Isaan city of Khon Kaen. In the confrontation with security forces, many red shirts were killed.

The symbolism of the red shirt movement was strongly and deliberately provocative, through the attire and the label. Some red shirt activists believe that "red" is simply the color of resistance (Taylor 2012, 137); other observers speculate on deeper connotations. Salamat (2011, 5) ventures:

There is no vivid proof as to the reason for UDD to hold red as symbolic colour, but it is presumably because red is simply and explicitly contrast to yellow. Moreover, while yellow has been accepted as the throne or royal colour, along

---

[8] As a unitary state, Thailand's central government appoints governors and city officials in most provinces. Therefore, the municipal building was a symbol of the central government.

178   *Lessons from Pro-Poor Policy Instruments*

with other countries in Asia, it is also the King's symbolic birthday colour, which is hostile to red, according to Thai astrology.

Whatever the interpretation, the choice of red certainly has been an anti-state symbolic act, and to a certain degree represents a distancing from the late King Bhumibol Adulyadej. Thais concerned about maintaining stability had elevated the King to a status of reverence, without explicitly acknowledging the limited discretion he had vis-à-vis the armed forces. The draconian *lese majeste* restrictions, and the banning of books critical of the King, reveal the fear of disintegration of the existing political formula, with the possibility of much heightened conflict. In all likelihood, these fears contribute to the military's opposition to the electoral participation of the Shinawatra movement.

In the aftermath of Thaksin's ouster, some outside observers warned that Thailand was on the brink of civil war (Chambers 2010). Despite martial law and the banning of Thaksin's Thai Rak Thai Party, Thaksin loyalists remained mobilized. When, after considerable turmoil, a centrist civilian coalition government led by the Democrat Party took office in 2008, the red shirts engaged in a prolonged series of marches, sit-ins, and other anti-government actions as discussed previously. By 2011, in the face of continued disruptions and the unraveling of the centrist coalition, the Prime Minister dissolved parliament and called for new elections. The military did not ban the relabeled Shinawatra party from running, resulting in a quite clear red shirt victory: Thaksin's party, relabeled and running Thaksin's sister as its prime ministerial candidate, won in 2011.

One might expect that the charges of corruption, nepotism, authoritarian actions, and undermining the authority of the King would erode the support of the Shinawatras among followers, especially in light of the moralistic aspects of conservative Buddhism. It may be that corruption is considered to be so pervasive that Thaksin's actions would be considered as normal, or that the criticisms against him were false. The cognitive dissonance[9] between adulating Thaksin and Yingluk, and accepting the validity of corruption charges, would be high. In addition, the perception of the "Thai elite" as untrustworthy can reinforce the belief that the charges are false. Of course, these dynamics exacerbate the antagonism across regions.

In addition, Yingluk Shinawatra continued the same populist vein as her brother, and, in terms of regional development, devoted far greater

---

[9] The discrepancy between preexisting information, attitudes, or emotions and new information can cause psychological distress, often leading to rejection of the new information. See Festinger (1957).

Regional Development Targeting the Poorest Areas 179

central government funds to Isaan, triggering a building boom and higher wages reflecting a higher minimum wage. This was on top of remarkable growth from 2007 to 2011, during which Isaan's cumulative economic growth was 40 percent, compared to 23 percent for Thailand as a whole and 17 percent for the Bangkok area. The Yingluk government promised an infrastructure program that was to total US$71 billion, with a high-speed railroad, intended to connect Thailand to China through Thailand's Northeast, as the centerpiece (Carsten and Temphairojana 2013).

The disruptions that the red shirts undertook during the period before Yingluk was elected were replaced by agitation by the yellow shirts and accusations by centrist leaders of corruption in the Yingluk government. The military deposed her in 2014. The fears of a civil war between red shirts and yellow shirts have subsided. Both Thaksin and Yingluk are living abroad; the Thai military is still indirectly in power, through electoral and legislative manipulations ensconcing the dominance of a party largely handpicked by the military leaders.

It is perhaps surprising that red shirt disruption since the 2014 coup has been quite limited. Of course, military repression plays some role, but equally important is the fact that the military government continued to prioritize Isaan's development. Sabpaitoon and Theparat (2017) reported that in August 2017 "[t]he cabinet allocated 1.7 billion baht for the construction of the Thai-Sino Bangkok-Nakhon Ratchasima high-speed train, 33 billion baht for a Public-Private Partnership (PPP) venture for the operation and maintenance of a Bangpa-in-Nakhon Ratchasima motor-way, and 2.6 billion baht to elevate the double-track railway in a down-town section of Nakhon Ratchasima."[10] The junta also revived the decentralization initiative, focusing on devolution plans for the Northeast, the North, and the South to cover agriculture, transport planning, environment management, health care, economic development, finance, education, industry, and training. Presumably, military leaders have had a strong incentive to placate Isaanese. The government installed in 2019, with strong representation of the Shinawatra party despite the military's manipulation to dominate the government, is likely to continue in the same vein.

The improvements resulting from the regional development targeting of Isaan certainly contribute to the economic growth and the reduction in poverty in the region. Confirming the convergence dynamic, the gross

---

[10] Roughly equivalent to US$50 million, $1 billion, and $80 million, respectively.

180 *Lessons from Pro-Poor Policy Instruments*

regional product per capita in the Northeast in 2015 was 3.77 times as great as in 1995, compared to 3.27 for the North, 2.51 for the South, 3.26 for the East, 2.87 for the West, 3.08 for the Central region, and only 1.79 for Bangkok and vicinities.[11] Isaan's internationally recognized poverty headcount, at 69 percent in 1990, was reduced to 13 percent in 2016 (Durongkaveroj and Ryu 2018, 28).

Thaksin's mobilization of the rural population, particularly in Isaan, dramatically changed the self-perception of villagers as passive subjects to the guidance of the military and the state. The red shirt movement belies the narrative of northeasterners as immature "villagers," that is so clearly an insult to their self-esteem. Regardless of whether the Shinawatra populists and other political elites have been manipulating the movement, the formerly largely passive people, particularly Isaanese, concluded that they could organize, make demands, influence policy, and elect legislators – as long as the military lets them.

Prior to the turn of the century, Isaanese levels of political activity, beyond the representation by elected officials of centrist, Bangkok-centered parties and provincial governors appointed by the central government's Interior Ministry, were very low. Before the Thaksin regimes, rural villagers and low-income peri-urban residents throughout Thailand were subjected to overtly paternalistic treatment by the Thai state. Elinoff (2012, 383) characterizes the mentality – though possibly in overly stark terms – as follows:

"Villagers" … need to be protected from both the external world and from themselves via various types of state and non-state government, especially those rooted in the technologies of development and visions of improvement. In short, "villagers" [chaoban] are the nation's most governable subjects because they are "not yet" prepared to act as full citizens …. [I]t is this "not yet" that marks villagers as critical but volatile subjects in need of government intervention. The always impending transformation from "not yet" to "now" is precisely what enables a whole host of development-based interventions that never actually fulfil the promises embedded in these temporal politics.

This is not to say that Isaan was the only region to experience this paternalism. The armed forces and the Bangkok-centered elite have been committed to modernization throughout the country, led by centrist politicians when government has been in their hands. When the military has ruled, modernization has been pursued through bureaucratic

---

[11] Statistics are from the Government of Thailand 2016.

authoritarianism – the coalition between the bureaucracy and the modernizing military.

This is complicated by the fact that the Thai military leadership has long viewed its role as both guardian and guide to civilian society – including the civilian elite. The role of the military as the overseer of Thai affairs, reflecting its penetration into the national administration, is remarkably strong (Lee 1999). Heiduk (2011, 264) concludes: "The Thai military see themselves as the guardians of the monarchy and of a very patriarchal concept of democracy and ultimately as genuine political actors .... Corresponding with its doctrine, the military's operational tasks went far beyond external defense and included the provision of internal security, political stability, and national development."

Yet the elections of the Shinawatras altered expectations in profound ways. The prior heuristic-based assumption of low influence, based on many previous instances, no longer seemed accurate. A new script emerged: organizing the poor under a populist leader, and resorting to aggressive confrontation, could bring the previously ignored people into the political game.

Although the military intervened against the Yingluk government and the red shirt movement, it is likely that the mobilization will endure, both in the consciousness that the potential for disruption can be effective and in the political imperative for the regime to accommodate Isaanese demands. These demands, for the continuation of social programs and greater physical infrastructure investment, have not been disappointed. The quiescence of the red shirt movement in recent years is, in part, due to regional development initiatives targeted to Isaan. Although it was tragic that people were killed during the red shirt uprisings, the silver lining is that the paternalism toward the "villagers" is now confronted with political maturation of rural ties, Isaanese included. They have progressed beyond the *parochial* orientation of nonengagement with politics and policy beyond the locale, and many have adopted a *participant* orientation of engagement with the possibility of making demands effectively.[12] As Anderson (1964) pointed out in the Latin American context, the credible threat of significant disruption has often been the only way that

---

[12] The classic developmental construct of Almond and Verba (1963) on political maturation posits a transition from the parochial orientation, to a subject orientation to the participant orientation. The sudden mobilization by Thaksin seems to have skipped the intermediate orientation.

182   *Lessons from Pro-Poor Policy Instruments*

previously marginalized groups have been able to become actors in the policy process.

The Multiple Bases of Resentment in Isaan

The first level of red shirt anger is the intertwined combination of the apparent neglect of the Isaan economy and the political exclusion of the red shirt movement upon the ouster of first Thaksin and then Yingluk. The red shirt movement derived its mobilizing capacity from the belief that Thai governments – with the exception of the Shinawatra regimes – neglected Isaan in term of regional development.

The reality, however, is that subregions within Isaan indeed had been favored by regional development initiatives well before the Shinawatras.[13] Ouyyanont (2017, 322) notes that during the government of General Chatichai Choonhavan (1988–1991), physical infrastructure development in Nakhon Ratchasima Province, Isaan's economic center, was particularly important in stimulating economic growth: "The industrial sector's growth was 19.6 percent in 1980 and it increased to 21.9 percent and 27.3 percent in 1985 and 1990, respectively. Wholesale and retail trade increased by 18.8 percent, 18.3 percent, and 17.3 percent during the same period." In addition, the feasibility of Isaanese working in the Bangkok area, and sending remittances back to Isaan, while still maintaining family connections back home, has improved with the expansion of physical infrastructure.

The fact that these advances were largely ignored requires further explanation. To be sure, Isaan still is Thailand's poorest region, but the climate, topography, poor soils, and tradition-bound farming practices largely account for the existing poverty, and economic diversification faces the handicaps of geographic isolation and skilled labor shortages. Other bases of discontent in Isaan must be sought. One of the primary bases is the Isaanese identity that gives rise to resentment against Central Thais.

How Isaanese Identity Became So Salient
The red shirt insurrection would have been less likely if the Isaanese identity, as distinct from "Thai," had been less salient (Volpe 2015). This identity, insofar as it is defined in contrast with the characteristics that

---

[13] For background on this, see Pansuwan and Routray (2011) and Seng-Arun (2013).

Isaanese attribute to Central Thais, focuses attention on the perceived economic differences between Isaan and the wealthier, more industrialized, more politically important central region (Buchanan 2013).

Isaan is indeed distinctive, because of its proximity, historic connections, cuisine, religious ceremonies, and cultural-linguistic similarity to impoverished Laos. However, it is also distinct from Laos, and some argue that the state has promoted Isaan identity as "a tool to distance Northeasterners from the feeling of Lao-ness" (Alexander and McCargo 2014, 64). Yet every region has some degree of distinctiveness, because any particular aspect of distinctiveness may or may not be important enough to be a core aspect of identity. In the case of Isaan, the interrelated aspects begin with the historic and cultural ties with Laos, and the expansion of the Kingdom of Thailand. The Laotian legacy and the expansion of Thailand are jointly responsible for the distinctiveness of Isaanese speech. Speech patterns of most Isaanese, roughly somewhere between central Thai (near Bangkok) and Laotian, are regarded by central Thais as unsophisticated.

In addition, the poverty of the region, despite the heroic effort to farm despite harsh conditions for agriculture, and the nonstandard speech compared the more cosmopolitan central region, are responsible for the development of identity as neglected and disdained. McCargo and Hongladarom (2004, 233), based on fieldwork soliciting attitudes of university students in Isaan, reported: "Most interviewees argued that Bangkokians and central Thais looked down on Isaan people, seeing them as provincial, poor, low class, old fashioned and uneducated."

To understand the full extent of Isaanese resentment of central Thais and, by extension, the central government, it is useful to employ the parallel concepts of "meta-stereotypes" and "metaperceptions" that Vorauer et al. (2000) and Techakesari et al. (2015) respectively use to refer to what members of one group believe to be how members of another group perceive them, and the reactions to these perceptions. Techakesari et al. (2015, 456) argue that

negative contact prompts individuals to focus on the differences between their own and the outgroup's perspectives and worldviews, and thus elevate intergroup anxiety .... [N]egative metaperceptions vary as a function of intergroup anxiety .... In particular, the more anxiety individuals experience in intergroup contexts, the more they hold beliefs that the outgroup evaluates them negatively.

Although both the Vorauer and Techakesari research teams focused on attitudes of majority groups vis-à-vis minority groups, the concept is equally useful to understand other intergroup perceptions. For Isaan, the key point is that many Isaanese believe that central Thais hold them in contempt; that central Thais hold them as unsophisticated, that Laotian attributes of Isaanese are regarded as a sign of backwardness, and that Isaanese who work in central Thailand are relegated to low-level jobs. Many Isaanese experience keen resentment over the fact that they are stereotyped in that way, and therefore are more likely to hold negative attitudes toward central Thais.

This is in sharp contrast with the self-perception of many Isaanese of being more devout as Buddhists, less grasping, and more honest than central Thais. Farming is seen as honorable; the excesses of Bangkok businesspeople and the non-Isaanese, who interact with the farmers, are not as honorable. The compensatory attribution dynamic (see Chapter 3) is clearly in play.

One indication is that Isaanese, particularly youth, are leery about speaking with the Isaanese accent in the presence of central Thais. McCargo and Hongladarom (2004, 227) concluded that: "For the time being, Isaan remains mostly the language of personal communication for in-groups of Isaan people, and not a language to be used with (or in front of) central Thais. This is clearly the case for many young Isaan people, who seek to emulate the behaviour of their Bangkok counterparts, and whose use of local language was declining."

It may be that many people native to central Thailand find it mildly amusing that Isaanese seem unsophisticated, speak Thai "poorly," and need training to be neat.[14] The fact that people of Isaan can and do seek work in the Bangkok area also colors the perceptions of deservingness of Isaanese who remain in Isaan. Perhaps, a Bangkokian might believe the people of the Isaan are content with their farming, even though knowledgeable people would be aware that the soils and climatic conditions of Isaan do not promise very prosperous farming.

It is important to note that ethnographic research reveals that many Isaanese are ambivalent about their relation to Central Thais and Laotians. In some respects, Isaanese attitudes toward central Thais fit the mindset of acknowledging the superiority of others. For the Isaanese, Alexander and McCargo (2014, 80) conclude that they "share sociocultural values with the mainstream Thai society that are conducive to the juxtaposition of Central Thai and *phasa isan* [the Isaanese variety of the

---

[14] Isaanese and other migrants who serve as the cleaning staff in upscale Bangkok malls are required to attend training sessions to learn how to be clean.

Thai-Lao language cluster] in such a way that Central Thai connotes prestige and power and *phasa isan* inferiority and humbleness."

Reinforcing this image of greater rectitude was a proclamation by the late King Bhumibol Adulyadej that Thais must be content with "sufficiency" and must be honest even when tempted by problematic opportunities to gain wealth. His proclamation of December 4, 1997, came on the heels of the 1997 economic collapse, which many Thais attributed to the reckless speculation in real estate and other businesses. Mongsawad (2010, 127) recounts:

King. Bhumibol Adulyadej proposed the philosophy of sufficiency economy (PSE) .... The following is a synthesis of the philosophy, with royal approval:

"Sufficiency economy" is a philosophy that stresses the middle path as the overriding principle for appropriate conduct by the populace at all levels. This applies to conduct at the level of the individual, families, and communities, as well as to the choice of a balanced development strategy for the nation so as to modernize in line with the forces of globalization while shielding against inevitable shocks and excesses that arise. "Sufficiency" means moderation and due consideration in all modes of conduct, as well as the need for sufficient protection from internal and external shocks .... At the same time, it is essential to strengthen the moral fibre of the nation, so that everyone, particularly political and public officials, technocrats, businessmen and financiers, adhere first and foremost to the principles of honesty and integrity. In addition, a balanced approach combining patience, perseverance, diligence, wisdom and prudence is indispensable to cope appropriately with the critical challenges arising from extensive and rapid socio-economic, environmental and cultural changes occurring as a result of globalization.

To single out "political and public officials, technocrats, businessmen and financiers" as lacking sufficient moral fiber is striking. The regions – including Isaan – that did not experience the rapid and speculative pre-1997 growth were closer to this standard of rectitude.

Thus, the Isaanese mindset vis-à-vis central Thais is an uncomfortable dialectic of inferiority and superiority, along dimensions that are common for rural people in many other parts of the world. Feelings of ethical superiority – reinforced by official doctrine – combined with the perception of being disrespected, is a potent source of moral indignation.

Grievance-Based Identity and Attribution of Responsibility for Isaan's Poverty

Whom to blame for Isaan's relative poverty? The growth of the Bangkok area from the 1960s through the 1990s was fueled by factors beyond the control of anyone in Thailand. Globalization, which brought in capital for manufacturing, much of which was profitable only in coastal or near-coastal areas, has obviously been a major factor (Phongpaichit and Baker 2016, 8). The global decline of agricultural prices cut into the profitability of Thai agriculture (Phongpaichit and Baker 2016, 8). Nevertheless, the impulse to attribute effects to more proximate actors elevates the consequences of the perceptions of government actions over more remote trends, such as shifts in the world economy.

The need to explain adverse events or circumstances and to find someone to blame for problems, is certainly one facet of Isaanese resentment against the national government. In addition, however, holding the central government and the people of the central region responsible reinforces the status of victimhood as an important part of the Isaanese self-conception. The idea that Isaan has been subject to internal neocolonialism, regardless of whether this idea is to be considered meaningful, is an element of a fairly widely accepted perspective that casts Isaanese as victimized.

These identity-based orientations are the context for the economic grievances, which since the early 2000s added an additional economic "victimhood" element of identity. In distinction from the more common social identity theory scenario of identity groups emphasizing their strength and accomplishments, some group discourse centers on its victimhood (Bar-Tal 2009; Confino 2005; Jacoby 2015). McCargo and Hongladarom (2004, 221) note that the

combination of economic deprivation, ethnic minority status and seasonal residence patterns serves to enhance the self-image of Isaan people as a marginalised and disadvantaged group which has missed out on the benefits of Thailand's remarkable economic growth since the early 1960s .... This sense of marginality is somewhat offset by a strong sense of ethnoregional pride.

Rallying around a grievance based on victimhood, whether arising from personal experience or through leaders or provocateurs, may strengthen collective identity, especially if some aspect of identity is believed to be threatened. Confino (2005, 51) notes that:

Some notions of victimhood are based on tangible aspects such as territory ..., property, or physical brutality .... But there is always an intangible component in notions of rights and victimhood: the component of identity. It happens when one side experiences the actions of a second side as detrimental to its natural rights and inalienable character. For every perceived notion of victimhood there was a perceived notion of rights.

The point of "ethnoregional pride" is an important insight, in that shared victimhood is a unifying force. This is consistent with the combination of "common history, common fate, and close interaction" (Campbell 1958) in the context of mutually reinforcing perceptions of deprivations of both respect and material well-being.

One component of grievance arises from the stereotype of the central Thais as prosperous, despite the fact that Isaanese migrants to the Bangkok area can see central Thais living in poverty. Yet the abstract characterization of the central Thai prevails in establishing the comparison between Isaan and the central region. In short, just as central Thais may hold stereotypes of Isaanese, Isaanese have stereotypes of central Thais.

Another component of resentment has been the belief that Thai governments, if genuinely committed to the regional development of Isaan, could have followed through with the periodic promises of massive irrigation development. The framing of irrigation as a heroic way to overcome agricultural deficits maintains the characterization of Isaan as the region of farmers, rather than a region in transition. Molle (2009, 254) point out the widespread allure of irrigation:

Planners and politicians in dry countries have frequently been captivated by the "desert bloom" syndrome, whether this led them to embracing small-scale irrigation or large-scale river engineering. Irrigation is still often seen as a redemptive solution and politicians have long seized the promise of water and the pledge to "green the desert" as an electoral trump card. It has also been the favoured option of governments seeking to ensure national food security, alleviate poverty and control potential social unrest.

In fact, ambitious plans for hydroelectric and irrigation dams have been extensively studied and proposed for Isaan. When the plans fizzle, the blame is typically attributed to environmentally based opposition, corruption, and changes in government. Yet Molle et al. (2009) depict the promise of "greening" Isaan through massive irrigation as an illusion, in light of the natural impediments of poor soil, topography, drought, and flooding.

The socioeconomic impacts of regional development are, of course, not all positive, and, in fact, in some respects contribute to resentment and conflict. The shifts from subsistence to commercial agriculture, the expansion of manufacturing, and the greater ease of working in the central region can corrode the esteem of traditional Isaanese folkways. The dignity of hardscrabble farming is diminished as it is demonstrated to be a poor way to provide for one's family in light of other opportunities

188   *Lessons from Pro-Poor Policy Instruments*

that have emerged.[15] Boonmathya (2003, 284) "observed that some villagers responded by taking advantage of the expanding market. Others, however, were clearly disadvantaged by such participation, and some openly resisted certain development policies. By criticizing state-led development policies and practices, some villagers made attempts to counter the hegemonic view of development."

It is also possible that the resentments against central Thailand are displacements of the anger toward local moneylenders and other influential, higher-income groups within Isaan. Lasswell (1930/1960, 159) formulated the displacement hypothesis that individuals displace private motives onto public objects; this can reduce both interpersonal risk and psychological distress.

The incomes of Isaanese also became more vulnerable to the volatility of urban employment. The possibility of another economic meltdown, such as that which occurred in 1997, cannot be dismissed. Following that collapse, the jobs for migrants dried up as construction projects and factories closed. Ouyyanont (2017, 327) cites official statistics estimating that return laborers numbered 800,000 to 1 million.

In summary, regional development balances in Thailand turned in favor of Isaan once the red shirt movement reduced the likelihood that the government, even out of the hands of populists, could ignore the disparities between Isaan and wealthier regions of Thailand. With all of the complex issues of political competition, insurgency in the South, trade arrangements, social programs, financial precariousness, pollution, and so on, allocating development resources to poor Isaan has not been a cause célèbre for policy critics. When the Shinawatras were in power, the controversies were over free trade, corruption, and deep conflicts with unions, university students, the monarchy, bureaucrats marginalized by the Shinawatra party, and no-longer-connected business cliques (Kongkirati 2019; Pye and Schaffer 2008). What is crucial for Isaan's infrastructure is not a high priority on the politicized policy

---

[15] Boonmathya (2003: 279) concluded that:

> Following modernizing projects of the country, many rural family farms, especially poor family farms, find it difficult to survive economically from the rural agricultural sector alone due to low farm produce prices and expensive farm inputs. Also, they have expenses relating to child education, medical care, clothes, food and household items, and social activities. Thus, they need to look for other sources of income to ensure the survival of their families. Many young couples tend to leave their children in the care of their aged parents in the villages and migrate to work in major cities or abroad.

Regional Development Targeting the Poorest Areas 189

agenda. If the Isaanese can take advantage of greater resources, take on nontraditional occupations and overcome the aspects of identity that disparage the entrepreneurship denounced in the King's doctrine, the region may prosper. Whether the resentment against central Thailand will abate depends on changes in the self-identity of the Isaanese, and whether Thai governments will continue to treat Isaanese as empowered citizens.

The cost of these gains – in access to the policymaking process and the elevated status of villages as political participants – is the polarization rising from the confrontations between the Shinawatras and their opposition, between the red shirts and the yellow shirts. In the midst of it – two years before Yingluk was ousted – Saxer (2012: 6) lamented:

The traditional symbolic order is losing its ability to define identities and find social cohesion …. Social cohesion may be strengthened by opening up more channels for citizens to participate in political, social and cultural life. However, no such process of broad societal deliberation has emerged over the past year. On the contrary, public debate is poisoned by polarization, hate speech, character assassinations and cyber mobbing on the one side, as well as censorship and prosecution on the other.

The polarization continues. The 2019 election gave the Shinawatra party enough seats to control the legislature, until the military manipulated the rules to put a pro-military party in control. With the Shinawatra movement again denied control, the years of being out of office, and the decline of the centrist parties that lack the support of the military, the prospect of further conflict remains high. Parpart (2019), writing after the 2019 election, concludes "that nothing close to a reconciliation of political conflicts has been accomplished … The lack of reconciliation also shows that coups did not solve the deeply rooted political turmoil."

The positive result of polarization in Thailand, in contrast with Argentina's stagnation, provides an insight into the timing related to identities and mobilization. As mentioned earlier in this chapter, the mobilization of the red shirts marks the new identity of Isaanese and the other rural poor as participants. Yet the Argentine poor, at least those who were the mobilizable urban poor, gained policymaking status in the 1940s. The polarization, without a new, mutually respectful equilibrium of high- and low-status groups, has existed into the present. In Thailand, whether reconciliation could establish a mutually respectful equilibrium also remains to be seen.

PART IV

OVERCOMING OBSTACLES IN THE POLICY PROCESS

9

How the Wealthy React to Pro-Poor-Labeled Initiatives

So much of the research on poverty alleviation has focused on the poor and the capacity to mobilize them. Undoubtedly the actions of people who would gain from poverty alleviation are important, but it is crucial to find the bases of negative reactions to pro-poor initiatives on the part of prosperous people. If some prosperous people wish to undermine a government's economic programs, they often have the capacity to do so. Even if a government with a pro-poor agenda is elected by a majority of voters sympathetic to this agenda, the non-poor frequently have tools to undermine specific policy initiatives or the economy itself. Compared to the poor, the wealthy do tend to invest more of their incomes into economic activities, but not necessarily within their own countries, especially if they see a threat to their investments or their persons. Capital flight has been, in many countries, a major reason for recessions, which in turn undercut the prospects for poverty alleviation. The obvious implication is that there is a threshold of the perceived threat from redistributive policies beyond which faltering economic growth undermines poverty-alleviation efforts. In addition to blocking these initiatives, the prosperous, in their opposition to higher taxes, may turn to destructive conflict.

It is easy to overlook the multiplicity of cognitive and affective elements that underlie a pro-poor predisposition. Of course, the multiplicity adds to the challenge of persuading pro-poor sacrifices.

First, a particular individual must be aware that some people are deprived. This may seem obvious, but in fact the belief that the poor are deprived depends on both sufficient empathetic awareness and the assessment that the condition of the poor is truly a deprivation.

194 *Overcoming Obstacles in the Policy Process*

Second, the individual either must believe that these people deserve to be helped by the individual's actions or that helping others would provide psychological or material gratifications for the individual. It should be noted that the commitment to act on a judgment of deprivation does not necessarily mean that those attributed as deprived regard themselves as such. Consider, for example, the missionaries' presumption that people of the "wrong" religions would be better off converting.

Third, the individual must believe that his or her actions could improve the situation of the deprived people. These actions may be direct transfers to these others, or through stances vis-à-vis government policy (either pushing for pro-poor policies or acquiescing to them).

Fourth, the individual must believe that not enough is being done for the poor; people may be pro-poor, willing to make sacrifices, and yet believe that they already are making the sacrifices. After all, the non-poor pay various taxes, and, if interested, can find out about the pro-poor programs that virtually every government claims to be undertaking.

BASES OF RESISTANCE TO PRO-POOR INITIATIVES DESPITE PRO-POOR PREDISPOSITIONS

But what of people who are, in principle, in favor of assisting the poor, but in practice resist pro-poor initiatives? It is reasonable to posit three characteristics of those not targeted for benefits would support pro-poor policies: having high cognitive and affective empathy, belief that the targeted populations are deserving, and belief that their support is not unacceptably threatening to their own well-being. As mentioned previously, the status of these untargeted people, in terms of their own incomes and vulnerabilities, is obviously important. Those who are economically insecure – often those who are also of moderate or fairly low income, but are not targeted for benefits, are least supportive. The Latin American Public Opinion Project, the best source of attitude surveys that distinguish between less-prosperous and more-prosperous respondents,[1] reveal the general, in-principle support for serious pro-poor policy initiatives, by prosperous and less-prosperous alike. As Table 9.1 indicates, survey results of the Latin America Public Opinion Project 2014 round indicate at least verbal agreement with the statement that "The government should

---

[1] Attitude surveys that cover other regions, such as the World Values Survey and Project Globe, include questions on judgments of laziness, but do not partition less-prosperous and more-prosperous respondents, which is so important to determine whether the prosperous support pro-poor policies.

How the Wealthy React to Pro-Poor-Labeled Initiatives 195

TABLE 9.1 *Agreement of the need for strong government policies to reduce income inequality, six most populous Latin American countries, 2014*

	Percent of less-prosperous respondents agreeing to the need for government to implement strong policies to reduce income inequality between the rich and the poor (LAPOP 2014) (%)	Percent of more-prosperous respondents agreeing to the need for government to implement strong policies to reduce income inequality between the rich and the poor (%)	Ratio of less-prosperous to more-prosperous respondents agreeing to the need for government to implement strong policies to reduce income inequality between the rich and the poor
Argentina	65	67	0.97
Brazil	89	85	1.05
Chile	90	93	0.97
Colombia	87	92	0.95
Mexico	84	89	0.94
Peru	77	92	0.84

Source: Latin American Public Opinion Project 2014

implement strong policies to reduce income inequality between the rich and the poor." Argentina has the smallest proportion of endorsers, but even there the two-thirds of respondents agreed with the statement. The most striking result is larger proportions of the more-prosperous respondents affirm this need in all but Brazil.

On the basis of this affirmation, one would expect that pro-poor initiatives would be embraced on a consistent basis. Yet initiatives claimed to be pro-poor are often rejected out of hand by prosperous people, and governments actually enacting pro-poor programs are often vulnerable to being cast out. Seven reasons are worth considering:

(1) doubt that the initiative is sincere;
(2) concern that the initiative, even if sincere, will not have the intended positive consequences;
(3) fear that the initiative would cause unacceptable degrees of deprivation for the more prosperous;
(4) fear that even if the particular initiative is not so costly, it would be a precursor to more damaging initiatives;
(5) concern that the recipients of the pro-poor policies are not the appropriate ones;

196 *Overcoming Obstacles in the Policy Process*

(6) preference for other pro-poor policies regarded as better-targeted, more effective; and

(7) agent's opposition in order to represent non-poor "clients'" interests.

Doubt Regarding the Sincerity of the Leaders

The policies promised by the initiative may be seen as simply rhetoric. Any announcement of a pro-poor policy initiative by Argentina's centrist President Macri is likely to be dismissed as insincere by the Left; any promises made by the military-backed government in Thailand to favor Isaan through state investment is likely to be doubted by many Isaanese. Skepticism toward the motives of leaders proposing what they claim are pro-poor initiatives can depend, of course, on the political divisions between a particular individual and those proposing reforms. Yet it also depends on the track record of the leaders as interpreted by the individual. The heuristics literature points most prominently to the possibility that the leaders' reputation for sincerity depends on either the broad range of actions known to the individual or to one or more highly prominent cases.[2] What is seen as "typical" insincerity of the initiators may be the basis of the individual's rejection of the initiative, or a single past "betrayal" may poison any faith in the initiator's sincerity.

Doubt can undermine even the soundest of measures. The same heuristic dynamics may account for the doubt regarding the likely effectiveness of the particular kind of pro-poor measure that has been proposed. Isaanese, believing that past regional development efforts have failed to lift the region, are likely to be dubious of current initiatives even if the initiatives are regarded as sincere. If prosperous people believe that the proposed pro-poor measures will undermine overall economic growth, and would therefore harm the poor,[3] then opposing the government's policies could be seen as pro-poor.

These beliefs may be deepened by accepting not just the broad categorization of the current case, but a "script" of causal chains (Abelson 1976) that is more integrated than single judgments. For example, the representativeness heuristic may yield a negative affect, such as dread or disdain,

---

[2] The "representativeness heuristic" and the "availability heuristic" respectively (Kahneman and Tversky 1972; Tversky and Kahneman 1973).

[3] Recall the Dollar and Kraay (2002) and Dollar, Kleineberg, and Kraay (2016) findings that overall economic growth is key to the income growth of the poor.

or a policy-relevant attitude, such as skepticism toward pro-poor subsidies. Yet it may also yield a script consisting of beliefs that the subsidies escape the poor, because fewer poor people are allowed to qualify, wealthier people would cheat to take the subsidies, and the limited volume of subsidized goods would create a black market that brings the prices out of reach of the poor. Or the script may be that some of the very poor sell their quotas, because they have even greater needs for the cash.

The expectation of the effectiveness of a pro-poor policy often depends on an overall assessment of the government's strength or that of the relevant enacting agency. In many countries, ranging from relatively wealthy ones such as Argentina to very poor countries such as Malawi, a widespread perception prevails that the government is generally ineffective.

The credibility of the initiatives also depends, at least in part, on whether potentially affected people believe that the initiative is in the self-interest of the initiators. The paradox is that despite the typical disdain for leaders who are acting in their own interests, the skepticism toward the sincerity of an initiative is likely to be less insofar as the initiative is believed to serve the leaders' interests. A key point is the potential clash between the credibility of the initiative and, as Kelley and Thibaut (1985, 32) note, the risk of cynicism arising from the presumption that people act out of self-interest. Therefore, leaders face the dilemma of gaining support for an initiative by strengthening its credibility by noting their political gains if the initiative is successful, at the risk of seeming more self-interested.

Fear of Unacceptable Deprivation due to the Proposed Initiative

Even pro-poor prosperous people must take into account the risks facing their own economic standing, or that of others they care about. High levels of contention, in the absence of a tacit understanding that adjustments will be made if a particular prosperous group suffers high levels of unanticipated damage, can seriously erode pro-poor predispositions.

Fear of Unacceptable Deprivation due to Future Policies Enabled by the Current Initiative

A common script is based on the "slippery slope" fear that not resisting initiatives that redistribute benefits away from the ingroup will make even more damaging redistribution more likely. One might think that *if our*

198   *Overcoming Obstacles in the Policy Process*

group acquiesces to a policy that mildly redistributes benefits from our group to others, this would be taken as an indication that our group is willing to make larger sacrifices, or cannot resist efforts by the government to force us to sacrifice. Therefore, we could not fend off policies that would redistribute from our group more harshly. This fear may persist even if the initiators have no intention of following the current initiative with a more extreme one. However, vulnerable stakeholders may not be in a position to presume that the current initiative is the farthest that the government leaders intend to go. Doubts that "mutual adjustment" (as described in Chapter 2) will be sufficient increases risk aversion

This fear is most likely to occur when top government leaders take on the mantle of populists. Many populists, through their grandiose rhetoric, typically appear to be either incompetent as economic managers, or as insincere in terms of pursuing truly pro-poor initiatives. Second, the prosperous have to worry that extreme redistributive rhetoric is serious and that support of, or even acquiescence to, moderately populist initiatives may increase the power of the populist and the likelihood of more extreme populist measures.

Reactions to populists are also exacerbated by the dynamic of reciprocal disrespect. As the case of Thailand's Isaan region demonstrates, the populist's condemnation of the "elite" as selfish, corrupt, and disdainful of other people results in disrespect for the populist as dishonest, crass, and self-serving.

Concern over Inappropriate Recipients

The beneficiaries of pro-poor policies often are diverse; some of them may not be regarded as deserving, or as insufficiently deserving. Opponents to pro-poor policies that benefit a wide range of people may highlight the possibility that some benefits would go to those of debatable deservingness. After all, some of the poor are criminals; others may have given indications that they are not prepared to use the benefits productively.

Preference for Other Pro-Poor Initiatives

Progress toward enacting pro-poor policies may be stalled by disagreements among pro-poor advocates as to the right approach. The existence of so many potential poverty-alleviation measures means that proponents may fasten on different measures. Leaders of different political groups, and of different segments of the poor, may find advantage in contesting over particular policy preferences. As mentioned in Chapter 4, pro-poor advocates in Brazil have been deeply split over the CCT program.

Agent's Commitment to Represent Non-Poor Interests Rather than Preferences

Representatives of interest groups are typically committed to defending their group's economic interests, rather than whatever altruistic impulses are held by those represented. This is an important contrast to leaders of political parties or movements who aspire to broaden their bases and reflect encompassing ideologies. Interest groups, in fulfilling their principal-agent obligation, may fail to convey the empathy and altruism of their members. Union representatives are less likely to push for greater benefits for the unorganized than union members may desire.

STRATEGIES TO OVERCOME RESISTANCE TO PRO-POOR INITIATIVES AND REDUCE DESTRUCTIVE CONFLICT

This chapter explores how psychological understandings can guide approaches to promote pro-poor initiatives, overcome resistance to these initiatives, and avoid provoking destructive conflict that undermines overall economic growth for extended periods. When credible pro-poor policies are absent, the frustration of the poor and its advocates may lead to aggressive actions (Gurr 1970). When redistributive initiatives are launched, the perception of threat, frequently exacerbated by uncertainty as to how far the redistribution will go, may provoke defensive aggression by prosperous stakeholders.

While there is no panacea for high levels of destructive conflict, such conflict can often be reduced through careful strategies to deploy knowledge of the dynamics of identifications, attributions, deservingness, credibility, norm creation, and the policy process. Governments and activists have both communications and concrete actions to shape all of these elements.

A clarification is needed before launching this exploration. Pro-poor initiatives are not confined to establishing new programs or poverty-reduction policies; they can encompass opposition to programs or policies that would reduce the existing benefits going to the poor. For example, Chapter 7 notes that in India, opposing the other backward classes' (OBC) affirmative action eligibility for wealthy subcastes is a pro-poor

Overcoming Policy Process Malfunctions

initiative, insofar as the university applicants of wealthy families crowd out needier applicants.

Empathy, altruism, and in-principle pro-poor predispositions are not enough if the relatively prosperous reject the legitimacy or likely success of the decision processes involved in ostensibly pro-poor policies or programs. A common problem that accounts for resistance to initiatives claiming to be pro-poor is the skepticism as to whether the initiative is soundly designed or that it would be enacted. To address such a challenge, the policy sciences framework is useful for identifying what aspects of the policy process give rise to these negative judgments. The decision process can be understood as a set of functions,[4] each potentially subject to malfunctions that could undermine the confidence that support of the initiative would yield positive results.

Intelligence Function

In needing to combine knowledge of trends and conditions with the exercise of projecting the possible outcomes of policy options, the intelligence function is often beset with deficits of facts and analysis. Basic knowledge of the nature and incidence of poverty is often deficient, to the detriment of pro-poor programs. Simply identifying the magnitude of families eligible for Brazilian or Mexican CCTs is a huge challenge for allocating sufficient resources for the programs.

The projection task of the intelligence function is heavily engaged by psychological dynamics. New policies or programs are, by definition, less anchored in previous experience within the country. With weak analytic capacity and a history of poorly designed policies, heuristics and scripts will lead to skepticism or even cynicism toward the capacity for policies to reduce poverty and constrain destructive conflict. Useful information and insights that run counter to existing beliefs run the risk of rejection due to the disconfirmation bias (Chapter 3). The possibility that the analysis is politicized adds to the doubts about the effectiveness of the policy. The presumption of malice attributed to policymakers in disagreement with a

---

[4] The most illuminating set of decision functions, in terms of identifying political and technical issues as well as malfunctions, is the Lasswell and Kaplan (1950) categorization: intelligence, promotion, prescription, invocation, application, termination, and appraisal.

group's positions would impart an exaggerated pessimism to the projections.

However, invoking the successes of other countries can reinforce the confidence in policy and program design. Perhaps the best case is the remarkable dissemination of CCT programs through the publications, international conferences, and workshops organized by the World Bank and the regional development banks.

Promotion Function

It is common for people of a particular income level to underestimate their own influence in the policy process. This increases their concern that their interests will be underrepresented and heightens their defensiveness. More prosperous people may fear that the expanded participation of lower-income people will result in unacceptably high levels of redistribution. This increases the likelihood that the more prosperous will oppose the expansion of participation or would oppose pro-poor policies, in general, on the grounds that these policies may be precursors to more threatening policies.

The balance of influence in pressing for preferred policies and outcomes is often skewed by stereotypes of marginalized ethnicities and women, in judging them as inadequately sophisticated to be able to advocate sensible policies. Groups also may be excluded or disregarded in the promotional function through negative judgments of deservingness. For example, the policy influence of Sri Lankan Tamils has been minimized by the dominant Sinhalese, by maintaining that the Tamils do not belong in Sri Lanka. Similar sentiments have long been prevalent in Malaysian Malays' attitudes toward Malaysian Chinese and Indians.

The promotional strategy of deliberately exaggerating goals, as Thaksin did in Thailand with respect to a huge gamut of pro-poor objectives (as recounted in Chapter 8), is likely to arouse cynicism among people doubting the feasibility of these goals. It also encourages a stereotype of leaders as naïve, manipulative, or both.

Prescription Function

Formalizing a policy or program per se (the "prescription") poses dilemmas for the policymakers if they hold negative stereotypes toward the population and the bureaucracy. Often policies ultimately are too rigid or too vague to be effective. If the officials attribute naivete to the groups potentially affected by the policy, claiming implausibly broad ranges of potential beneficiaries would make the initiative – and the leaders themselves – more attractive.

If policymakers stereotype the officials who are responsible for implementing the policies as corrupt, captured by particular interests, or simply disobedient, the policies may be written to minimize the discretion open to implementers. The problem is that different circumstances require policy adaptations to be effective. The implementers, faced with the dilemma of applying inappropriate policies or defying the policymakers, typically face considerable anxiety.

Even if a policy proposal seems reasonable on the face of it, it may be rejected because of the heuristic sway of past experiences. To the degree that past experiences regarded as similar are seen as negative – whether a whole set of experiences (e.g., the multiple tax reform efforts over the past decade) or the most prominent experiences (e.g., most recent, most contentious, or most problematic tax reform effort)[5] – the stance toward the next initiative will have to overcome the heuristic-based negativity. In a country with such a dismal policy record as Argentina, the possibility of a broad consensus over a major economic policy is practically nil.

In addition to the obvious rationale for policymakers to limit the participation of others in order to preserve their own policy preferences, the common tendency of policymakers to dominate decision-making may arise from a basic impulse to control. This may reflect a primal drive, or the motive of enhancing their self-esteem as powerful people.

Invocation Function

The decision to consider a particular rule (e.g., law or regulation) as applicable to a specific case is very important in determining whether pro-poor policy or program enactments are perceived as appropriate. The leeway in determining whether a given family or individual is eligible for a pro-poor program, reflecting the ambiguity of criteria, engages the implementer's judgments of deservingness in borderline cases. To a large degree, this accounts for the large volume of "inclusion" and "exclusion" errors in CCT eligibility in Mexico and Brazil (Chapter 4), and the inconsistent eligibility decisions in Brazil's Afro-Brazilian affirmative action (Chapter 7). More generally, the flexibility in determining who qualifies for benefits gives room for implementers to favor those of shared identity. Feelings of fraternal deprivation can focus attention on such

---

[5] Corresponding to the representativeness and availability heuristics, respectively.

How the Wealthy React to Pro-Poor-Labeled Initiatives   203

people even if implementers are unaware of the bias. This ambiguity, and the inconsistencies that it creates, especially if groups sharing identity with the implementers are favored, can sour the attitudes of untargeted people who believe that the programs are being abused.

Application Function

The actual delivery of pro-poor policy goods and services, as opposed to decisions on who should receive them, is the challenge of administrative capacity.

"Poor implementation" is typically the most common diagnosis of policy and program failure, even when, in fact, the root problem is vague, overly rigid, underfunded, or otherwise problematic policy or program design. This attribution error, leading to negative stereotyping of the bureaucracy, exacerbates skepticism toward the capacity to implement effectively, often accompanied by expectations of corruption.

Termination Function

One of the biggest problems for the sustained progress of the poor is the termination of existing programs, a frequent occurrence when governments change hands, and the new policymakers downgrade the deservingness of those who have been receiving benefits; "they have enjoyed their benefit; let others benefit now." In many cases, poor people have altered their livelihoods in response to opportunities provided by existing pro-poor policies (e.g., Thailand's Million Baht Village Fund microcredits that has encouraged small-scale businesses), such that cutting off access could be highly damaging.

Conversely, often it is difficult to terminate policies or programs even after they have been shown to be ineffective or damaging. The fear that damaging policies may not be eliminated even if the damage becomes apparent can add to the risks perceived by the prosperous as well as the poor. Of course, termination may be resisted if government leaders believe that their support would erode if the policies or programs are cut short. Yet beyond that political consideration, the self-esteem of top policymakers may be jeopardized if their policies are dropped.

Appraisal Function

Ex-post evaluation (appraisal in the Lasswellian nomenclature) shares with the intelligence function the risk of cynicism as to whether the analysis of past or current policies is politicized. If stakeholders seek a rationalization for opposing existing or proposed pro-poor policies, negative appraisals of past experiences, or of administrative weakness, can be the pretext.

A core problem is that appraisals themselves are often judged to be deficient, short-circuiting the essential process of adapting policies on the basis of their results. Without trust in whether past assessments are valid, or whether an initiative underway is succeeding or faltering, prosperous people are loath to make strong commitments. In the Philippines, for example, Swamy (2016, 80), judging the Philippine cash transfer program (NHTS) as fairly well-targeted, found a huge divergence in other evaluations.[6]

Deservingness is also at stake in how the actions of the poor are evaluated. The question is whether aggressive behavior by the poor is regarded as legitimate. This hinges on the deservingness criteria of current discrimination, particularly in exclusion from the policy process, and blamelessness for their poverty and exclusion. Appraisal of the actions of the poor to press for pro-poor policies is fundamentally shaped by attributions: are they overreaching in their demands, overly aggressive in pressing their demands, and so on?

Most importantly – and thus meriting detailed attention – is how progress in poverty alleviation is evaluated. It is far more problematic than one might suppose from the rather impressive methodology used to estimate income levels. Relying on household surveys to determine the poverty headcount[7] may be the most feasible way the incomes of the poor in developing countries can be broadly documented. However, two segments of the overall population may be seriously underrepresented. One is the isolated minorities, typically living in remote areas that would take extraordinarily committed enumerators to reach. The other is internally

---

[6] Swamy (2016, 80) writes:

> What are we to make of these divergent views on the selection process? Some of the scepticism regarding the NHTS probably reflects justifiable cynicism stemming from long experience with past clientelist practices rather than evidence of current malfeasance …. [W]e can say … [that] for social protection to reduce demand for clientelism by providing subsistence guarantees, what matters more is reducing exclusion errors. While including non-poor recipients due to political interference indicates the continued relevance of clientelism and undermines political support for the programme, a social protection programme that guaranteed the poor were covered would weaken the structural foundations of clientelist demand. From that point of view, it is significant that the main sources of exclusion error seem to be structural – migrants without a physical address and families without children – rather than political.

[7] That is, the proportion of people with incomes below specified levels.

displaced persons, who, unless the displacement occurred many years ago, may not be employed, and may or may not be receiving support from the government or from NGOs or external donors. For example, in Sri Lanka the household surveys on which the income-distribution estimates are based have excluded the people in displacement camps. In the late 2000s, nearly half a million Sri Lankans were internally displaced persons (IDPs), out of a population of roughly 20 million. Most of these 2.5 percent of the Sri Lankan population were in a situation of very little income earning capacity. IDPs had to sell jewelry in order to sustain themselves; a clear indication of very low-income levels. The 2015 household survey report (Government of Sri Lanka, 2015) fails to mention this. Until 2012, the surveys did not even cover the entire country.[8] Obviously, temporal trends based on different coverage are likely to be highly misleading.

Yet, even more problematic are the appraisals of trends in income distribution, as mentioned in Chapter 1. *How* people conclude what income differences exist among different groups has not been extensively researched, nor has the understanding of how people attribute income differences. These attributions can make a huge difference as to whether groups are aggressive toward one another.

In contrast to poverty headcounts (i.e., the proportion of the population living below a given poverty line), measures of income disparity are more complicated and obscure. For the commonly used Gini index, represented by a single number reflecting the degree of deviation from equal incomes of all, quite different distributions can yield the same Gini value. Moreover, the standard overarching evaluative measures themselves are often fraught with errors.

An equally relevant income-distribution evaluation issue is the salience of dimensions other than the national distribution, whether regional, ethnic, religious, and so on. Economists and political scientists have written literally thousands of articles and books about income distribution based on national-level indicators of overall income distribution. This may seem appropriately comprehensive, but it carries the implicit message that the national distribution, covering all income earners regardless of region, ethnicity, or other differences, is the politically relevant dimension. Yet, people may be more focused on quite different dimensions reflecting a combination of salient identities and

---

[8] Personal communication, Professor Dileni Gunewardena, January 26, 2017.

available information, whether accurate or not. For example, relatively prosperous Malays may care much more about the fact that Malaysian Chinese are even wealthier than the overall distribution of income and wealth among Malays, Chinese, and Indians within Malaysia. The most explosive conflict potentials in Thailand are based on the resentment toward central Thailand of both the Isaanese in the Northeast, who regard themselves as ethnically and linguistically distinctive though Buddhist, and the Muslims in the South. For many in India, it is the income differences among different subcastes among those eligible for affirmative action. In Middle Eastern Muslim countries, it may be the relative incomes of Sunni and Shia. Stewart (2002) emphasizes the importance of conflicts over "horizontal inequalities" among people of roughly similar economic levels but differing along other dimensions such as ethnicity or religion.

Because distributional data are systematically and reliably collected and analyzed for few dimensions besides the national trends,[9] appraisals of income-distribution trends across many dimensions are subject to serious attribution distortions. The wealthy region, occupational group, or religious sect is assumed to be very wealthy or very poor. These exaggerations can have positive effects if they induce the prosperous to have greater sympathy for the poor; yet they can exacerbate conflict if the less prosperous are aggrieved due to their distorted perceptions of the wealth of others. The media, in particular, tend to cover "more interesting" stories of very wealthy or very poor people, contributing to stereotypes based on the availability heuristic.

Another pattern that can lead to presumptions of one's group's disadvantage in income-distribution trends is the strikingly common negative evaluation of the government's current treatment of the ingroup compared to other groups. This may reflect a script based on the premise that government is powerful: *If government is powerful, it must have effected changes that have benefited some groups. One's own group has not been benefited very much. Therefore, the government must have benefited others more. Therefore, the incomes of others are probably growing faster than one's own group.* These distortions can hold for groups at any income level; a particularly explosive scenario emerges if multiple groups hold the same worry of lower growth.

---

[9] For some countries, such as Thailand, reliable regional distribution studies exist (Ouyyanont 2017), but even the boundaries of regions can be ambiguous.

APPEALS BASED ON PSYCHODYNAMIC INSIGHTS

Psychodynamic insights complement social identity theory, which is tethered to the premises that group members seek to maximize group esteem through contrasts with outgroups, and that cognitive elements – most basically attributions – are the core. The broader treatment of affect also can be organized around classes of appeals based on the Freudian distinctions among id, ego, and superego (Lasswell 1932). The "triple-appeal principle" of these three personality divisions is based on the premise that "the meaning of any social object to any particular person is to be interpreted in terms of its appeal to one or more of these main divisions" (Lasswell 1932, 525). The principle has implications for the meaning of identifications and attitudes toward ingroups and outgroups that may impact pro-poor predispositions positively or negatively.

For understanding opposition to pro-poor support, raw impulses (i.e., Freud's *id*) are most relevant; ingroup provocateurs may try to mobilize these impulses for reasons other than enhancing ingroup esteem. The more primitive impulses, preexisting or established very early in life, are often visceral reactions that operate apart from instrumental logic of enhancing group esteem or accomplishing other goals. Thus, while some id impulses, such as competitive rivalry, can be consistent with the social identity theory's core premise of enhancing ingroup self-esteem, in other circumstances they will not be. Aggressive impulses against an outgroup may be rationalized by disdain toward that group, undermining belief in the outgroup's deservingness. Punitive impulses may have the same result.

Raw impulses include aggressiveness, dominance, lust, punitiveness, and submissiveness. The emotional reactions to fear, particularly if they result in hatred, clearly may exaggerate negative outgroup stereotypes as well as fueling destructive conflict. The impulse to dominate, often accompanied by feelings of superiority (even if as reactions against humiliation and shame), may culminate in punitiveness rationalized by moral indignation toward individuals or groups believed to have transgressed in some manner. Thus, when poor people engage in behaviors, or express beliefs, that more-prosperous people regard as immoral, the emotional reaction may overwhelm the sense of responsibility to assist the needy. Insofar as the prosperous would resent rewarding the poor together, the moral outrage might undermine the support for pro-poor policies in general. Opponents of pro-poor policies may try to arouse moral indignation against segments of the poor by highlighting beliefs or behaviors likely to arouse indignation. For example, the Dayaks of West

208 *Overcoming Obstacles in the Policy Process*

Kalimantan have been subjected to contempt by some of the migrant groups, a factor that also has contributed to violence between Dayaks and Madurese (Davidson 2003). In contrast, submissiveness, which may be rooted in infantile urges, may contribute to accepting prevailing stereotypes, rather than assessing their validity. Ingroup provocateurs may try to take advantage of the primal impulse of submissiveness to gain unquestioned acceptance of negative stereotypes attributed to the poor.

Even so, the impulses of superiority and dominance – the less noble drives behind noblesse oblige – may motivate support for pro-poor policies that place the beneficiaries in subservient positions, such as adhering to particular conditions to maintain eligibility. These dynamics also alert us to the possibility that negative stereotypes can be harnessed in the service of pro-poor policies. Referring back to the impetus behind the original affirmative action focus on Dalits ("untouchables") and Adivasis ("tribals"), the provision of benefits to virtually powerless groups raises the question of why higher-status Indians, in an extremely impoverished country overall, would countenance yielding job and university opportunities. Although ethical commitments of the independence movement played a role, yet impulses of dominance often go hand-in-hand with noblesse oblige. It is also worth noting that "noblesse oblige" is typically based on the self-conception of being in a "noble" position. Again, this reinforces the likelihood that people who cannot see themselves as "noble" may be less disposed to make sacrifices than those in higher income levels.

Regarding the "ego" (instrumental rationality) appeal, support of pro-poor initiatives by untargeted people might have the instrumental benefit of enhancing the ingroup's deference.[10] And instrumental rationality may dictate that a prosperous group would support pro-poor policies in order to reduce the likelihood of conflict that would damage their material well-being. On the other hand, threats to material well-being may induce ingroup members to sacrifice their deference esteem (respect, affection, and rectitude) to fend off the threats in a heavy-handed way, neglecting what they otherwise might consider to be altruistic obligations.

Superego appeals also may run counter to the net increase in ingroup self-esteem, in that rectitude self-demands may prevail even if acting on them diminishes ingroup standing. For example, acceding to significant income losses lowers the group's capacity to rise economically, educate its

---

[10] Deference values are power, respect, affection, and rectitude; the welfare (material) values are wealth, skill, and enlightenment and (physical) well-being (Lasswell 1947, 26).

children, and so on. However, the ego-defense mechanism of "reaction formation," through which rigid superego norms to fend off distress about an individual's own weaknesses (Baumeister Dale, and Sommer 1998), may be projected onto others, including the poor, or at least segments of the poor. Strict religious orthodoxy may induce greater disdain toward the poor if the latter are believed to be irreligious or to hold the "wrong" beliefs.

Similarly, policies claiming to be pro-poor may fail because of perceptions – valid or not – that the policies would inflict harm on groups capable of blocking them. Perceptions that income inequality is increasing, even where it is not, often lead to levels of conflict that undermine the economic growth that would lift up both the poor and the non-poor. Although the dominant emphasis of social identity theory on the tendency to denigrate other groups goes far in explaining the denial of the worthiness of the poor, the possibility that the ingroup's self-esteem would be enhanced by charitable treatment of the poor is typically neglected. Misperceptions of the relationship between the economic growth of the non-poor and that of the poor, stoked by provocateurs on both the left and the right, exacerbate antagonisms.

10

Lessons and Conclusions

THE PSYCHOLOGY OF INSTRUMENT SELECTION

Assuming that a modicum of pro-poor sentiment exists, and the government's sincerity and ability are not cynically rejected out of hand, a pro-poor initiative has the potential for feasibility, sustainability, and long-term integrity in maintaining its progressivity. However, each class of pro-poor instruments will have a different potential depending on the psychology of both nontargeted and targeted people. These dynamics are worth outlining, as long as it is remembered that the specific history and current context of any given country must be taken into account.

Subsidizing for the Sake of the Poor

Where enhancing noblesse oblige is more crucial to the identity of relatively prosperous people than typically modest material gains, the possibility of protecting programs of subsidized goods and services from untenable levels of benefit leakage is feasible. This is especially promising if the recognition of estimable behavior is apparent.

Some subsidy programs, such as the Indian LPG program described in Chapter 6, are particularly appealing to self-esteem because individuals can demonstrate *voluntary* relinquishment of benefits in order to assist poorer people, rather than making sacrifices dictated by government policy. However, if the gains to relatively prosperous people of taking advantage of the subsidy exceeds a particular magnitude, voluntary relinquishment is likely to dry up.

Affirmative Action Programs

The feasibility of establishing a pro-poor affirmative action program, maintaining its pro-poor targeting, and avoiding destructive conflict depends first on whether untargeted groups attribute deservingness to those formally eligible according to the initiative's criteria. Interpretations of history can be crucial, particularly if untargeted groups engage in denial of the deprivation suffered by those who are potentially eligible. Because well-targeted affirmative action programs require restraint by those who ought not to be eligible but could force their way into eligibility, appropriate targeting is more likely if the esteem of relatively prosperous people demanding eligibility would be threatened, as in the case of Indian *jatis* denounced as greedy.

Affirmative action programs predicated on the self-serving interpretations of a politically dominant group's history, as in the cases of Malaysia and Sri Lanka, can be used to rationalize predatory affirmative action programs. Similar self-serving interpretations that exaggerate past or existing deprivation of groups lobbying for affirmative action benefits have undermined the pro-poor targeting of India's affirmative action program.

Even when clearly ineligible people accept that another group warrants special privileges, affirmative action programs based on ethnic criteria are vulnerable to conflict and subversion when the identities of potentially eligible beneficiaries are subject to ambiguity, for both the potentially eligible and nontargeted groups. Affirmative action in Brazil, for example, has foundered on the ambiguity of Afro-Brazilian identity.

Cash Transfers

The psychological conditions most fertile for successful cash transfers rest, in large part, on deservingness attributions, and the strength of the impulses of control and punitiveness of nontargeted groups. Where self-esteem of untargeted people rests heavily on broad charitability, helping the poor directly through unconditional cash transfers may be most attractive, in keeping with the "basic income" normative commitment. Unconditional transfers may have the virtue of reducing conflict among low-income people when some meet the eligibility criteria but others do not. People skeptical of bureaucratic expansion also may find unconditional transfers as more efficient.

In contrast, where judgments of deservingness require demonstrations of compliance to satisfy relatively prosperous people who hold generally negative stereotypes of the poor, conditional cash transfer programs are more likely to be supported. A strong future orientation also could make additional cash transfers more attractive insofar as long-term human capital are appreciated.

Social-Sector Spending Targeting the Poor

The general predisposition to support budget diversions for greater pro-poor spending is enhanced by a high priority of charitability in the self-esteem of the relatively prosperous. It also depends on optimistic attributions of government competence and expectations that the poor would benefit from higher service levels. In short, deservingness is based on not only need, but also potential for improvement. Obviously, the prevalence of stereotypes of the poor as unambitious, unteachable, irresponsible, or otherwise incapable of benefiting from increased social services would undermine support for greater pro-poor spending.

Regional Development Targeting the Poorest Areas

Positive attributions regarding the people of poorer regions would bolster the willingness of people in relatively wealthy regions to acquiesce to explicit favoritism for poorer regions. Similarities of identifications also are likely to induce greater support. Reducing the conflict due to resentment of groups from other regions would benefit from awareness of the deprivations suffered in the poorest regions, and, among those with pro-poor predispositions, also by optimism that the investments would be effective. The capacity to debias the heuristics based on past failures in those regions would be important. Widespread awareness of ethnic differences across regions, negative stereotypes held toward the poorer regions, and obviously antagonism among regionally identified groups are likely to reduce the acceptance of explicit regional development policies targeting the poorest regions.

The paradox is that high-profile government initiatives to target poor regions run the risk of causing resentment not only among people of other regions, but also among people of the poor regions. Often, investments targeted to the poorest regions do not result in clear improvements, and knowledge is limited as to whether other regions are benefiting equally or even more. The sense of victimization that frequently is prevalent in poorer regions is hard to overcome.

MAPPING THE APPROACHES TO CONFLICT-SENSITIVE POVERTY ALLEVIATION

The policy sciences framework categories of identifications, demands, and expectations (Lasswell and Kaplan 1950; Lasswell and McDougal 1992) is useful for organizing recommendations in light of the complex factors that shape the predispositions of the prosperous and the poor. The category and scope of identifications has been explained sufficiently; as displayed in Figure 10.1, the scope of demands and expectations needs further elaboration.

Demands encompass both demands on others and self-demands. Demands on others include demands on members of one's ingroup, on members of outgroups, and on the government. Self-demands are often a component of identifications; for example, the self-demand to help the poor is a component of the identification as "fully observant Muslim" because of the commitment to *zakat*. The extremeness of the demands influences the impetus to both support or oppose pro-poor policies, and the strength of reactions to the outcomes of pro-poor policy initiatives.

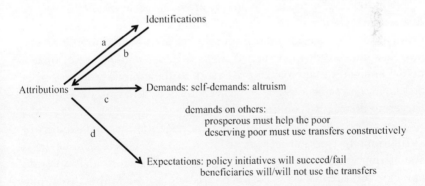

a. Positive/negative esteem, power, etc. attribution of potential identity groups
b. Positive ingroup attribution to enhance ingroup esteem; negative outgroup attributions to enhance ingroup esteem through contrast
c. Some of the poor have compelling needs
d. The prosperous should help the poor because some poor are deserving and would use transfers constructively

FIGURE 10.1 Attributions and perspective components

214 *Overcoming Obstacles in the Policy Process*

Expectations are projections of possible outcomes, whether specific, such as the success of a program, or very broad, such as a mood of general optimism. Expectations may or may not be conditioned on other events or circumstances such as, "*if* the government initiates a given pro-poor policy, it is likely to increase the income share of the lowest quintile by X percentage points."

Identifications may explicitly include self-demands in their very definition (e.g., "devout Muslim") or in self-demands to engage in behavior that would enhance the esteem of the ingroup; and demands on other members of the ingroup to do the same. Self-demands can induce an individual to identify with a particular ingroup. For example, an altruistic commitment may induce an individual to identify with the political party of the strongest altruistic reputation. Insofar as identification with a particular ingroup induces positive attitudes toward that group, the expectations of the group's behavior may be more positive. The tendency to have higher esteem toward one's ingroup by holding outgroups in lower esteem may lead to expectations that those groups would behave badly. Identifications with particular ingroups with a history of cooperation or conflict with other groups often will shape expectations of the behavior of these groups. Optimistic or pessimistic expectations may encourage stronger or weaker self-demands to engage in pro-poor actions. Expectations of outgroup actions may drive self-demands for cooperation or confrontation.

Attributions, covered in Chapter 3, provide one source of connective tissue among the perspective components of identifications, demands, and expectations, and the potential approaches to promoting pro-poor predispositions and averting destructive conflict. Understanding these connections illuminates many of the precursors to these predispositions, from beliefs of deservingness and esteem-motivated behavior to animosity triggering destructive conflict.

The approaches that can take advantage of the malleability of attributions rest on the reciprocal relationship between identifications and attributions, such as ingroup attributions of altruism that do or do not call for sacrifices by members wishing to be faithful to group identity. Influencing the attributions of deservingness of potential beneficiaries can alter the demands on oneself and others to support pro-poor policies. Attributions of government sincerity to carry out effective pro-poor initiatives also can influence whether altruistic impulses are worth pursuing.

RECOMMENDATIONS

Fundamental Recommendations for Growth and Poverty Alleviation

Two fundamental points are emphasized in the first two chapters of this book. First, overall economic growth, necessary to raise the incomes of the poor, requires some moderation in redistributive demands to avoid high levels of destructive conflict. Second, growth, poverty alleviation, and the containment of conflict require policies that provide the wherewithal for the poor to increase their productivity and their sociopolitical standing. Supply-side policies will not accomplish this. The challenge is to identify pro-poor policies that complement sustainable overall growth policies.

Recommendations to Promote Altruistic Predispositions

Gathering and Publicizing Evidence

Research on the disparities among different segments of the poor is essential not only to guide policymakers in formulating balanced pro-poor approaches, but also in identifying and publicizing the most compelling needs for poverty alleviation.

The inventory of the people constituting a relatively prosperous ingroup often will reveal greater diversity of income and other resources than the ingroup's self-stereotype. This may heighten sympathy toward the poor out of sentiments of fraternal deprivation and soften harshness of deservingness judgments. If possible, this can be reinforced by communications that establish broader definitions of the group to include more of the poor. This can contribute to debiasing simplistic negative attributions of characteristics of the poor.

Highlighting the self-help success of at least some of the poor may dispel the attribution of lack of capacity or willingness to take advantage of benefits. In addition, to counter the stereotype of the poor's contentment, research can help us by demonstrating that few of the poor are content with poverty, and they would be vulnerable to illness and other emergencies without additional resources.

When unconstructive debates over alternatives block a sound policy, analysis demonstrating that the initiative is likely to do as well as alternatives may expedite the initiative's enactment. Building adaptability into the policy can strengthen its support from otherwise skeptical stakeholders.

The approaches that can take advantage of the potential for an individual's identifications to create self-demands for altruism include publicizing the prevalence of altruism among other members of the ingroup and demonstrating how the ingroup's self-esteem would be enhanced if its members engage in altruism. It is also useful to publicize that disliked prosperous outgroups are less altruistic than ingroup(s), in order to strengthen the support of pro-poor initiatives to enhance the ingroup(s)' esteem. Focusing attention on highly respected/beloved ingroup members who are known for their pro-poor actions can induce the emulation of these actions. Communications that broaden the meaning of an identification ought to include the attribute of altruism, and moderation as a key facet of the meaning of salient identifications.

For largely prosperous groups, communications ought to highlight any existing pro-poor commitments. Communications also can focus attention on events that demonstrate self-esteem enhanced by pro-poor actions (such as the relatively prosperous Indians who relinquished their right to purchase fuel at subsidized prices for the sake of the poor).

Redefining Norms

Because many norms are broad, and the terms that define them are open to multiple interpretations, it is often possible to recast norms to become more clearly pro-poor. Broad norms such as "love of country" can be elaborated as "love of all segments of the country's population"; "commitment to democracy" can be refined as "commitment to inclusive democracy."

Selecting Pro-Poor Programs to Enhance Deservingness Judgments

The psychology associated with different broad pro-poor policy instruments, as presented earlier in this chapter, ought to be combined with context-specific conditions of particular cases: the magnitude of available funds, administrative capacity, the socioeconomic status of potential targets, and the political atmosphere. For example, selecting program designs such as conditional cash transfers that benefit recipients who demonstrate their striving for improvement may reduce skepticism about deservingness, but sometimes such programs simply are not feasible for political, administrative, or other reasons.

Inducing Pro-Poor Engagement

Engaging relatively prosperous people in even minor or largely symbolic pro-poor activities can shape corresponding self-demands. As mentioned in Chapter 3, self-attributions are, to a certain degree, retrospective. Instilling a pro-social identity is often a goal in youth education, but it may need to be supplemented for relatively prosperous adults who understand that pro-poor policies entail sacrifices.

Engaging the Poor in Responsible Activities

To dispel the stereotype of the poor as lazy or incapable of taking advantage of pro-poor policies, it is sometimes possible to engage the poor in activities, such as constructing or managing important public facilities, that demonstrate their reliability.

Recommendations to Reduce Skepticism toward Sound Pro-Poor Policies

Gathering and Publicizing Evidence

Identifying government accomplishments that would be widely considered to be positive could counter cynicism toward government capabilities. More specifically with respect to pro-poor policies, identifying past or current successful pro-poor efforts may be able to offset cynical expectations about the prospects for pro-poor initiatives. If the initiative has no successful precedent in the country, experiences in other countries may be useful. This helps to explain the proliferation of programs throughout the developing world. Having the imprimatur of highly respected institutions, such as the Asian Development Bank, can reinforce the optimism toward the likelihood of success.

Insofar as skepticism is based on heuristics that overweight prior negative experiences, the minimal and obvious debiasing effort would be to communicate the differences between the current and previous efforts. This should be reinforced by any available evidence of improved policymaking quality, such as greater transparency, more ample administrative resources, and so on.

Pilot Programs

If serious reservations about a major program proposal seem to threaten the initiative, an alternative is to begin with a pilot program to reduce the uncertainty and risk. In Thailand, the Ministry of Social Development and Human Security and the Ministry of Public Health launched the modest pilot Child Support Grant Programme in 2015 (Chanmorchan et al. 2015). The outcomes were sufficiently promising to warrant the establishment of a broader, regular program. Whether a pilot program

218 *Overcoming Obstacles in the Policy Process*

can be scaled up successfully is by no means guaranteed, yet successful pilot programs can go for refocusing from past to present.

Hands-Tying

Arrangements that persuasively limit the future impact of a pro-poor initiative can dispel fears that the initiative would damage potential supporters beyond the explicit content of the initiative. If the framing of the initiative clarifies that leaders will face severe political costs if they go beyond stated limits of redistributive measures, such hands-tying could enable support of relatively prosperous groups willing to make only some degree of sacrifice.

Linking the Initiative's Success to the Leaders' Success

Conveying that top leaders have legitimate personal incentives (such as reelection) for the initiative to succeed can help to dispel the cynicism that the initiative is insincere. This may be counterintuitive to many leaders who try to present themselves as above personal considerations, but few people believe that leaders are without personal motivation.

Diagnosing and Addressing Decision-Process Malfunctions

Because the skepticism toward the success of a pro-poor initiative may in fact be valid if the decision process is functioning badly, addressing these problems could both improve the outcomes and offset negative expectations about their prospects. Chapter 9 has laid out the framework for identifying these malfunctions.

Recommendations to Reduce the Potential for Destructive Conflict

Gathering and Publicizing Evidence

Clarifying the economic vulnerability of contending groups is important for sensitizing all contenders of the risks of conflict escalation. Publicizing past experiences of the damage of destructive conflict posed by demands for drastic redistribution can encourage the moderation of the demands of the poor and their provocateurs. Enumerating the trends in benefits going to the poor can demonstrate – where appropriate – that the poor are not as neglected as some provocateurs try to convey. This would have helped to defuse the conflict between Isaanese and central Thais. Similarly, highlighting serious obstacles and trade-offs of improving the well-being of the poor, such as environmental limitations to expansions of physical

Lessons and Conclusions

infrastructure, may make the leaders of the poor less hostile when government leaders are in fact sincere about poverty alleviation.

To reduce the risk that rigid stereotypes would contribute to vicarious retribution, identifying the variations of characteristics of all contending groups should be a high priority. This includes the possibility of demonstrating that particular groups are not as uniformly wealthy as may be commonly believed.

Emphasizing the positive attributions of contesting groups may be able to reduce aggressive behavior induced by antagonism toward outgroups. Bringing attention to pro-social behavior of relevant groups may be able to moderate expectations of threats to the ingroup's well-being by these groups. Publicizing the cases of highly respected individuals who espouse moderation (e.g., Nelson Mandela) can elevate the esteem of moderation.

Because the disputes arising out of interactions between internal migrants and host communities frequently create acute conflict, it is worthwhile to improve the often inaccurate "scripts" (see Chapter 3) that people hold toward historical settlement patterns. Clarifying the complexity of previous migration patterns can erode the radicalizing "sons of the soil" identifications that provoke aggressive confrontation.

Designing pro-poor policies and programs that avoid demeaning the recipients (e.g., requiring stigmatizing documents or designations) could reduce the resentment of the recipients that otherwise might trigger aggressive confrontation.

Broad Participation in Policymaking

Inclusiveness of policymaking access across income levels not only ensures that poverty alleviation will be on the policy agenda, it also provides an alternative to confrontation outside of the formal process.

FINAL THOUGHTS

Our point of departure is that *sometimes* relatively prosperous people can be induced to sacrifice some of their benefits by supporting, or at least acquiescing to, pro-poor government policies. We know, from such cases as India's initial affirmative action and its more recent voluntary relinquishment of fuel subsidies, that pro-poor sentiment exists in some contexts and can be mobilized. Yet, the risks of cynicism vis-à-vis government, negative stereotypes, and the decay of initially sound pro-poor policies have to be addressed.

The social identity theory and other psychological insights, in their emphasis on ingroup solidarity and the prevalence of outgroup prejudice, raise the question of whether compassion is limited to the ingroup. In some of the cases examined in this book (Malaysian and Sri Lankan affirmative action), ingroup favoritism is indeed powerful enough to preclude compassion to outgroups. Yet, the dynamics of enhancing ingroup esteem through acts of noblesse oblige or other means of elevating ingroup standing, and the possibility of enhancing identities that go across income levels, account for successful pro-poor policies. In short, particular contexts and psychologically informed strategies, might permit pro-poor leaders to overcome narrow ingroup self-centeredness.

The fact that psychology has much to say about how poverty alleviation can be more effectively pursued is very encouraging. With ample opportunities for the well-being of the poor to be wedded to the well-being of society in general, relying on psychological insights to instill pro-poor predispositions among relatively prosperous people ought to be a high priority among policymakers and advocates. Relying on such insights to moderate demands by both rich and poor so as to avert destructive conflict is equally important. Thus, understanding how best to enact poverty-alleviation efforts requires appreciating that the impacts depend not only on the identities and perspectives of relatively prosperous people, but also on the profound effects on the identities of the beneficiaries of these policies. This book has offered a framework and illustrative cases to assist in the necessary integration of psychological, economic, and sociopolitical considerations.

References

Abad, Leticia Arroyo, and Peter H. Lindert. 2017. Fiscal redistribution in Latin America since the nineteenth century. In Luis Bertola and Jefferey Williamson, eds., *Has Latin American inequality changed direction*, pp. 243–282. New York: Springer.

Abelson, Robert P. 1976. Script processing in attitude formation and decision making. In John W. Payne and John S. Carroll, eds., *Cognition and social behavior*, pp. 33–46. Mahwah, NJ: Lawrence Erlbaum Associates.

Acemoglu, Daron, and Simon Johnson. 2007. Disease and development: The effect of life expectancy on economic growth. *Journal of Political Economy* 115(6): 925–985.

Acemoglu, Daron, and James Robinson. 2009. Foundations of societal inequality. *Science* 326(5953): 678–679.

Agénor, Pierre-Richard. 2017. Caught in the middle? The economics of middle-income traps. *Journal of Economic Surveys* 31(3): 771–791.

Agénor, Pierre-Richard, Otaviano Canuto, and Michael Jelenic. 2012. *Avoiding middle-income growth traps*. World Bank Economic Premise Series. Washington, DC: World Bank.

Al Ramiah, Ananthi, Miles Hewstone, and Katharina Schmid. 2011. Social identity and intergroup conflict. *Psychological Studies* 56(1): 44–52.

Al Ramiah, Ananthi, and Thillainathan Ramaswamy. 2013. Exploring the relationship between development and conflict: The Malaysian experience. In William Ascher and Natalia Mirovitskaya, eds., *Development strategies, identities, and conflict in Asia*, pp. 183–208. New York: Palgrave Macmillan.

Alexander, Saowanee, and Duncan McCargo. 2014. Diglossia and identity in Northeast Thailand: Linguistic, social, and political hierarchy. *Journal of Sociolinguistics* 18(1): 60–86.

Almond, Gabriel, and Sidney Verba. 1963. *The civic culture: Political attitudes and democracy in five nations*. Princeton: Princeton University Press.

Alzate, Maria. 2006. *La estratificación socioeconómica para el cobro de los servicios públicos domiciliarios en Colombia: ¿Solidaridad o focalización?* Bogotá: CEPAL.

References

Amann, Edmund, Nektarios Aslanidis, Frederick Nixson, and Bernard Walters. 2006. Economic growth and poverty alleviation: A reconsideration of Dollar and Kraay. *The European Journal of Development Research* 18(1): 22–44.

Ames, D. R. 2004. Mental state inference in person perception: Everyday solutions to the problem of other minds. *Journal of Personality and Social Psychology* 87: 340–353.

Anas, M. U. M., and Seetha Wickremasinghe. 2010. Brain drain of the scientific community of developing countries: The case of Sri Lanka. *Science and Public Policy* 37(5): 381–388.

Anderson, Charles W. 1964. Toward a theory of Latin American politics. The Graduate Center for Latin American Studies, Vanderbilt University Occasional Paper No. 2. Nashville, TN: Vanderbilt University.

Anisimova, Alla, and Olga Echevskaya. 2012. "Sibiriak": Community, nationality, or "state of mind"? *Laboratorium* 4(3): 11.

Balakrishnan, Ravi, Chad Steinberg, and Murtaza H. Syed. 2013. The elusive quest for inclusive growth: Growth, poverty, and inequality in Asia. No. 13-152. Washington, DC: International Monetary Fund.

Balatchandirane, G. 2000. State and education: India's failures and Japanese lessons. *Minamiajiakenkyu* 12: 175–202.

Balisacan, Arsenio. 1994. Demand for food in the Philippines: Responses to price and income changes. *Philippine Review of Economics and Business* 31(2): 137–163.

Barrera-Osorio, F., M. Bertrand, L. Linden, and F. Perez-Calle. 2008. Conditional cash transfers in education design features, peer and sibling effects evidence from a randomized experiment in Colombia. Working Paper 13890. Cambridge, MA: National Bureau of Economic Research.

Barro, R. J., and X. Sala-i-Martin. 1992. Convergence. *Journal of Political Economy* 100: 223–251.

Barron, Robert. 2018. Conference report: Building pluralistic and inclusive states post-Arab Spring. Baker Institute for Public Policy. Houston: Rice University. https://scholarship.rice.edu/bitstream/handle/1911/102748/cme-pub-carnegie conf-beirut-042618.pdf?sequence=1.

Bar-Tal, Daniel, Lily Chernyak-Hai, Noa Schori, and Ayelet Gundar. 2009. A sense of self-perceived collective victimhood in intractable conflicts. *International Review of the Red Cross* 91: 229–258.

Baruah, Sanjib. 1986. Immigration, ethnic conflict, and political turmoil – Assam, 1979–1985. *Asian Survey* 26(11): 1184–1206.

Bass, Jeffrey. 2006. In exile from the self: National belonging and psychoanalysis in Buenos Aires. *Ethos* 34(4): 433–455.

Batson, C. Daniel. 2011. These things called empathy: Eight related but distinct phenomena. In Jean Decety and William Ickes, eds., *The social neuroscience of empathy*, pp. 3–16. Cambridge, MA: MIT Press.

Batson, C. Daniel, Bruce D. Duncan, Paula Ackerman, Terese Buckley, and Kimberly Birch. 1981. Is empathic emotion a source of altruistic motivation? *Journal of Personality and Social Psychology* 40(2): 290–302.

Batson, C. Daniel, Jim Fultz, and Patricia A. Schoenrade. 1987. Distress and empathy: Two qualitatively distinct vicarious emotions with different motivational consequences. *Journal of Personality* 55(1): 19–39.

References

Batson, C. Daniel, and Laura L. Shaw. 1991. Evidence for altruism: Toward a pluralism of prosocial motives. *Psychological Inquiry* 2(2): 107–122.

Baumeister, R. F., K. Dale, and K. L. Sommer. 1998. Freudian defense mechanisms and empirical findings in modern social psychology: Reaction formation, projection, displacement, undoing, isolation, sublimation, and denial. *Journal of Personality* 66: 1081–1124.

Bayly, Susan. 1999. *Caste, society and politics in India.* Cambridge: Cambridge University Press.

Bem, Darryl. 1967. Self-perception: An alternative interpretation of cognitive dissonance phenomena. *Psychological Review* 7: 183–200.

Benton, Allyson. 2009. What makes strong federalism seem weak? Fiscal resources and presidential–provincial relations in Argentina. *Publius: The Journal of Federalism* 39(4): 651–676.

Beteille, Andre. 2003. Poverty and inequality. *Economic and Political Weekly* 2003: 4455–4463.

Bevilaqua, Ciméa Barbato. 2015. The institutional life of rules and regulations: Ten years of affirmative action policies at the Federal University of Paraná, Brazil. *Vibrant* 12(2): 193–232, doi:10.1590/1809-43412015v12n2p193.

Bhavnani, Rikhil R., and Bethany Lacina. 2015. The effects of weather-induced migration on sons of the soil riots in India. *World Politics* 67(4): 760–794.

Biernat, Monica, Diane Kobrynowicz, and Dara Weber. 2003. Stereotypes and shifting standards: Some paradoxical effects of cognitive load. *Journal of Applied Social Psychology* 33(10): 2060–2079.

Blattman, C., and E. Miguel. 2010. Civil war. *Journal of Economic Literature.* 48(1): 3–57.

Bogliacino, Francesco, Laura Jiménez Lozano, and Daniel Reyes. 2018. Socio-economic stratification and stereotyping: Lab-in-the-field evidence from Colombia. *International Review of Economics* 65(1): 77–118.

Bonilla, J., D. López, and C. Sepúlveda. 2014. Estratificación socioeconómica en Colombia: Contexto general y diagnóstico. In C. Sepúlveda, D. López, and J. Gallego, eds., *Los límites de la estratificación: en busca de alternativas.* Bogota: Editorial Universidad del Rosario.

Boonmathya, Ratana Tosakul. 2003. A narrative of contested views of development in Thai society: Voices of villagers in rural Northeastern Thailand. *Southeast Asian Studies* 41(3): 269–298.

Boräng, Frida, Agnes Cornell, Marcia Grimes, and Christian Schuster. 2014. Bureaucratic politicization, and politicized knowledge: Implications for the functioning of democracy. Gothenburg: Quality of Government and the Performance of Democracies Conference, May 20–22, 2014, University of Gothenburg. https://qog.pol.gu.se/digitalAssets/1530/1530009_bor–ng–cor nell–grimes—schuster.pdf.

Bormann, Nils-Christian, Lars-Erik Cederman, and Manuel Vogt. 2017. Language, religion, and ethnic civil war. *Journal of Conflict Resolution* 61(4): 744–771.

Bourdieu, Pierre. 1986. The forms of capital. In J. G. Richardson, ed., *Handbook of theory and research for the sociology of education,* pp. 241–258. New York: Greenwood.

Bourdieu, Pierre. 1990. *The logic of practice.* Palo Alto, CA: Stanford University Press.

Brady, H. E., and Sniderman, P. M. 1985. Attitude attribution: A group basis for political reasoning. *American Political Science Review* 79: 1061–1078.

Brewer, Marilynn B. 1999. The psychology of prejudice: Ingroup love and outgroup hate? *Journal of Social Issues* 55(3): 429–444.

Brewer, Marilynn B., and Roderick M. Kramer. 1985. The psychology of intergroup attitudes and behavior. *Annual Review of Psychology* 36(1): 219–243.

Britto, Tatiana. 2008. The emergence and popularity of conditional cash transfers in Latin America. In Armando Barrientos and David Hulme, eds., *Social protection for the poor and the poorest: Concepts, policies and politics*, pp. 181–193. London: Palgrave Macmillan.

Buarque, Cristovam, Vida A. Mohorčič Špolar, and Tiedao Zhang. 2006. Introduction: Education and poverty reduction. *International Review of Education* 52(3–4): 219–229.

Buchanan, James. 2013. Translating Thailand's protests: An analysis of Red Shirt rhetoric. *ASEAS-Austrian Journal of South-East Asian Studies* 6(1): 60–80.

Bull, Benedicte. 2013. Social movements and the "Pink Tide": Governments in Latin America: Transformation, inclusion and rejection. In Kristian Stokke and Olle Törnquist, eds., *Democratization in the Global South*, pp. 75–99. London: Palgrave Macmillan.

Camacho Solis, Luis Antonio. 2012. The political origins of support for redistribution: Argentina and Peru in comparative perspective. Doctoral dissertation, University of Texas, Austin. Austin, TX: University of Texas.

Cambon, Laurent, Vincent Yzerbyt, and Sonya Yakimova. 2015. Compensation in intergroup relations: An investigation of its structural and strategic foundations. *British Journal of Social Psychology* 54: 140–158.

Campbell, Donald T. 1958. Common fate, similarity, and other indices of the status of aggregates of persons as social entities. *Behavioral Science* 3: 14–25.

Campbell, Donald T. 1967. Stereotypes and the perception of group differences. *American Psychologist* 22(10): 817–829.

Canuto, Otaviano. 2019. *Traps on the road to high income.* Rabat, Morocco: Policy Center for the New South.

Carsten, Paul, and Pairat Temphaorpjana. 2013. Thailand's boom: To the northeast, the spoils. *Reuters*, June 16.

Castro-Leal, F., J. Dayton, L. Demery, and K. Mehra. 2000. Public spending on health care in Africa: Do the poor benefit? *Bulletin of the World Health Organization* 78(1): 66–74.

Chambers, Paul. 2010. Thailand on the brink: Resurgent military, eroded democracy. *Asian Survey* 50(5): 835–858.

Chanmorchan, Proudfong, Teppawan Pornwalai, Christina Popivanova, and Nard Huijbregts. 2015. *Thailand's child support grant programme.* Bangkok: UNICEF and the Thailand Development Research Institute.

Chatterji, Saubhadra. 2016. History repeats itself as yet another Central govt faces a Jat stir. *Hindustan Times*, February 22.

Chauvel, R. H. 1990. *Nationalists, soldiers and separatists: The Ambonese Islands from Colonialism to Revolt, 1880–1950.* Verhandelingen van het

References

Koninklijk Instituut voor Taal-, Land- en Volkenkunde; 143. Leiden: KITLV Press.

Confino, Alon. 2005. Remembering the Second World War, 1945–1965: Narratives of victimhood and genocide. *Cultural Analysis* 4: 46–75.

Cookson, Tara Patricia. 2016. Working for inclusion? Conditional cash transfers, rural women, and the reproduction of inequality. *Antipode* 48(5): 1187–1205.

Corona, Mónica E. Orozco, and Sarah Gammage. 2017. Cash transfer programmes, poverty reduction and women's economic empowerment: Experience from Mexico. ILO Working Paper No. 1/2017. Geneva: International Labour Organization.

Corrêa, Diego Sanches, and José Antonio Cheibub. 2016. The anti-incumbent effects of conditional cash transfer programs. *Latin American Politics and Society* 58(1): 49–71.

Costa, Sergio. 2018. Entangled inequalities, state, and social policies in contemporary Brazil. In M. Ystanes and I. Å. Strønen, eds., *The social life of economic inequalities in contemporary Latin America*, pp. 59–80. London: Palgrave Macmillan.

Courtis, Corina, María Inés Pacecca, Diana Lenton, Carlos Belvedere, Sergio Caggiano, Diego Casaravilla, and Gerardo Halpern. 2007/trans 2009. Racism and discourse: A portrait of the Argentine Situation. In Teun van Dijk, ed., *Racism and discourse in Latin America* (Elisa Barquin and Alexandra Hibbett, trans), pp. 13–55. Lanham, MD: Lexington Books.

Cutrona, Sebastián. 2018. Violence and security in Argentina: Major trends and policy responses. In Hannah Kassab and Jonathan Rosen, eds., *Violence in the Americas*, pp. 1–12. Lanham, MD: Lexington Books.

Dahana, A. 1997. Comments. In Leo Suryadinarta, ed., *Ethnic Chinese as Southeast Asians*, pp. 66–72. London: Palgrave Macmillan.

Daniel, E. Valentine. 1989. Three dispositions towards the past: One Sinhala Two Tamil. *Social Analysis: The International Journal of Social and Cultural Practice* 25: 22–41.

Das, Pauline. 2013. The Irula language and literature. *The Criterion* 4(2): 1–7.

Dasgupta, Abhijit. 2003. Repatriation of Sri Lankan refugees: Unfinished tasks. *Economic and Political Weekly* 38(24): 2365–2367.

Dasgupta, Indraneel, and Ravi Kanbur. 2011. Does philanthropy reduce inequality? *The Journal of Economic Inequality* 9(1): 1–21.

Davidson, Jamie S. 2003. The politics of violence on an Indonesian periphery. *South East Asia Research* 11(1): 59–89.

Davis, Thomas. 2014. Affirmative action in Brazil: Its recent developments and the argument for a narrow Federalism Doctrine. *University of Miami Race & Social Justice Law Review* 4: 72–97.

Dawis, Aimee. 2009. *The Chinese of Indonesia and their search for identity: The relationship between collective memory and the media*. Amherst, NY: Cambria Press.

de Oliveira, Cleuci. 2017. Brazil's new problem with blackness. *Foreign Policy*, April 5.

del Rio, Vicente. 2010. Guest Editorial. *Urban Design International* 15(2): 71–72.

Denson, T., B. Lickel, M. Curtis, D. Stenstrom, and D. R. Ames. 2006. The roles of entitativity and essentiality in judgments of collective responsibility. *Group Processes and Intergroup Relations* 9: 43–62.

Deshpande, Ashwini, and Rajesh Ramachandran. 2016. The changing contours of intergroup disparities and the role of preferential policies in a globalizing world: Evidence from India. Delhi: Delhi School of Economics Centre for Development Economics Working Paper No. 267, December.

Deshpande, Satish, and Yogendra Yadav. 2006. Redesigning affirmative action: Castes and benefits in higher education. *Economic and Political Weekly* 41(24): 2419–2424.

Devarajan, Shantayanan, Tuan Minh Le, and Gaël Raballand. 2010. Increasing public expenditure efficiency in oil-rich economies: A proposal. World Bank Policy Research Working Paper 5287. Washington, DC: World Bank, April.

DeVotta, Neil. 2016. A win for democracy in Sri Lanka. *Journal of Democracy* 27(1): 152–166.

DeWalt, Billie, and Kathleen DeWalt. 1980. Stratification and decision making in the use of new agricultural technologies. In Peggy Bartlett, ed., *Agricultural decision-making: Anthropological contributions to rural development*, pp. 289–315. New York: Academic Press.

Dhanaraj, Sowmya, and Smit Gade. 2013. Universal PDS: Efficiency and equity dimensions. *Journal of Social and Economic Development* 15(3): 1–15.

Diaz Cayeros, Alberto, and Beatriz Magaloni. 2003. The Programa Nacional de Solidaridad (PRONOSAL) in Mexico. Background Paper for the 2004 World Development Report, April. Washington, DC: World Bank. http://documents .worldbank.org/curated/en/512011468774653301/pdf/269490v120Caye1s1 of1public1spending.pdf.

Dollar, David, Tatjana Kleineberg, and Aart Kraay. 2015. Growth, inequality and social welfare: Cross-country evidence. *Economic Policy* 30(82): 335–377.

Dollar, David, Tatjana Kleineberg, and Aart Kraay. 2016. Growth still is good for the poor. *European Economic Review* 81: 68–85.

Dollar, David, and Aart Kraay. 2002. Growth is good for the poor. *Journal of Economic Growth* 7(3): 195–225.

Doron, A. 2010. The intoxicated poor: Alcohol, morality and power among the boatmen of Banaras. *South Asian History & Culture* 1: 282–300.

Doyle, David. 2015. Remittances and social spending. *American Political Science Review* 109(4): 785–802.

Drèze, Jean, and Reetika Khera. 2015. Understanding leakages in the public distribution system. *Economic and Political Weekly* 50(7): 39–42.

Dunning, David, Dale W. Griffin, James D. Milojkovic, and Lee Ross. 1990. The overconfidence effect in social prediction. *Journal of Personality and Social Psychology* 58(4): 568.

Dupper, Ockert. 2014. Affirmative action in comparative perspective. In Ockert Dupper and Kamal Sankaran, eds., *Affirmative action: A view from the Global South*, pp. 7–42. Bloemfontein: African Sun Media.

Durongkaveroj, W., and Taehyun Ryu. 2018. Trade liberalisation and poverty: Evidence from Thailand. ARTNeT Working Paper Series No. 180, June. Bangkok: ESCAP.

References

The Economist. 2017. Deformation action: Malaysia's system of racial preferences should be scrapped. May 20.

Edwards, Kari, and Edward E. Smith. 1996. A disconfirmation bias in the evaluation of arguments. *Journal of Personality and Social Psychology* 71(1): 5–24.

Eelapalan. 2013. Did the British divide & rule Ceylon? April 23. http://sangam.org/british-divide-rule-ceylon/.

Effron, Daniel, and Eric Knowles. 2015. Entitativity and intergroup bias: How belonging to a cohesive group allows people to express their prejudices. *Journal of Personality and Social Psychology* 108(2): 234–253.

Eisenberg, Nancy, and Paul Miller. 1987. Empathy and prosocial behavior. *Psychological Bulletin* 101: 91–119.

Elinoff, Eli. 2012. Smouldering aspirations: Burning buildings and the politics of belonging in contemporary Isan. *South East Asia Research* 20(3): 381–398.

Epley, N., B. Keysar, L. Van Boven, and T. Gilovich. 2004. Perspective taking as egocentric anchoring and adjustment. *Journal of Personality and Social Psychology* 87: 327–339.

Epple, Dennis, Richard E. Romano, and Miguel Urquiola. 2017. School vouchers: A survey of the economics literature. *Journal of Economic Literature* 55(2): 441–492.

Evans, Peter. 2004. Development as institutional change: The pitfalls of monocropping and the potentials of deliberation. *Studies in Comparative International Development* 38(4): 30–52.

Fanselow, Frank. 2015. Indigenous and anthropological theories of ethnic conflict in Kalimantan. *Znbun (Kyoto University)* 45: 131–147.

Fearon, James, and David Laitin. 2011. Sons of the soil, migrants, and civil war. *World Development* 39(20): 199–211.

Fernando, Srimal, and Pooja Singh. 2018. Sri Lanka's shifting politics: 2018 marks a turning point for SLFP. *Modern Diplomacy*, November 13. http://dspace.jgu.edu.in:8080/xmlui/bitstream/handle/10739/2007/Sri%20Lanka%E2%80%99s%20Shifting%20Politics.pdf?sequence=1&isAllowed=y.

Festinger, Leon. 1957. *A theory of cognitive dissonance.* Palo Alto, CA: Stanford University Press.

Fetni, Hocine. 2009. Citizenship divided: Muslim subjects, citizens, democratic dilemmas. In Jose V. Ciprut, ed., *The future of citizenship*, pp. 167–190. Cambridge, MA: MIT Press.

Fontes, Paulo. 2016. *Migration and the making of industrial São Paulo.* Durham, NC: Duke University Press.

Freedom House. 2019. Sri Lanka report. https://freedomhouse.org/report/freedom-world/2019/sri-lanka.

Frey, D. 1986. Recent research on selective exposure to information. In Leonard Berkowitz, ed., *Advances in experimental social psychology*, vol. 19, pp. 41–80. New York: Academic Press.

Gandhi, Mohandas. 1936. *Harijan* 4, December 19.

García-Colín, Jacqueline, and Santiago Sordo Ruz. 2016. Giving Mexico: Giving by individuals. *VOLUNTAS: International Journal of Voluntary and Nonprofit Organizations* 27(1): 322–347.

Gezici, Ferhan, and Geoffrey Hewings 2004. Regional convergence and the economic performance of peripheral areas in Turkey. *Review of Urban and Regional Development Studies* 16(2): 113–132.

Ghildiyal, Subodh. 2015. OBC panel backs off, won't make "creamy layer'" reservation criteria stringent. *Times of India*, October 27. https://timesofindia.indiatimes.com/india/OBC-panel-backs-off-wont-make-creamy-layer-reservation-criteria-stringent/articleshow/49545470.cms.

Gimpelson, Vladimir, and Daniel Treisman. 2018. Misperceiving inequality. *Economics & Politics* 30(1): 27–54.

Gino, Francesca, Shahar Ayal, and Dan Ariely. 2013. Self-serving altruism? The lure of unethical actions that benefit others. *Journal of Economic Behavior & Organization* 93: 285–292.

Giurata, Lauren. 2018. *La polarización política y socioeconómica en la Argentina: Las bases psicológicas y soluciones potenciales.* Claremont, CA: Claremont McKenna College.

Global Financial Integrity. 2017. *Illicit financial flows to and from developing countries: 2005–2014.* Washington, DC: Global Financial Integrity.

González de la Rocha, M. 2006. Los hogares en las evaluaciones cualitativas: Cinco años de investigaciones. In M. González de la Rocha, ed., *Procesos domesticos y vulnerabilidad: Perspectivas antropologicas de los hogares con oportunidades,* pp. 87–172. Mexico City: CIESAS. www.oportunidades.gob.mx:8010/en/docs/docs2006.php.

Gooptu, Nandini. 1997. The urban poor and militant Hinduism in early twentieth-century Uttar Pradesh. *Modern Asian Studies* 31(4): 879–918.

Gould, Carlos, and Johannes Urpelainen. 2018. LPG as a clean cooking fuel: Adoption, use, and impact in rural India. *Energy Policy* 122: 395–408.

Government of Sri Lanka. 2015. Department of Census and Statistics, Ministry of Policy Planning Economic Affairs, Child Youth and Cultural Affairs. Colombo: Government of Sri Lanka.

Government of Thailand, National Economic and Social Development Board. 2016. *Table of gross regional and provincial product 2015.* Bangkok: Government of Thailand, www.nesdb.go.th/nesdb_en/search_result.php.

Graham, Carol. 2002. Public attitudes matter: A conceptual frame for accounting for political economy in safety nets and social assistance policies. World Bank Social Protection Discussion Paper 0233. Washington, DC: World Bank.

Grosh, Margaret, Carlo de Ninno, Emil Tesliuc, and Azedine Ouerghi. 2008. *For protection and promotion.* Washington, DC: World Bank.

Guan, Lee Hock. 2005. Affirmative action in Malaysia. *Southeast Asian Affairs* 1: 211–228.

Gunawardena, Chandra. 1979. Ethnic representation, Regional imbalance and university admissions in Sri Lanka. *Comparative Education* 15(3): 301–312.

Gurr, Ted. 1970. *Why men rebel.* Princeton, NJ: Princeton University Press.

Haryono, Endi, and Samihah Khalil. 2018. Malaysia's governance reforms under PM Najib Razak. *Aegis: Journal of International Relations* 2(1): 5–10.

Hashim, Ahmed. 2013. *When counterinsurgency wins: Sri Lanka's defeat of the Tamil Tigers.* Philadelphia: University of Pennsylvania Press.

References

Haslam, Nick, and Steve Loughnan. 2014. Dehumanization and infrahumanization. *Annual Review of Psychology* 65: 399–423.

Haslam, S. Alexander, Clare Powell, and John Turner. 2000. Social identity, self-categorization, and work motivation: Rethinking the contribution of the group to positive and sustainable organisational outcomes. *Applied Psychology* 49(3): 319–339.

Hassan, Golam, Ali Asan, and Mohd Muszafarshah. 2011. Regional disparities, income inequality, and poverty: A cumulative causation from Malaysia's experience. In Aris Ananta and Richard R. Barichello, eds., *Poverty and global recession in Southeast Asia*, pp. 106–152. Singapore: Institute of Southeast Asian Studies.

Haughton, James. 2009. Building modern communities in capitalist Thailand. In Andrew Walker, ed., *Tai lands and Thailand: Community and state in Southeast Asia*, pp. 41–63. Honolulu: University of Hawaii Press.

Hawley, Emily. 2017. ISIS crimes against the Shia: The Islamic State's genocide against Shia Muslims. *Genocide Studies International* 11(2): 160–181.

Heider, Fritz. 1958. *The psychology of interpersonal relations*. Hillsdale, NJ: Lawrence Erlbaum Associates.

Heiduk, Felix. 2011. From guardians to democrats? Attempts to explain change and continuity in the civil–military relations of post-authoritarian Indonesia, Thailand and the Philippines. *The Pacific Review* 24(2): 249–271.

Heilman, Bruce, and Paul Kaiser. 2002. Religion, identity and politics in Tanzania. *Third World Quarterly* 23(4): 691–709.

Hernandez, Tanya Kateri. 2005. To be brown in Brazil: Education and segregation Latin American style. *New York University Review of Law and Social Change* 29: 683–707.

Heyer, Judith, and Nirajah Jayal. 2012. The challenge of positive discrimination. In Graham Brown, Armin Langer, and Frances Stewart, eds., *Affirmative action in plural societies: International experiences*, pp. 54–79. Basingstoke, Hampshire: Palgrave Macmillan.

Hickey, Sam, and Giles Mohan. 2008. The politics of establishing pro-poor accountability: What can poverty reduction strategies achieve? *Review of International Political Economy* 15(2): 234–258.

Higgins, Sean, and Claudiney Pereira. 2014. The effects of Brazil's taxation and social spending on the distribution of household income. *Public Finance Review* 42(3): 346–367.

Hoff, Karla, and Joseph Stiglitz. 2001. Modern economic theory and development. In Gerald Meier and Joseph Stiglitz, eds., *Frontiers of development economics*, pp. 389–460. New York: Oxford University Press.

Hogg, Michael, and Dominic Abrams. 1998. *Social identifications*. London: Routledge.

Horowitz, Donald L. 1989. Incentives and behaviour in the ethnic politics of Sri Lanka and Malaysia. *Third World Quarterly* 11(4): 18–35.

Hossain, Naomi, and Mick Moore. 1999. Elite perceptions of poverty: Bangladesh. *IDS Bulletin* 30(2): 106–116.

Htun, Mala. 2004. From "racial democracy" to affirmative action: Changing state policy on race in Brazil. *Latin American Research Review* 39(1): 60–89.

Huber, Evelyne, Thomas Mustillo, and John D. Stephens. 2008. Politics and social spending in Latin America. *The Journal of Politics* 70(2): 420–436.

Huddy, Leonie. 2013. From group identity to political cohesion and commitment. In Leonie Huddy, David O. Sears, and Jack Levy, eds., *Oxford handbook of political psychology*, pp. 737–773. New York: Oxford University Press.

Jacoby, Tami. 2015. A theory of victimhood: Politics, conflict and the construction of victim-based identity. *Millennium* 43(2): 511–530.

Jaffrelot, Christophe. 2006. The impact of affirmative action in India: More political than socioeconomic. *India Review* 5(2): 173–189.

James, Daniel. 1993. *Resistance and integration: Peronism and the Argentine working class, 1946–1976*. Cambridge: Cambridge University Press.

Jan, Wan, and Wan Saiful. 2011. Malaysia's New Economic Model: Is the Malaysian government serious about economic liberalisation? Background Paper 14, September. Potsdam: Friedrich Naumann Stiftung für die Freiheit. www.researchgate.net/publication/265235480_Malaysia%27s_New_Economic_Model_Is_the_Malaysian_government_serious_about_economic_liberalisation.

Jayawardene, Kumari. 1983. Aspects of class and ethnic consciousness in Sri Lanka. *Development and Change* 14: 1–18.

Jenkins, Laura, and Michele S. Moses. 2014. Affirmative action initiatives around the world. *International Higher Education* 77: 5–6.

Jessel, Ella. 2017. "If I'm stratum 3, that's who I am": Inside Bogotá's social stratification system. *Guardian* November 9. www.theguardian.com/cities/2017/nov/09/bogota-colombia-social-stratification-system.

Johannesen, Niels, and Jukka Pirttilä. 2016. Capital flight and development: An overview of concepts, methods, and data sources. No. 2016/95. WIDER Working Paper 2016/95.

Jomo, K. S., and Wee Chong Hui. 2003. The political economy of Malaysian federalism: Economic development, public policy and conflict containment. *Affirmative-Action Journal of International Development* 15(4): 441–456.

Jost, John, Mahzarin Banaji, and Brian Nosek. 2004. A decade of system justification theory: Accumulated evidence of conscious and unconscious bolstering of the status quo. *Political Psychology* 25(6): 881–919.

Justino, Patricia. 2011. Poverty and violent conflict: A micro-level perspective on the causes and duration of warfare. *London: IDS Working Papers* 2011(38): 1–25.

Kahneman, Daniel, and Shane Frederick. 2002. Representativeness revisited: Attribute substitution in intuitive judgment. In *Heuristics and biases: The psychology of intuitive judgment*, Thomas Gilovich, Dale Griffin, and Daniel Kahneman, eds., pp. 49–81. Cambridge: Cambridge University Press.

Kahneman, Daniel, and Amos Tversky. 1972. Subjective probability: A judgment of representativeness. *Cognitive Psychology* 3(3): 430–454.

Kaboski, Joseph, and Robert Townsend. 2009. The impacts of credit on village economies. https://ndigd.nd.edu/assets/172922/impacts_of_credit_on_village_economies.pdf.

Katz, Daniel. 1960. The functional approach to the study of attitudes. *Public Opinion Quarterly* 24: 163–204.

References

Kaufman, Robert, and Guilermo Trejo, Guillermo. 1996. Regionalismo, Transformación del Régimen y Pronasol: la Política del Programa Nacional de Solidaridad en Cuatro Estados Mexicanos. *Política y Gobierno* 3(2): 245–280.

Kearney, Robert. 1978. Language and the rise of Tamil separatism in Sri Lanka. *Asian Survey* 18(5): 521–534.

Keen, Michael, and Joel Slemrod. 2017. Optimal tax administration. *Journal of Public Economics* 152: 133–142.

Kelley, Harold. 1973. The process of causal attribution. *American Psychologist* 28: 107–128.

Kelley, Harold, and John Thibaut. 1985. Self-interest, science, and cynicism. *Journal of Social and Clinical Psychology* 3(1): 26–32.

Keyes, Charles. 2014. *Finding their own voice: Northeastern villagers and the Thai state.* Eastbourne, East Sussex: Silkworm Press.

Kidd, Stephen. 2016. To condition or not to condition? What is the evidence? *Pathways Perspectives* 20: 1–5.

King, Elizabeth, Peter Orazem, and Darin Wolgemuth. 1999. Central mandates and local incentives: The Colombia education voucher program. *World Bank Economic Review* 13(3): 467–491.

King, E., L. Rawlings, M. Gutierrez, C. Pardo, and C. Torres. 1997. Colombia's targeted education voucher program: Features, coverage, and participation. Series on Impact Evaluation of Education Reforms Working Paper No. 3. Development Research Group Washington DC: World Bank.

Knörr, Jacqueline. 2010. Contemporary Creoleness: Or, the world in pidginization? *Current Anthropology* 51(6): 731–759.

Koenig, Anne M., and Alice H. Eagly. 2014. Evidence for the social role theory of stereotype content: Observations of groups' roles shape stereotypes. *Journal of Personality and Social Psychology* 107(3): 371.

Kongkirati, Prajak. 2019. From illiberal democracy to military authoritarianism: Intra-elite struggle and mass-based conflict in deeply polarized Thailand. *The Annals of the American Academy of Political and Social Science* 681(1): 24–40.

Kopper, Moisés. 2015. Designing Brazil's new middle class: Economic science and welfare policies in the making of a social category. *Urbanities – Journal of Urban Ethnography* 5(2): 20–31.

Koski, Alissa, Erin C. Strumpf, Jay S. Kaufman, John Frank, Jody Heymann, and Arijit Nandi. 2018. The impact of eliminating primary school tuition fees on child marriage in sub-Saharan Africa: A quasi-experimental evaluation of policy changes in 8 countries. *PLoS One* 13(5): e0197928.

Kozicka, Marta, Regine Weber, and Matthias Kalkuhl. 2016. *Public distribution system vs. market: Analysis of wheat and rice consumption in India.* No. 40. The Hague: Foodsecure.

Krueger, Joachim, and Russell W. Clement. 1994. Memory-based judgments about multiple categories: A revision and extension of Tajfel's accentuation theory. *Journal of Personality and Social Psychology* 67(1): 35–47.

Kühn, Thomas. 2014. Construction of belongingness in late modernity: National pride in Brazil from a social inequality research perspective. In Gavin Sullivan, ed., *Understanding collective pride and group identity: New directions in emotion theory, research and practice*, pp. 161–172. East Sussex: Routledge.

Kuznets, Simon. 1955. Economic growth and income inequality. *The American Economic Review* 45(1): 1–28.

Lasswell, Harold D. 1930/1960. *Psychopathology and politics*. New York: Viking.

Lasswell, Harold D. 1932. The triple-appeal principle: A contribution of psycho-analysis to political and social science. *American Journal of Sociology* 37: 523–538.

Lasswell, Harold D. 1935/1965. *World politics and personal insecurity*. New York: The Free Press.

Lasswell, Harold D. 1947. The data of psychoanalysis and the social sciences. *The American Journal of Psychoanalysis* 7(1): 26–35.

Lasswell, Harold D. 1965. The world revolution of our time: A framework for basic policy research. In Harold D. Lasswell and Daniel Lerner, eds., *World revolutionary elites*, pp. 64–68. Cambridge, MA: MIT Press.

Lasswell, Harold D., and Abraham Kaplan. 1950. *Power and society*. New Haven: Yale University Press.

Lasswell, Harold D., and Myres McDougal. 1992. *Jurisprudence for a free society*. New Haven: New Haven Press.

Latin American Public Opinion Project. 2012. Argentine questionnaire.

Latinobarómetro. 2018. Latinobarometro data base. www.latinobarometro.org/latOnline.jsp.

Layton, Matthew, and Amy Smith. 2017. Is it race, class, or gender? The sources of perceived discrimination in Brazil. *Latin American Politics and Society* 59(1): 52–73.

Le, Tuan Minh, Blanca Moreno-Dodson, and Nihal Bayraktar. 2012. *Tax capacity and tax effort: Extended cross-country analysis from 1994 to 2009*. Washington, DC: World Bank.

Lee, Hwanbum. 1999. The role of public administration and bureaucracy in Thailand. *International Area Review* 2(2): 137–152.

Lee, Hwok-Aun. 2017. Majority affirmative action in Malaysia: Imperatives, compromises and challenges, March. Ottawa: Global Centre for Pluralism. www.pluralism.ca/wp-content/uploads/2017/10/Malaysia_Case_Note_EN.pdf.

Leftwich, Adrian, and Kunal Sen. 2011. "Don't mourn; organize": Institutions and organizations in the politics and economics of growth and poverty-reduction. *Journal of International Development* 23(3): 319–337.

Leichtman, Mara. 2005. The legacy of transnational lives: Beyond the first generation of Lebanese in Senegal. *Ethnic and Racial Studies* 28(4): 663–686.

Lessmann, Christian. 2012. Regional inequality and decentralization: An empirical analysis. *Environment and Planning A* 44: 1363–1388.

Levitsky, Steven. 2003. *Transforming labor-based parties in Latin America: Argentine Peronism in comparative perspective*. Cambridge: Cambridge University Press.

Lickel, B., D. L. Hamilton, and S. J. Sherman. 2001. Elements of a lay theory of groups: Types of groups, relational styles, and the perception of group entitativity. *Personality and Social Psychology Review* 5: 129–140.

References

Lickel, B., D. L. Hamilton, G. Wieczorkowska, A. Lewis, S. J. Sherman, A. N. Uhles. 2000. Varieties of groups and the perception of group entitativity. *Journal of Personality and Social Psychology* 78: 223–246.

Lickel, B., N. Miller, D. M. Stenstrom, T. F. Denson, and T. Schmader. 2006a. Vicarious retribution: The role of collective blame in intergroup aggression. *Personality and Social Psychology Review* 10: 372.

Lickel, B., A. Rutchick, D. L. Hamilton, and S. J. Sherman. 2006b. Intuitive theories of group types and relational principles. *Journal of Experimental Social Psychology* 42: 28–39.

Limpanonda, Suphannada. 2015. Provincial disparities, convergence and effects on poverty in Thailand. *Singapore Economic Review* 60(2): 1550015-1-25.

Lindblom, Charles. 1965. *The intelligence of democracy: Decision making through mutual adjustment*. New York: Free Press.

Lindblom, Charles. 1977. *Politics and markets*. New York: Basic Books.

Lodola, Germán, and Mitchell Seligson. 2011. *Cultura política de la democracia en Argentina, 2010: Consolidación democrática en las Américas en tiempos difíciles*. Buenos Aires: Universidad Torcuato Di Tella.

Lolayekar, Aparna, and Pranab Mukhopadhyay. 2017. Growth convergence and regional inequality in India (1981–2012). *Journal of Quantitative Economics* 15(2): 307–328.

Longva, Anh Nga. 2006. Nationalism in pre-modern guise: The discourse on hadhar and badu in Kuwait. *International Journal of Middle East Studies* 38(2): 171–187.

López, Matias. 2013. The state of poverty: Elite perceptions of the poor in Brazil and Uruguay. *International Sociology* 28(3): 351–370.

Loxton, James, and Steven Levitsky. 2018. Personalistic authoritarian successor parties in Latin America. In James Loxton and Scott Mainwaring, eds., *Life after dictatorship: Authoritarian successor parties worldwide*, pp. 113–141. Cambridge: Cambridge University Press.

Lustig, Nora, Luis F. Lopez Calva, and Eduardo Ortiz Juarez. 2014. Declining inequality in Latin America in the 2000s: The cases of Argentina, Brazil, and Mexico. *World Development* 44: 129–141.

Martin, P. 1998. Can regional policies affect growth and geography in Europe? *World Economy* 21(6):757–774.

McCargo, Duncan, and Krisadawan Hongladarom. 2004. Contesting Isan-ness: Discourses of politics and identity in Northeast Thailand. *Asian Ethnicity* 5(2): 219–234.

McConahay, John, and Joseph Hough, Jr. 1976. Symbolic racism. *Journal of Social Issues* 32: 23–45.

McGraw, Kathleen M. 2000. Contributions of the cognitive approach to political psychology. *Political Psychology* 21(4): 805–832.

Means, Gordon P. 1991. *Malaysian politics: The second generation*. Oxford: Oxford University Press.

Mearns, D. 1996. Class, status, and habitus in Ambon. In D. Mearns and C. Healey, eds., *Remaking Maluku: Social transformation in Eastern Indonesia*, pp. 95–105. Darwin: Northern Territory University.

Medrano, Anahely. 2013. Elites and poverty in the neoliberal era: The case of Mexico. *Poverty & Public Policy* 5(2): 203–223.

Minguez, Guia. 1978. *An historical evaluation of governmental attempts to achieve self-sufficiency in rice production in the Philippines*. Ithaca: Cornell University.

Mitchell, J. P. 2009. Inferences about mental states. *Philosophical Transactions of the Royal Society of London* 364: 1309–1316.

Mittal, Neeraj, Anit Mukherjee, and Alan Gelb. 2017. Fuel subsidy reform in developing countries: Direct benefit transfer of LPG cooking gas subsidy in India. Center for Global Development. Retrieved from www.cgdev.org/sites/default/files/fuel-subsidy-reformdeveloping-countries-india.pdf.

Mohamad, Maznah. 2012. Ethnicity and inequality in Malaysia: A retrospect and a rethinking. In Graham Brown, Armin Langer, and Frances Stewart, eds., *Affirmative action in plural societies*, pp. 151–181. Basingstoke, Hampshire: Palgrave Macmillan.

Molina Millán, Teresa, Tania Barham, Karen Macours, John A. Maluccio, and Marco Stampini. 2018. Long-Term impacts of conditional cash transfers: Review of the evidence. Paris School of Economics, March. www income region.parisschoolofeconomics.eu/docs/macours-karen/long-term-impacts-of-cct-review-of-the-evidence31mar2018.pdf.

Molle, François, Philippe Floch, Buapun Promphakping, and David J. H. Blake. 2009. The "Greening of Isaan": Politics, ideology and irrigation development in the northeast of Thailand. In François Molle, Tira Foran, and Mira Kakonen, eds., *Contested waterscapes in the Mekong region: Hydropower, livelihoods and governance*, pp. 253–282. London: Earthscan.

Mongsawad, Prasopchoke. 2010. The philosophy of the sufficiency economy: A contribution to the theory of development. *Asia Pacific Development Journal* 17(1): 123–143.

Mugo, John, Peter Moyi, and Onesmmus Kiminza. 2016. The challenge of access, quality and equity: Education in Kenya. In Ishmael Munene, ed., *Achieving education for all*, pp. 81–106. London: Lexington Books.

Muralidharan, Sukumar. 2006. Religion, Nationalism and the state: Gandhi and India's engagement with political modernity. *Social Scientist: March* 1: 3–36.

Murray, Matthew, and Carole Pateman, eds. 2012. *Basic income worldwide: Horizons of reform*. London: Palgrave Macmillan.

Nagamadhuri, J. 2015. Fourth World in reality. *Human Rights International Research Journal* 3(2): 110–113.

NaRanong, Viroj, and Anchana NaRanong. 2006. Universal health care coverage: Impacts of the 30-Baht health-care scheme on the poor in Thailand. *TDRI Quarterly Review* 21(3): 3–10.

Navaratnam, Ramon. 2002. *Malaysia's economic sustainability: Confronting new challenges amidst global realities*. Selangor, Malaysia: Pelanduk Publications Sdn Bhd.

Neri, Marcelo. 2008. *A Nova Classe Média: O lado brilhante dos pobres*. Rio de Janeiro: CPS/FGV.

Neri, Marcelo. 2011. *A Nova Classe Média: O lado brilhante da base da pirâmide*. São Paulo: Editora Saraiva.

References

Nesiah, Devanesan. 1999. *Discrimination with reason? The policy of reservations in the United States, India and Malaysia*. New Delhi: Oxford University Press.

Newhouse, David, and Ani Silwal. 2018. The state of jobs in post-conflict areas of Sri Lanka. World Bank Poverty & Equity Global Practice Working Paper February 141. Washington, DC: World Bank.

Nickerson, R. S. 1998. Confirmation bias: A ubiquitous phenomenon in many guises. *Review of General Psychology* 2(2): 175–220.

Niño-Zarazúa, Miguel. 2016. Mexico's Progresa-Oportunidades-Prospera and the raise of social assistance in Latin America. UNU-WIDER Working Paper, February. www.researchgate.net/publication/320416721_Mexico%27s_Progresa-Oportunidades-Prospera_and_the_raise_of_social_assistance_in_Latin_America.

Nixon, Stewart, Hidekatsu Asada, and Vincent Koen. 2017. Fostering inclusive growth in Malaysia. OECD Economic Department Working Paper 1371.

Nordhaus, Ted, and Michael Shellenberger. 2007. *Break through: From the death of environmentalism to the politics of possibility*. Boston, MA: Houghton Mifflin Harcourt.

Norhashim, Mariati, and Kamarulzaman Aziz. 2005. Smart partnership or cronyism? A Malaysian perspective. *International Journal of Sociology and Social Policy* 25(8): 31–48.

North, Douglass. 1998. Five propositions about institutional change. In J. Knight and I. Sened, eds., *Explaining social institutions*, pp. 15–26. Ann Arbor: University of Michigan Press.

Oberst, Robert. 1988. Federalism and ethnic conflict in Sri Lanka. *Publius: The Journal of Federalism* 18(3): 175–194.

OECD. 2016. *OECD reviews of health systems: Mexico 2016*. Paris: OECD Publishing.

Oorschot, Wim van. 2000. Who should get what, and why? On deservingness criteria and the conditionality of solidarity among the public. *Policy and Politics* 28(1): 33–48.

Ostiguy, Pierre. 2007. Syncretism in Argentina's party system and Peronist political culture. In Dennis Galvan and Rudra Sil, eds., *Reconfiguring Institutions across time and space*, pp. 83–113. New York: Palgrave Macmillan.

Ouyyanont, Porphant. 2017. *A regional economic history of Thailand*. Singapore: ISEAS-Yusof Ishak Institute.

Page, Abigail, Tessa Minter, Sylvain Viguier, and Andrea Bamberg Migliano. 2018. Hunter-gatherer health and development policy: How the promotion of sedentism worsens the Agta's health outcomes. *Social Science & Medicine* 197: 39–48.

Palma, José Gabriel. 2011. Homogeneous middles vs. heterogeneous tails, and the end of the "inverted-U": It's all about the share of the rich. *Development and Change* 42(1): 87–153.

Pansuwan, A., and Routray, J. K. 2011. Policies and pattern of industrial development in Thailand. *Geo-Journal* 76(1): 25–46.

Paradise, Tom. 2016. The Bedouins of Petra, Jordan: A geographer's life with the Bdoul. *The Arab World Geographer* 9(3–4): 209–224.

Parpart, Erich. 2019. Army unwilling to yield to democracy. *Bangkok Post*, July 31.

Pathmanand, Ukrist. 2016. Network Thaksin: Structure, roles and reaction, in Pasuk Phongpaichit and Chris Baker, eds., *Unequal Thailand: Aspects of income, wealth and power*, pp. 1–31. Singapore: NUS Press.

Peebles, Patrick. 1990. Colonization and ethnic conflict in the Dry Zone of Sri Lanka. *The Journal of Asian Studies* 49(1): 30–55.

Perry, Guillermo, William F. Maloney, Osmar S. Arias, Pablo Fajnzylber, Andrew D. Mason, and Jaime Saavedra-Chanduvi. 2007. *Informality: Exit and Exclusion*. Washington, DC: The World Bank.

Pessino, Carola, and Ricardo Fenochietto. 2010. Determining countries' tax effort, *Hacienda Pública Española/Revista de Economía Pública* 195: 65–87.

Pessino, Carola, and Ricardo Fenochietto. 2013. Understanding countries' tax effort. International Monetary Fund Fiscal Department Working Paper. Washington, DC: International Monetary Fund.

Pettigrew, Thomas F. 1979. The ultimate attribution error: Extending Allport's cognitive analysis of prejudice. *Personality and Social Psychology Bulletin* 5 (4): 461–476.

Phadnis, Urmila. 1972. Infrastructural linkages in Sri Lanka-India relations. *Economic and Political Weekly* 7(32/33): 1493–1501.

Phongpaichit, Pasuk, and Chris Baker. 2008. Thaksin's populism. *Journal of Contemporary Asia* 38(1): 62–83.

Phongpaichit, Pasuk, and Chris Baker. 2016. Introduction: Inequality and oligarchy. In Pasuk Phongpaichit and Chris Baker, eds., *Unequal Thailand: Aspects of income, wealth and power*, pp. 1–31. Singapore: NUS Press.

Pillarisetti, Ajay, Dean T. Jamison, and Kirk R. Smith. 2017. Household energy interventions and health and finances in Haryana, India: An extended cost-effectiveness analysis. In Charles N. Mock, Rachel Nugent, Olive Kobusingye, and Kirk R. Smith, eds., *Injury prevention and environmental health*, pp. 223–237. Washington, DC: World Bank.

Pitch, Pongsawat. 2004. Senthang prachathippatai lae kan prap tua khong rat thai nai rabop thaksin' [The Path of Democracy and the Modification of the State under Thaksinism]. Fa dieo kan [Same Sky] 2(1): 64–91, cited in Phongpaichit, Pasuk, and Chris Baker (2008, 68).

Pochmann, M. 2014. *O mito da Grande Classe Média: Capitalismo e estrutura social*. São Paulo: Boitempo.

Potenza Dal Masetto, Fernanda, and Fabián Repetto. 2012. *Social protection systems in Latin America and the Caribbean: Argentina*. Santiago de Chile: UN Economic Commission for Latin America.

Prentice-Dunn, S. and R. W. Rogers. 1989/2015. Deindividuation and the self-regulation of behavior. In P. Paulus, ed., *Psychology of group influence*, 2nd ed., pp. 87–109. Hillsdale, NJ: Lawrence Erlbaum Associates.

Pritchett, Lant. 2005. The Political Economy of Targeted Safety Nets. Discussion Paper, World Bank Social Protection Unit, January.

Pye, Oliver, and Wolfram Schaffar. 2008. The 2006 anti-Thaksin movement in Thailand: An analysis. *Journal of Contemporary Asia* 38(1): 38–61.

References

Rapoza, Kenneth. 2017. World Bank: Brazil is the worst economy in Latin America. *Forbes*, June 6. www.forbes.com/sites/kenrapoza/2017/06/06/world-bank-brazil-is-the-worst-economy-in-latin-america/#534eee9a29fo.

Ravallion, Martin. 2002. Are the poor protected from budget cuts? Evidence for Argentina. *Journal of Applied Economics* 5(1): 95–121.

Rediff News. 2017. Income limit for OBC "creamy layer" raised, August 23.

Reicher, Stephen, Russell Spears, and S. Alexander Haslam. 2010. The social identity approach in social psychology. In M. S. Wetherell and C. T. Mohanty, eds., pp. 45–62. *Sage identities handbook*. London: Sage.

Reid, Ben. 2016. The geopolitical economy of social policy in the Philippines: Securitisation, emerging powers and multilateral policies. *Third World Quarterly* 37(1): 96–118.

Reis, Elisa. 2005. Perceptions of poverty and inequality among Brazilian elites. In Elisa Reis and Mick Moore, eds., *Elite perceptions of poverty and inequality*. London: Zed Books, 26–56.

Richardson, Harry W. 1982. Industrial policy and regional development in less-developed countries. In *Regional dimensions of industrial policy*, edited by Michael E. Bell and Paul S. Lande, pp. 93–120. Lexington, KY: Lexington Books.

Roberts, Michael. 1978. Ethnic conflict in Sri Lanka and Sinhalese perspectives: Barriers to accommodation. *Modern Asian Studies* 12(3): 353–376.

Rodrik, Dani. 2000. Participatory politics, social cooperation, and economic stability. *American Economic Review* 90(2): 140–144.

Romero, Simon. 2012. Brazil Enacts Affirmative Action Law for Universities. *New York Times*, August 30.

Rosenblatt, David. 2016. The credibility of economic policy making in Argentina, 1989–2015. World Bank Policy Research Working Paper 7870. Washington, DC: World Bank.

Rothbart, Myron, Solomon Fulero, Christine Jensen, John Howard, and Pamela Birrell. 1978. From individual to group impressions: Availability heuristics in stereotype formation. *Journal of Experimental Social Psychology* 14(3): 237–255.

Rudolph, Lloyd. 1965. The modernity of tradition: The democratic incarnation of caste in India. *American Political Science Review* 59(4): 975–989.

Sabbagh, Daniel. 2004. Affirmative action policies: An international perspective. Background paper for the human development report 2004. New York: UN Development Programme.

Sabpaitoon, Patpon, and Chatrudee Theparat 2017. Govt dangles B68bn development carrot. Bangkok Post, August 27. www.bangkokpost.com/news/gen eral/1311163/govt-dangles-b68bn-development-carrot.

Sáenz de Miera Juárez, Belén. 2017. The expansion of public health insurance in Mexico: Health, financial and distributional effects. PhD diss., The London School of Economics and Political Science (LSE).

Salamat, Patchrathanyarasm. 2011. The green body in red shirt yellow pants: A religio-political discourse over yellow-red conflict within Muslim Thai (cyber) society. *Jati: Journal of Southeast Asian Studies* 16(1): 3–21, August 27.

Saxer, Marc. 2012. How can Thailand overcome its transformation crisis? A strategy for democratic change. Friedrich Ebert Stiftung, Bangkok Thailand Analysis. www. fes-thailand. org.

Schwartzman, Luisa. 2009. Seeing like citizens: Unofficial understandings of official racial categories in a Brazilian university. *Journal of Latin American studies* 41: 221–250.

Seng-Arun, N. 2013. Development of regional growth centres and impact on regional growth: A case study of Thailand's Northeastern region. *Urbani Izziv* 24(1): 160–171.

Shapiro, Yakov, and Glen O. Gabbard. 1994. A reconsideration of altruism from an evolutionary and psychodynamic perspective. *Ethics & Behavior* 4(1): 23–42.

Sharma, Sangeeta V., and Vinod K. Sharma. 2016. Socio-economic impacts of an LPG subsidy removal on the household sector in India. In Han Phoumin and Shigeru Kimura, eds., *Institutional policy and economic impacts of energy subsidies removal in East Asia*, pp. 83–101. Jakarta: Economic Research Institute for ASEAN and East Asia.

Sharma, Sargam. 2018. Presidency University, Kolkata is dismantling affirmative action, September 5, 2018. http://raiot.in/presidency-university-kolkata-is-dismantling-affirmative-action/.

Shastri, Amita. 1999. Estate Tamils, the Ceylon Citizenship Act of 1948 and Sri Lankan politics. *Contemporary South Asia* 8(1): 65–86.

Sherif, Muzafer, ed. 1962. *Intergroup relations and leadership*. New York: Wiley.

Shrinivas, Aditya, Kathy Baylis, Ben Crost, and Prabhu Pingali. 2018. Do staple food subsidies improve nutrition? Ithaca: Cornell University. http://barrett.dyson.cornell.edu/NEUDC/paper_520.pdf.

Siddique, Sharon, and Leo Suryadinata. 1981. Bumiputra and pribumi: Economic nationalism (indiginism) in Malaysia and Indonesia. *Pacific Affairs* 54(4): 662–687.

Silveira, Fernando Gaiger, Fernando Rezende, Jose Roberto Afonso, and Jhonatan Ferreira. 2013. Fiscal equity: Distributional impacts of taxation and social spending in Brazil, Working Paper, International Policy Centre for Inclusive Growth, No. 115. Brasilia: International Policy Centre for Inclusive Growth. file:///D:/Inclusion/Silveira%20Fiscal%20Equity%20Brazil.pdf.

Simpson, Brent, and Robb Willer. 2015. Beyond altruism: Sociological foundations of cooperation and prosocial behavior. *Annual Review of Sociology* 41: 43–63.

Simson, Rebecca. 2018. Mapping recent inequality trends in developing countries. London: London School Of Economics and Political Science International Inequality Institute, Working Paper 24, May.

Sindic, Denis, and Susan Condor. 2014. Social identity theory and self-categorisation theory. In Paul Nesbitt-Larking, Catarina Kinnvall, and Tereza Capelos, eds., *The Palgrave handbook of global political psychology*, pp. 39–54. London: Palgrave Macmillan.

Singer, Marshall R. 1996. Sri Lanka's ethnic conflict: Have bombs shattered hopes for peace? *Asian Survey* 36(11): 1146–1155.

Skidmore, Thomas E. 1992. Fact and myth: Discovering a racial problem in Brazil. Kellogg Institute Working Paper #173, April. South Bend, IN: The Helen Kellogg Institute for International Studies, Notre Dame University.

Sniderman, P. M., R. A. Brody, and P. E. Tetlock. 1991. *Reasoning and choice: Explorations in political psychology.* New York: Cambridge University Press.

Soares, Benjamin F. 2004. Muslim saints in the age of neoliberalism. *Studies on Religion in Africa* 26: 79–105.

Soares, Fabio Veras. 2011. Brazil's Bolsa Família: A review. *Economic and Political Weekly* 46(21): 55–60, May 21.

Soares, Fábio Veras, Rafael Perez Ribas, and Rafael Guerreiro Osório. 2010. Evaluating the impact of Brazil's Bolsa Familia: Cash transfer programs in comparative perspective. *Latin American Research Review* 45(2): 173–190.

Soares, Sergei, Rafael Guerreiro Osório, Fabio Veras Soares, Marcelo Medeiros, and Eduardo Zepeda. 2009. Conditional cash transfers in Brazil, Chile and Mexico: Impacts upon inequality. *Estudios Económicos* 207–224.

Solt, Frederick. 2019. The Standardized World Income Inequality Database, Version 8. https://doi.org/10.7910/DVN/LM4OWF, Harvard Dataverse, V2.

Stampini, Marco, and Leopoldo Tornarolli. 2012. The growth of conditional cash transfers in Latin America and the Caribbean: Did they go too far? No. 49. Bonn: Institute for the Study of Labor Policy Paper No. 49.

Standing, Guy. 2008. How cash transfers promote the case for basic income. *Basic Income Studies* 3(1): 1–30.

Stewart, Frances. 2000. Crisis prevention: Tackling horizontal inequalities. *Oxford Development Studies* 28(3): 245–262.

Stewart, Frances. 2002. Horizontal inequalities: A neglected dimension of development. Vol. 5. Wider.

Stocks, Eric L., David A. Lishner, and Stephanie K. Decker. 2009. Altruism or psychological escape: Why does empathy promote prosocial behavior? *European Journal of Social Psychology* 39(5): 649–665.

Stürmer, Stefan, and Mark Snyder. 2010. Helping "Us" versus "Them": Towards a group-level theory of helping and altruism within and across group boundaries. In Stefan Stürmer and Mark Snyder, eds., *The psychology of prosocial behaviour: Group processes, intergroup relations, and helping*, pp. 33–58. Oxford: Wiley-Blackwell.

Sumner, Andy. 2018. *Revisiting Kuznets: Is rising inequality still inevitable during economic development?* London: ESRC GPID Research Network Briefing Paper 10.

Swamy, Arun Ranga. 2016. Can social protection weaken clientelism? Considering conditional cash transfers as political reform in the Philippines. *Journal of Current Southeast Asian Affairs* 35(1): 59–90.

Taber, Charles, and Milton Lodge. 2006. Motivated skepticism in the evaluation of political beliefs. *American Journal of Political Science* 50(3): 755–769.

Tajfel, Henri. 1969/1981. Cognitive aspects of prejudice. *Journal of Social Issues* 25(4): 79–97; reprinted in Henri Tajfel 1981, *Human groups and social categories*. New York: Cambridge University Press, pp. 127–142.

Tajfel, Henri. 1981. *Human groups and social categories: Studies in social psychology.* London: Cambridge University Press.

Tajfel, Henri. 1982. Social psychology of intergroup relations. *Annual Review of Psychology* 33(1): 1–39.

Tajfel, Henri, and John C. Turner. 1979. An integrative theory of intergroup conflict. In W. Austin and S. Worchel, eds., *The social psychology of intergroup relations*. Monterey, CA: Brooks/Cole.

Tajfel, Henri, and John C. Turner. 1986. The social identity theory of inter-group behavior. In Stephen Worchel and William Austin, eds., *Psychology of intergroup relations*. Chicago: Nelson-Hall.

Tan, Jeff. 2013. Running out of steam? Manufacturing in Malaysia. *Cambridge Journal of Economics* 38(1): 153–180.

Taylor, Jim. 2012. Remembrance and tragedy: Understanding Thailand's "Red Shirt" social movement. *SOJOURN: Journal of Social Issues in Southeast Asia* 27: 1.

Techakesari, Pirathat, Fiona Kate Barlow, Matthew J. Hornsey, Billy Sung, Michael Thai, and Jocelyn L. Y. Chak. 2015. An investigation of positive and negative contact as predictors of intergroup attitudes in the United States, Hong Kong, and Thailand. *Journal of Cross-Cultural Psychology* 46(3): 454–468.

TeleSur. 2016. Brazil Commission to Judge Darkness of State Officials' Skin, September 5.

Thorat, Amit, and Sonalde Desai. 2012. Social inequalities in education. In IDFC Foundation, ed., *India Infrastructure Report 2012*, pp. 82–89. Delhi: Routledge India.

Thyne, Clayton, and Erika Moreno. 2008. Squeaky wheels and unequal policy: Executive authority and education reform in Latin America. *Comparative Political Studies* 41(7): 921–946.

Tilly, Charles. 1998a. *Durable inequality*. Berkeley and Los Angeles: University of California Press.

Tilly, Charles. 1998b. Social movements and (all sorts of) other political interactions – local, national, and international – including identities. *Theory and Society* 27(4): 453–480.

Torche, Florencia. 2014. Intergenerational mobility and inequality: The Latin American case, *Annual Review of Sociology* 40: 619–642.

Turner, John C., Michael Hogg, Penelope J. Oakes, Stephen Reicher, and Margaret Wetherell. 1987. *Rediscovering the social group: A self-categorization theory*. Oxford: Basil Blackwell.

Turner, John C., and Penelope J. Oakes. 1986. The significance of the social identity concept for social psychology with reference to individualism, interactionism and social influence. *British Journal of Social Psychology* 25(3): 237–252.

Turner, John C., Penelope J. Oakes, S. Alexander Haslam, and Craig McGarty. 1994. Self and collective: Cognition and social context. *Personality and Social Psychology Bulletin* 20(5): 454–463.

Turner, John C., and Katherine J. Reynolds. 2012. Self categorization theory. In Paul A. M. Van Lange, Arie W. Kruglanski, and E. Tory Higgins, eds., *Handbook of theories of social psychology*, pp. 399–417. London: SAGE Publications Ltd.

Tversky, Amos, and Daniel Kahneman. 1973. Availability: A heuristic for judging frequency and probability. *Cognitive Psychology* 5(2): 207–232.

References

Tversky, Amos, and Daniel Kahneman. 1991. Loss aversion in riskless choice: A reference-dependent model. *Quarterly Journal of Economics* 106(4): 1039–1061.

United Nations. 2015. *The millennium development goals report.* New York: United Nations.

United Nations Development Programme. 2013. *Human development report.* New York: United Nations.

Upadhyay, V. S., and Gaya Pandey. 2003. *Tribal development in India (A critical appraisal).* Ranchi: Crown Publications.

Upmeyer, A., and H. Layer. 1974. Accentuation and attitude in social judgment. *European Journal of Social Psychology* 4: 469–488.

Uribe Mallarino, Consuelo. 2008. Estratificación social en Bogotá: de la política pública a la dinámica de la segregación social. *Universitas Humanística* 65: 139–171.

Verkholantseva, Alexandra. 2016. Translation of Argentinian literature as illustrated by the translations of Adolfo Bioy Casares's works. [Thesis in Spanish]. St. Petersburg: State University of St. Petersburg Departamento de lenguas románicas.

Vodopivec, Milan. 2013. Introducing unemployment insurance to developing countries. *IZA Journal of Labour Policy* 2(1). www.izajolp.com/content/2/1/1.

Volpe, Michael. 2015. Frame resonance and failure in the Thai red shirts and yellow shirts movements. PhD dissertation, George Mason University. Fairfex, VA: George Mason University.

Vorauer, Jacquie D., A. J. Hunter, Kelley J. Main, and Scott A. Roy. 2000. Meta-stereotype activation: Evidence from indirect measures for specific evaluative concerns experienced by members of dominant groups in intergroup interaction. *Journal of Personality and Social Psychology* 78(4): 690–707.

Walter, Henrik. 2012. Social cognitive neuroscience of empathy: Concepts, circuits, and genes. *Emotion Review* 4(1): 9–17. Malaysia's New Economic Model.

Warr, Peter. 2005. Thailand's paradoxical recovery. *Southeast Asian Affairs Volume* 2005: 385–404.

Weinreich, Peter. 2005. Identity exploration: Theory into practice. In Peter Weinreich and Wendy Saunderson, eds., *Analysing identity,* pp. 77–110. New York: Routledge.

Whah, Chin Yee, and Benny Teh Cheng Guan. 2017. Malaysia's protracted affirmative action policy and the evolution of the Bumiputera Commercial and Industrial Community. *SOJOURN: Journal of Social Issues in Southeast Asia* 2017: 336–373.

Whitt, Sam, and Rick Wilson. 2007. The dictator game, fairness and ethnicity in postwar Bosnia. *American Journal of Political Science* 51(3): 655–668.

Wickramasinghe, Nira. 2012. Democracy and entitlements in Sri Lanka: The 1970s crisis over university admission. *South Asian History and Culture* 3(1): 81–96.

Widianto, Bambang. 2007. Are budget support and cash transfer effective means of social protection? In *Forum on inclusive growth and poverty reduction in the new Asia and the Pacific.* Manila: Asian Development Bank.

Wilkins, Vicky M., and Jeffrey B. Wenger. 2014. Belief in a just world and attitudes toward affirmative action. *Policy Studies Journal* 42(3): 325–343.

Winant, Howard. 1992. Thinking race in Brazil. *Journal of Latin American Studies* 24(1) 173–192.

Wjuniski, Bernardo Stuhlberger. 2013. Education and development projects in Brazil (1932–2004): Political economy perspective. *Brazilian Journal of Political Economy* 33(1): 146–165.

World Bank. 2008. The road not traveled: Education reform in the Middle East and Africa. MENA Development Report. Washington, DC: World Bank.

World Bank. 2016a. *Migration and remittances factbook*, 3rd ed. Washington, DC: World Bank.

World Bank. 2016b. *Poverty and shared prosperity 2016: Taking on inequality.* Washington, DC: World Bank.

World Bank. 2017a. Global database of shared prosperity, circa 2009–2014. Washington, DC: World Bank. http://pubdocs.worldbank.org/en/611081509650237862/GDSP-circa-2009-14-Oct-11-2017.pdf.

World Bank. 2017b. Thailand overview. Washington, DC: World Bank. www.worldbank.org/en/country/thailand/overview.

World Bank. 2018a. World Bank database. https://data.worldbank.org/indicator/NY.GDP.PCAP.KD.ZG?locations=CN.

World Bank. 2018b. The World Bank in Thailand. www.worldbank.org/en/country/thailand/overview.

World Bank. 2018c. World Bank poverty and equity database. http://databank.worldbank.org/data/reports.aspx?source=poverty-and-equity-database.

World Bank. 2018d. *Poverty and shared prosperity 2018: Piecing together the poverty puzzle.* Washington, DC: World Bank.

World Bank. 2019a. *World Bank country and lending groups.* Washington, DC: World Bank. https://datahelpdesk.worldbank.org/knowledgebase/articles/906519-world-bank-country-and-lending-groups.

World Bank. 2019b. World Bank database. https://data.worldbank.org/indicator/SE.XPD.PRIM.PC.ZS?view=chart; https://data.worldbank.org/indicator/SE.XPD.TOTL.GB.ZS?view=chart.

Yadav, Ashok. 2009. Concepts of reservation. *Countercurrents.Org.* www.countercurrents.org/yadav051209.htm.

Yadav, Ashok. 2015. OBC quota division: States' job, not Centre's. *Forward Press.* www.forwardpress.in/2015/09/obc-quota-division-states-job-not-centres-2/.

Yu, Wusheng, Christian Elleby, and Henrik Zobbe. 2015. Food security policies in India and China: Implications for national and global food security. *Food Security* 7(2): 405–414.

Yusof, Zainal. 2012. Affirmative action in Malaysia: An overview of progress and limitations. In Graham Brown, Armin Langer, and Frances Stewart, eds., *Affirmative action in plural societies: International experiences*, pp. 128–150. Basingstoke, Hampshire: Palgrave Macmillan.

Index

1MDB Scandal (Malaysia), 160
30-Baht Health-care Scheme (Thailand), 133

Abad, Letitia Arroyo, 117
Abelson, R. P., 196, 221
Abrams, Dominic, 61, 229
Acemoglu, Daron, 33, 221
Adivasi (scheduled tribes, India), 63, 73, 79, 138–139, 141, 146–148
affection value, 65, 208
affective empathy, 86
affirmative action, 3–4, 13, 20–21, 23, 36, 63, 78–79, 85, 96–97, 119, 124, 135–146, 148–161, 164, 168, 199, 206, 208, 223, 225–226, 229–230, 232, 234, 237–238, 241–242
African ancestry, 47, 56, 148, 153
Afro-Argentines, 112, 114
Afro-Brazilians, 3, 53, 97, 119, 121, 138–139, 148–154, 169, 211
Agénor, Pierre-Richard, 32–33, 221
aggressiveness, 207
agriculture, 27, 34, 40
Agta (Philippines), 82, 235
Al Ramiah, Ananthi, 60, 155, 221
Alexander, Saowanee, 183–184
Algeria, 34, 54
Ali Baba syndrome (Malaysia), 158
Almond, Gabriel, 221
altruism, 4, 10, 15, 22, 65, 84–85, 87, 137, 140, 199–200, 214–216, 223, 228, 238–239

Alzate, Maria, 131, 221
Amann, Edmund, 26
Amazonia, 79
Ambedkar, Bhimrao Ramji (India), 139
Ambiguity in decision making, 23, 91, 94, 135–136, 151, 169–170, 203
Ambonese (Indonesia), 71, 224
Amerindians, 112
Ames, D. R., 76
Anas, M. U. M., 34
Anderson, Charles W., 181, 222
Andhra Pradesh (India), 73, 129
Anisimova, Alla, 53, 56, 222
application function, 200, 203
appraisal function, 24, 200, 203–204
Arabs, 57, 64, 235
Argentina, 3, 12, 16–17, 20–22, 27, 33, 36, 38, 41–44, 47–48, 53, 81, 84, 92–93, 103, 107, 109–110, 112–114, 116, 153, 195–197, 202, 223–225, 228, 233, 235–237
Ariely, Dan, 16, 228
Armenians, 68, 72
armed forces, 37, 121, 144, 164
Asada, Hidekatsu, 156, 235
Asan, Ali, 154, 229
ascriptive identifications, 5, 15, 52, 55–58, 61, 64, 82, 84, 137, 215
Asian Development Bank, 217, 241
Assam (India), 62, 129, 222
assimilation effect, 71
attitude-based identifications, 59–60

243

Index

attributions, 18, 21, 23, 51, 55–56, 58, 60–61, 68–75, 77, 82, 84, 114, 135, 199, 204–205, 207, 214–215, 219
Australia, 16
availability heuristic, 70, 196, 202
Ayal, Shahar, 16, 228
Aziz, Kamarulzaman, 160

Baker, Chris, 134, 174, 176, 186, 222, 236
Balakrishnan, Ravi, 173, 222
Balatchandirane, G., 105, 222
Balisacan, Arsenio, 125, 222
Banaji, Mahzarin, 74, 230
Bangkok, 172, 174, 177, 179–180, 182–185, 187, 224, 226, 228, 237
Bangladesh, 48, 86, 229
bankers, 69
Barrera-Osorio, F., 132
Barro, R. J., 171, 222
Barron, Robert, 37, 222
Bar-Tel, Daniel, 186
Baruah, Sanjib, 62, 222
basic income approach, 96
basic universal rights, 96
Bass, Jeffrey, 112, 119, 222
Batson, C. Daniel, 85, 87, 222
Baumeister, R. F. K., 59, 209, 223
Baweanese (Malaysia), 80
Bayly, Susan, 143, 223
Bayraktar, Nihal, 40–41, 48, 232
Bedouins, 64, 78, 235
Bem, Darryl, 54, 223
benefit leakage, 210
Benton, Allyson, 109, 223
Beteille, Andre, 14, 223
Bevilaqua, Ciméa, 151, 153, 223
Bhavnani, Rikhil, 83, 223
Biernat, Monica, 71, 117
Bihar (India), 128
blamelessness criterion, 81
Blattman, C., 7
Bogliacino, Francesco, 131, 223
Bogotá, 4, 130, 221, 223, 241
Bolivians, 27, 84, 113
Bolsa Familia Program (Brazil), 66, 95–97, 119, 153, 239
Bonilla, J., 131, 223
Boonmathya, Ratana Tosakul, 188
Boräng, Frida, 109, 223
Bormann, Nils-Christian, 55, 223
Bourdieu, Pierre, 54, 62, 223

Brady, H. E., 55, 224
Brahmins (India), 62, 140–142, 144
Brasília (Brazil), 121
Brazil, 3, 12, 16–17, 21–22, 27–28, 32–33, 36, 41–43, 45, 47–48, 66, 81, 91–92, 94–97, 100, 103, 105, 117–121, 135–136, 139, 148–149, 151–153, 158, 161, 168, 195, 199, 202, 211, 223, 225, 229, 231–233, 237–240, 242
Brewer, Marilyn, 63, 73
British Malaya, 80
British rule, 139, 154
Britto, Tatiana, 94, 96
Brody, R. E., 81, 239
Brunei, 44
Buarque, Cristovam, 121, 224
Buchanan, James, 183
Buddhists, 6, 164, 167, 172, 178
Buenos Aires, 111–113, 119, 222, 233
Bull, Benedicte, 119, 224
Bumiputeras (Malaysia), 156–157
bureaucratic authoritarianism, 180
bureaucrats, 72, 93, 137, 139, 146, 166, 180
Burma, 53
Butonese (Indonesia), 71

Calcutta, 58
Cambodia, 16, 37, 42, 92
Cambon, Laurent, 74, 224
Cameroon, 105
Campbell, Donald, 68, 72, 187, 224
Campinas (Brazil), 95
Canada, 16, 98
Canuto, Otaviano, 31–33, 221, 224
capital flight, 8, 20, 30, 159
Cardoso, President Fernando (Brazil), 148, 153
Carnegie Endowment for International Peace, 95
Carsten, Paul, 179, 224
cash transfers, 13, 21, 28, 95, 99, 101, 106, 128, 130, 222, 224, 234, 239
caste system (India), 139–140, 143
Catholics, 68
Cederman, Lars-Erik, 55, 223
Central Thais, 182, 184
Ceylon Tamils, 165
Chanmorchan, Proudfong, 217, 224
charitability, 6, 51, 62

Index

Chatichai Choonhavan, General (Thailand), 182
Chatterji, Sauhadra, 143
Chauvel, R. H., 71, 224
Cheibub, José Antonio, 225
Chhattisgarh (India), 128–129
child labor, 96
child welfare, 101
Chile, 28, 81, 95, 117, 121, 153, 195, 236, 239
China, 15, 25, 30, 32–33, 38, 139, 177, 179, 242
Chinese Indonesians, 67, 84
Chinese Malaysians, 157, 159, 206
Christians, 6, 53, 55, 223, 232, 242
citizenship, 56, 96, 156, 160, 163, 165
City Population, 174
class, 73, 93, 101, 105, 108, 111–112, 114, 118–121, 131, 138, 151–152, 157–158, 173, 183, 230–232
Clement, Russell, 71, 231
cognitive empathy, 86–87
cognitive limitations, 68
cognitive load, 71, 86, 117, 223, 230, 239–240
cognitive theories, 71
collective action, 53, 57–58, 168
Colombia, 16–17, 21, 23, 28, 41–45, 47–48, 81, 121, 123, 130, 132, 134, 195, 221–223, 231
Condor, Susan, 60, 168, 238
Confino, Alon, 186, 225
consociational systems, 37
constitutive arrangements, 76
contrast effect, 71
Cookson, Tara, 92
Corona, Monica, 92
Corrêa, Diego Sanches, 94, 225
Costa Rica, 46
Costa, Sergio, 28, 120, 137, 225
Côte d'Ivoire, 106
Courtis, Corina, 113–114, 225
credibility, 110, 197, 199, 237
crime, 153, 161
crisis reactions, 8, 66, 100, 108, 153
cross-subsidies, 125, 133
cultural capital, 62
Cutrona, Sebastián, 111, 225
cynicism, 12, 21, 23, 60, 92, 107, 109, 144, 176, 197, 200–201, 203–204, 217–219, 231

Dahana, A., 84, 225
Dale, K., 59
Dalits (scheduled castes; India), 63, 74, 138–141, 146–147, 208
dāna (charity), 6
Daniel, E. Valentine, 167
Das, Pauline, 225
Dasgupta, Abhijit, 161
Dasgupta, Indraneel, 6
Davidson, Jamie, 58, 208, 225
Davis, Thomas, 169
Dawis, Aimee, 84, 225
Dayaks (Indonesia), 58, 72, 207
de la Rúa, President Fernando (Argentina), 109
de Oliveira, Cleuci, 151, 225
De Votta, Neil, 38
de-biasing, 215
decision process, 218
Decker, Stephanie, 87, 239
defensiveness, 51
deference values, 208
deindustrialization, 158
del Rio, Vicente, 119
demands (component of perspectives), 18–19, 23, 80, 93, 150, 156, 171, 180–181, 208, 213–216, 218
democracy, 35, 37, 149, 160, 181, 216, 221, 223–224, 226, 231, 233, 236
Democrat Party (Thailand), 178
Denson, T., 68, 226, 233
depersonalization, 65
Desai, Sonalde, 147
Desert Campaign (Argentina), 112
deservingness judgments, 4–5, 9, 12, 18, 21–22, 51, 56, 66, 69, 76–85, 91, 93–94, 96–97, 100–101, 114, 135–136, 143, 146, 153, 165, 184, 194, 198–199, 201–204, 207, 211–212, 214–216, 235
Deshpande, Ashwini, 140–141, 144–145, 226
Deshpande, Satish, 145
destructive conflict, 16, 30, 199
Devarajan, Shantayanan, 41, 226
DeWalt, Billie, 82
DeWalt, Kathleen, 82
Dhanaraj, Sowmya, 128, 226
Diaz Cayeros, Alberto, 98
disconfirmation bias, 71

Index

discrimination, 11, 63, 66, 79, 83, 113, 118, 132, 136, 138–139, 148–149, 152–153, 160–161, 165, 167, 204, 229, 232
disinvestment, 11, 154
displacement hypothesis, 188
disruptive capacity, 23
Dollar, David, 14, 29–30
dominance impulse, 19, 142, 144, 158, 164–165, 207–208
Dominican Republic, 28
Doron, A., 80, 226
Drèze, Jean, 127–128, 226
Dunning, David, 72
Dupper, Ockert, 136, 226
Durban (South Africa), 138
Durongkaveroj, W., 180, 226

Eagly, Alice, 70, 231
East Asia, 30, 225, 227, 238
East Asian financial crisis, 155
Echevskaya, Olga, 53, 56, 222
economic elites, 57, 76
economic roles, 57, 59, 70, 111
economic withdrawal, 17, 20
The Economist, 110, 155–157, 159–160, 227
Ecuador, 27
education, 7, 35, 66, 75, 78, 82, 85, 91–93, 95–96, 100, 103–105, 111, 118, 121, 125, 132, 138–139, 141–142, 144–146, 151–152, 155, 158, 167–169, 179, 188, 222, 226, 231, 234, 240
Edwards, Kari, 71
Eelapalan (Sri Lanka), 167, 227
Effron, Daniel, 69, 227
ego-defensive function, 59
Egypt, 34
Eisenberg, Nancy, 87
El Salvador, 28
Elinoff, Eli, 180, 227
Elleby, Christian, 127, 242
emotive identifications, 54
empathy, 5, 9, 22, 65, 77, 83, 85–87, 194, 199–200, 222, 227, 239, 241
employment, 70, 79, 103, 106–107, 147, 151, 164, 166, 188
enlightenment value, 208
entitativity, 68, 226, 232

Epley, N. B., 76
Epple, Dennis, 132
Estate Tamils (Sri Lanka), 162–163, 165, 167, 238
esteem motive, 10, 13, 51–52, 54, 58, 60–61, 63, 71, 73, 82, 91, 101, 103, 121, 123, 135, 139, 142, 144, 187, 207–208, 214, 216
Ethiopia, 105
ethnicity, 5–6, 14, 18, 21, 38, 40, 47–48, 52–53, 55–57, 62, 64, 69–70, 72, 80, 84, 108, 111–112, 114, 119, 135–136, 138, 154, 156–157, 160, 163–164, 166, 168, 186, 205, 222–223, 227, 229–230, 235–236, 238, 241
ethnocentrism, 65
ethnoregional pride, 186–187
Eurocentricism, 113
European heritage, 70
Evans, Peter, 34–35, 227
exasperation crisis, 153
exclusionary politics, 66
expectations (component of perspectives), 6, 19–20, 23, 157, 171, 181, 203, 213–214, 217–219
expropriation, 31
extreme poverty line, defined, 4

Fanselow, Frank, 58, 72, 227
farmers, 57, 69–70, 82, 99, 184, 187
Fearon, James, 164, 166, 227
Fenochietto, Ricardo, 41, 66, 236
Fernández de Kirchner, President Cristina (Argentina), 110
Fernando, Srimal, 38
Festinger, Leon, 178, 227
Fetni, Hocine, 34, 227
floods, 62, 125
Fontes, Paulo, 152, 227
food subsidies, 22, 96, 99, 110, 127–128, 130, 155, 157, 187–188, 222, 238, 242
forced displacement, 78
formal sector, 27, 106, 111
foundations, 82, 204, 224, 238
Fox, President Vicente (Mexico), 99
framing effects, 17, 127, 187
France, 64
fraternal deprivation, 60, 82, 153
Frederick, Shane, 69, 222

Index

Freud, Sigmund, 19, 207
Frey, D., 72
fuels, 124–126, 219
Fultz, Jim, 87, 222
functional approach, 59, 230

Gabbard, Glen, 86, 238
Gade, Smit, 128, 226
Gammage, Sarah, 92
Gandhi, Mohandas, 140, 227, 234
García-Colín, Jacqueline, 6, 227
gauchos (Argentina), 112
Gelb, Alan, 126–127, 234
Gestalt theory, 75, 114
Gezici, Ferhan, 171, 228
Ghana, 105–106
Ghildiyal, Subodh, 145, 228
Gilovich, Thomas, 230
Gimpleson, Vladimir, 40
Gini coefficient, 157
Gino, Francesca, 16
Giurata, Lauren, 114–115, 228
González de la Rocha, M., 92
Gooptu, Nandini, 143, 228
Gould, Carlos, 125, 127, 228
governance, 76, 113, 119, 228, 234
government competence, 74
government employment, 146, 166
Graham, Carol, 93, 107, 111, 228–229, 234, 242
grains, 125, 127–128
Great Recession, 36
grievance-based identity, 185
Griffin, Dale, 230
Grosh, Margaret, 91
group solidarity, 16, 18
Guan, Benny Teh Cheng, 159
Guangdong (China), 177
Guinea, 106
Gujarat (India), 129, 141
Gunawardena, Chandra, 164, 228
Gunewardena, Dileni, 205
Gurr, Ted, 199, 228

Hamilton, D. L., 68, 232–233
handicrafts sellers, 84
hands-tying strategy, 218
Haryana (India), 129, 141, 143, 236
Haryono, Endi, 156
Hashim, Ahmed, 167, 228

Haslam, S. Alexander, 53, 60, 115, 229, 237, 240
Hassan, Golan, 154, 229
Haughton, James, 175
Hausa-Fulani (Nigeria), 55
Hawley, Emily, 57, 229
healthcare, 7, 78, 85, 91, 93, 95–96, 100, 103, 106, 118, 125, 133, 174, 179, 188, 224, 234–236
Heider, Fritz, 68, 75, 117, 229
Heiduk, Felix, 181, 229
Heilman, Bruce, 55, 229
helplessness criterion, 79
herders, 69
heuristics, 9, 68–69, 181, 196, 200, 202, 206, 237, 240
Hewing, Geoffrey, 171
Hewstone, Miles, 60, 221
Heyer, Judith, 141, 229
Hickey, Sam, 36, 229
Higgins, Sean, 92, 117, 229, 240
high schools, 132–133, 149, 168
Himachal Pradesh (India), 128–129
Hindus, 58, 140, 142, 145, 147, 160, 164
Hoff, Karla, 34, 39
Hogg, Michael, 61, 229, 240
holiness criterion, 80
hollow democracy, 33–34
hollow growth, 33–34
Honduras, 46
Hongladarom, Krisadawan, 63, 183–184, 186, 233
horizontal inequality, 15
Horowitz, Donald, 38, 163, 166, 229
Hossain, Naomi, 86, 229
Hough, Joseph, 114, 233
Htun, Mala, 148–149, 153, 229
Huber, Evelyne, 117
Huddy, Leonie, 60, 230
Hui, Wee Chong, 157
hyperinflation, 109
hyper-politicization, 144

identifications and identity, 6, 9–10, 15, 17, 20–23, 52–67, 73, 83, 112, 119, 135, 142, 151, 153, 155, 168, 177, 199, 207, 213–214, 216, 219, 229
income distribution, 5, 9, 13–16, 25, 28–30, 60, 71, 79, 100, 118–119, 121, 152, 172–173, 205–206

Index

India, 3, 16–17, 21, 25, 32, 36, 43–44, 46–48, 62–63, 67, 73, 79–80, 83–85, 105, 123, 125, 127–128, 135–136, 138–145, 147, 154–155, 158, 161–163, 165, 167, 171, 199, 206, 208, 222–223, 226, 228, 230–231, 233–238, 240–242
Indians (Malaysia), 63, 83, 85, 128, 139, 144, 154–155, 159–160, 216
Indios, 137
Indonesia, 16, 42, 48, 58, 71–72, 80, 84, 92–94, 99, 225, 229, 233, 238
industrial workers, 57
industrialists, 64
infantile urges, 208
inferior goods, 124, 127
inferiority feelings, 63, 73, 185
informal sector, 57, 69
infrahumanization, 115, 229
ingroup favoritism, 66
insecurity crisis, 153
Instituto de Pesquisa Econômica Aplicada (Brazil), 95
Instituto Nacional de Estadística y Censos (Argentina), 109
instrumental rationality, 208
intelligence function, 200
intentionality, 18, 75
Inter-American Development Bank, 99
internally displaced persons (IDPs), 205
International Monetary Fund (IMF), 110
intermarriage, 113
inter-regional resentment, 172
intra-household bargaining, 130
invocation function, 200, 202
Iran, 34, 57
Iraq, 34
Irish, 72
irrigation, 187, 234
Irulas (India), 73
Isaan (Thailand), 198
ISIS, 57
Islam, 6, 145

Jacoby, Tami, 186, 230
Jaffrelot, Christophe, 142–143, 230
Jains (India), 67
Jakarta, 56, 238
Jammu and Kashmir (India), 128–129
Jan, Wan, 156
Japan, 16, 32

jatis (India), 140–145
Jats (India), 141, 143
Javanese (Indonesia), 80
Jayal, Nirajah, 141, 229
Jayawardene, Kumari, 166–167
Jelenic, Michael, 33, 221
Jenkins, Laura, 138
Jessel, Ella, 131, 230
Jews, 53
Jharkhand (India), 128–129, 146
Jiménez Lozano, Laura, 131, 223
Johannesen, Niels, 30, 230
Jomo, K. S., 157
Jost, John, 74, 230
journalists, 118
Justino, Patricia, 7

Kaboski, Joseph, 175, 230
Kahneman, Daniel, 9, 67–70, 196, 230, 240
Kaiser, Paul, 55, 229
Kalimantan (Indonesia), 58, 227
Kalkuhl, Matthias, 128, 231
Kanbur, Ravi, 6–7, 225
Kaplan, Abraham, 52, 150, 200, 213, 232
Karnataka (India), 73, 83, 129
Katz, Daniel, 59–60, 68, 230
Kaufman, Robert, 99, 231
Kearney, Robert, 166, 231
Keen, Michael, 41, 231
Kelley, Harold, 75, 197, 231, 241
Kenya, 105, 234
Kerala (India), 73, 83, 129
Keyes, Charles, 173
Khalil, Samihah, 156, 228
Khera, Reetika, 127–128, 226
Khon Kaen (Thailand), 177
Kidd, Stephen, 231
Kiminza, Onesmus, 105, 234
King Bhumibol (Thailand), 172, 178, 185
King, Elizabeth, 132, 172, 185, 231
Kirchner period (Argentina), 108, 110–111, 114–115, 117
Kirchner, President Nestor (Argentina), 110
Kirchneristas (Argentina), 115
Kleineberg, Tatjana, 7, 14, 24–25, 27, 29–30, 196, 226
Knörr, Jacqueline, 56, 231
knowledge function, 59
Knowles, Eric, 69, 227
Kobrynowicz, Diane, 71, 117, 223
Koen, Vincent, 156

Index

Koenig, Anne, 70, 231
Kongkirati, Prajak, 188, 231
Kopper, Moisés, 120, 231
Koreans, 53, 56
Kraay, Aart, 7, 14, 24–26, 29–30, 196, 222, 226
Kramer, Roderick, 73, 224
Krueger, Joachim, 71, 231
Kshatriyas castes (India), 140–141
Kühn, Thomas, 118–119, 231
Kurds (Iraq), 61
Kuwait, 64, 233
Kuznets, Simon, 27, 46, 232

labor income, 95
labor markets, 28
Lacina, Bethany, 83, 223
Laitin, David, 164, 166, 227
language, 5, 56–57, 61, 63, 73, 75, 83–84, 143, 161, 164, 166, 183–184, 225
Laos, 16, 42, 63, 173, 183–184
Lasswell, Harold D., 52, 66, 150, 153, 188, 200, 203, 207–208, 213, 232
Latin America, 5, 20–21, 27–28, 30, 41–42, 44, 46, 66, 70, 81, 92–94, 98, 105, 107, 109, 111–113, 117, 119–122, 131, 137, 181, 194–195, 221–222, 224–225, 229, 232–233, 235–236, 238–240
Latin America Public Opinion Project, 81, 108, 194–195, 232
Latinobarómetro surveys, 109
Layer, H., 71
Layton, Matthew, 152, 232
laziness criterion, 81, 194
Le, Tuan Minh, 40–41, 48, 226, 232
Lebanese, 72, 232
Lee, Hwanbum, 160, 181
leftists, 76, 96, 119
Leftwich, Adrian, 39, 232
Leichtman, Mara, 72, 232
Lessmann, Christian, 171, 232
Levitsky, Steven, 116, 232–233
Liberation Tigers of Tamil Eelam (Sri Lanka), 164
Lickel, B., 68, 232–233
Limpananonda, Suphannada, 173, 233
Lindblom, Charles, 36, 39, 233
Lindert, Peter H., 117, 221

liquified petroleum gas (LPG; India), 125
Lishner, David, 87, 239
livestock technologies, 82
Lodge, Milton, 71–72, 239
Lodola, Germán, 108, 233
Lolayekar, Aparna, 171, 233
Longva, Anh Nga, 64, 233
Lopez Calva, Luis, 28
López, D., 131, 223
López, Matias, 94
Loughnan, Steve, 115, 229
Lula da Silva, President Luiz Inácio (Brazil), 120, 154
Lustig, Nora, 16, 28, 66, 98, 233
Luzon (Philippines), 82

Ma ethnicity (China), 139
Macri, President Mauricio (Argentina), 115
macroeconomic policy, 110
Madagascar, 106
Madurese (Indonesia), 72, 208
Maduro, President Nicolás (Venezuela), 65
Madya Pradesh (India), 146
Magaloni, Beatriz, 98, 226
Maharashtra (India), 129, 141
majoritarian favoritism, 154
Malawi, 105, 197
Malays, 53–54, 59, 64, 80, 138–139, 154–161, 201, 206
Malaysia, 4, 16–17, 21, 23, 33, 36, 38, 42–48, 59, 64, 80, 83, 135–136, 138–139, 154–157, 159–162, 168, 172, 201, 206, 211, 220–221, 227–230, 232–235, 238, 240–242
malfunctions in the decision process, 218
malleability of identifications, 62, 64, 214
Mandal Commission (India), 142
Mandela, President Nelson (South Africa), 219
Mapuches (Chile), 58
Marathas (India), 141
Marcos, President Ferdinand (Philippines), 125
Martin, P., 171
McCargo, Duncan, 63, 183–184, 186, 221, 233
McConahay, John, 114, 233
McDougal, Myres, 213, 232
McGraw, Kathleen, 69, 233
Means, Gordon, 158
Mearns, D., 71, 233

memory load, 71
merchants, 69–70, 72, 140–141
mestizo ancestry, 113
metaperceptions, 183
Mexico, 6, 16–17, 21–22, 33, 41–45,
    47–48, 81, 91–92, 95, 97–100, 195,
    202, 225–228, 233, 235, 237, 239
Middle East, 105, 233, 242
middle-income trap, 32
migrants, 56, 72, 83, 113, 130, 148, 166,
    184, 187–188, 204, 208, 227
Miguel, E., 7
military (Thailand), 181
military rule (Brazil), 119
Millennium Development Goals, 4
Miller, Paul, 87
Million Baht Village Fund (Thailand), 175
Minangkabau (Malaysia), 80
Minguez, Guia, 125, 234
    minimal intergroup experiments, 70
Ministry of Public Health (Thailand), 217
Ministry of Social Development and Human
    Security (Thailand), 217
missionaries, 167, 194
Mitchell, J. P., 76
Mittal, Neeraj, 126–127, 234
mobilization, 18, 71, 149–150, 172–173,
    180–182
Mohamad, Maznah, 66, 234
Mohan, Giles, 36, 229
Molina Millán, Teresa, 92, 234
Molle, François, 187, 234
monetary policy, 44, 110
moneylending, 59
Mongsawad, Prasopchoke, 185
moods, 66, 121, 214
Moore, Mick, 86
moral indignation, 18, 60, 185, 207
Moreno, Erika, 105
Moreno-Dodson, Blanca, 40, 48, 232
Moses, Michele, 138
Movi, Peter, 105
Movimento Negro Unificado (Brazil), 150
Mugo, John, 105, 234
Mukherjee, Anit, 126–127, 234
Mukhopadhyay, Pranab, 171, 233
Muralidharan, Sukumar, 140, 234
Murray, Matthew, 79, 91
museums, 6, 78
Muslims, 55, 57–58, 64, 81, 147, 160, 162,
    206, 213–214, 229, 237, 239

Muslims (Sri Lanka), 38
Mustillo, Thomas, 117, 230
Muszafarshah, Mohd, 154, 229
mutual adjustment, 36–39, 198, 233
mutual disdain dynamic, 103

NAFTA (North American Free Trade
    Agreement), 98–99
Nagamadhuri, J., 74
Nakhon Ratchasima (Thailand), 179, 182
Namibia, 41, 105
NaRanong, Anchana, 133, 234
NaRanong, Viroj, 133, 234
National Food Security Act (India), 127
natural disasters, 26, 78, 106
natural-resource uses, 80
Navaratnam, Ramon, 159, 234
Nazis, 53
neediness criterion, 51, 78, 82
negative metaperceptions, 183
Nehru, Prime Minister Jawaharlal (India),
    140
Neri, Marcelo, 120
Nesiah, Devanesan, 140, 146–148,
    157–158, 235
New Economic Model (Malaysia),
    155–156, 230, 241
New Zealand, 16
Newhouse, David, 162, 235
Nickerson, R. S., 72, 235
Nigeria, 55
Niño-Zarazúa, Miguel, 99, 235
Nixon, Stuart, 156, 235
noblesse oblige, 51, 91, 93, 103, 123, 133,
    208, 210, 220
non-ascriptive identifications, 55
nongovernmental organizations (NGOs), 11
Nordhaus, Ted, 121, 235
Norhashim, Mariati, 160, 235
norm of responsibility, 85
norms, 64–65, 101, 209, 216
North Africa, 105
North, Douglass, 39
Northeast Brazil, 23, 55, 57, 63, 121, 129,
    148, 152, 175, 179, 206, 221, 233
Nosek, Brian, 74, 230
nutrition, 35, 100, 128, 238

Oakes, Penelope, 60, 64–65, 240
Oberst, Robert, 164, 235
occupationally-based attributions, 70

Odebrecht bribery scandal (Brazil), 154
Odisha (India), 128–129
Oorschot, Wim van, 76, 235
Oportunidades Program (Mexico), 97, 100, 235
optimism, 103, 212, 214, 217
Orazem, Peter, 132, 231
Organisation of Economic Cooperation and Development (OECD), 104
organized labor, 111–112
Ortiz Juarez, Eduardo, 16, 98, 233
Osório, Rafael, 97, 239
Ostiguy, Pierre, 116
Other Backward Classes (OBCs) (India), 140–142, 146, 199
outgroup identification, 91
Ouyyanont, Porphant, 182, 188, 206, 235
overlapping cleavages, 55, 164

Page, Abigail, 82, 235
PaHaL Program (India), 125–126
Palma, Jose Gabriel, 16, 235
Pandey, Gaya, 147
Pansuwan, A., 182, 235
Paradise, Tom, 65, 78, 235
Paraguayans (in Argentina), 113
Parpart, Erich, 189, 236
Partido de Acción Nacional (Mexico), 99
party affiliations, 17
past disadvantages criterion, 139
Patels (India), 141
Pateman, Carole, 79, 91
paternalism, 96, 101, 140, 180
Pathmanand, Ukrist, 174, 236
patronage, 97–100
peasants, 82
Peebles, Patrick, 162, 236
Pereira, Claudiney, 92
Perón, President Juan (Argentina), 111–112
Peronism (Argentina), 53, 109–112, 114
Perry, Guillermo, 107, 236
Peru, 27–28, 81, 92, 108, 195, 224
Pessino, Carola, 41, 66, 236
Pettigrew, Thomas, 117, 236
Phadnis, Urmila, 165, 167, 236
phenotype criterion, 113, 148, 152, 168
philanthropy, 6–7, 12–13, 59, 67, 225
Philippine cash transfer program (NHTS), 204
Philippines, 16, 42, 48, 82, 125, 159, 204, 222, 229, 234, 237, 239

Phongpaichit, Pasuk, 134, 174, 176, 186, 236
physical infrastructure, 143, 182
pilot programs, 217
pink tide (Latin America), 119
Pirttilä, Jukka, 30, 230
plasticity of identifications, 62
Pochmann, M., 120, 236
polarization, 3–4, 8, 10, 20–22, 32, 37–39, 44, 83, 103, 107–108, 112, 114–115, 117, 119, 121, 123, 153, 163, 172, 189
police, 37, 144, 174
policy process malfunctions, 200
policy sciences, 23, 200, 213
policy stalemate, 17, 20
policymakers' overconfidence, 72
political affiliation, 52
political mobilization, 172
political representation, 119
political stability, 160, 181
poor regions, 23, 170–171, 174
populism, 3, 12, 21–22, 76, 107, 110–111, 114, 120, 172, 174–178, 180–181, 188, 198, 236
Potenza Dal Masetto, Fernanda, 111, 236
poverty headcounts, 42, 205
Poverty Reduction Strategy Papers (World Bank), 36
poverty thresholds, 44
poverty trap, 31
Powell, Clare, 60
prejudice, 66, 85, 112, 131, 140
Prentice-Dunn, S., 19, 236
prescription function, 200–201
Presidency University in Kolkata (India), 146
PRI Party (Mexico), 98
price regulation, 125
principal-agent relationship, 199
Pritchett, Lant, 101, 236
PROCAMPO Program (Mexico), 99
Progresa Program (Mexico), 97, 99–100, 235
Project Globe, 194
promotion function, 200–201, 235
PRONASOL Program (Mexico), 98
pro-poor subsidies, 22, 123
pro-social behavior, 219
Prospera Program (Mexico), 97, 99–100, 235

Index

provocateurs, 18–19, 111, 167, 186, 207–209, 218
proxy means tests, 97
psychoanalytic theory, 19
psychodynamic approaches, 207
Public Distribution System (PDS) (India), 127–128, 130, 226
public hospitals (Thailand), 133
Public-Private Partnership (PPPs), 179
punitive impulses, 207
Punjab (India), 128–129
Pye, Oliver, 188

Raballand, Gaël, 41, 226
race riots (Malaysia), 160
race-blind selection, 121
racial democracy (Brazil), 118, 148, 229
racial project (Brazil), 150
racism, 114, 138, 148, 152, 225, 233
Raj Gonds (India), 147
Rajapaksha, President Mahinda (Sri Lanka), 38
Rajasthan (India), 128–129
Ramachandran, Rajesh, 139, 141, 226
Ramaswamy, Thillainathan, 155, 221
Rapoza, Kenneth, 121, 237
rational choice theory, 5
Ravallion, Martin, 33, 108, 237
reaction formation dynamic, 207
realistic group conflict theory, 84
recessions, 106, 193
rectitude value, 165, 185, 208
Red Shirts (Thailand), 8, 13, 177–180, 182, 237
Rediff News, 143
redistribution, 4, 7, 15, 18–19, 24, 28, 30, 64, 158, 171, 197, 199, 201, 218, 224
regional development, 13, 21, 23, 78, 147–148, 170–171, 178–179, 181–182, 187, 201, 212, 228, 237
regional inequality, 5, 14, 233
regulation, 11, 19, 69, 146, 151, 202, 223
Reicher, Stephen, 237, 240
Reid, Ben, 100
Reis, Elisa, 94
religion, 5–6, 18, 55–57, 61, 63, 80, 82, 84, 147, 164, 205–206, 209, 223
remittances, 97, 172, 182, 242
Repetto, Fabián, 111

resentment dynamic, 15, 18, 53, 141, 154–155, 157, 160, 172–173, 177, 182–184, 186–187, 189, 206, 219
reservation system (India), 139–140, 154
resistance to pro-poor initiatives, 194, 199
resource-dependent countries, 41
respect value, 7, 56, 63, 65–66, 68, 121, 140, 146, 187, 208
revolution of rising expectations, 5
Reyes, Daniel, 131, 223
Reynolds, Katherine J., 73
Ribas, Rafael, 97, 239
rice merchants (Chinese in SE Asia), 70
rice shortages, 125
Richardson, Harry, 170
righteousness, 80, 115
Rio de Janeiro, 121, 149, 234
riots, 93, 110, 164, 223
Roberts, Michael, 164
Rodrik, Dani, 35, 38, 237
Rogers, R. W., 19, 236
Rohingya (Burma), 53
Romano, Richard E., 132, 227
Romero, Simon, 151, 237
Rosenblatt, David, 110, 237
Rothbart, Myron, 71, 237
Rousseff, President Dilma (Brazil), 119
Routray, J. K., 182, 235
Rudolph, Lloyd, 143, 237
Russia, 56
Rwanda, 37, 105
Ryu, Taehyun, 180, 226

Sabbagh, Daniel, 155, 237
Sabpaitoon, Patpon, 179, 237
Sahai, Shambhavi, 143
Saiful, Wan, 156
Sala-i-Martin, X., 171, 222
Salamat, Patchrathanyarasm, 177, 237
salience of identifications, 14–15, 20, 53, 56, 61, 63, 205
Salinas de Gortari, President Carlos (Mexico), 99
Sanskritization (India), 143, 145
Saxer, Marc, 189
Schaffer, Wolfram, 188
Schmid, Katharina, 60, 221
Schoenrade, Patricia, 87, 222
scholarships, 82, 92, 155, 169
Schwartzman, Luisa, 148–149, 238
scripts, 18, 181, 196–197, 200, 206, 219

Index

secessionist movements, 32
self-categorization theory, 60–61, 66, 145, 240
self-demands, 213–214
self-deprivation, 66
self-esteem, 7, 59–61, 66, 82, 101, 137–139, 142, 144, 159, 180, 207–209, 216
self-perception, 65, 180, 184
self-stereotype, 215
Seligson, Mitchell, 108, 233
Sen, Amartya, 35
Sen, Kunal, 39
Senanayake, Prime Minister Dudley (Sri Lanka), 167
Senegal, 72, 232
Seng-Arun, N., 182, 238
Sepúlveda, C., 131, 223
Shapiro, Yakov, 86, 238
shared prosperity doctrine, 14, 29–30, 242
Sharma, Sangeeta, 126
Sharma, Sargam, 146
Sharma, Vinod, 126
Shastri, Amita, 165, 238
Shaw, Laura, 85, 223
Shellenberger, Michael, 121, 235
Sherif, Muzafer, 60, 84, 238
Sherman, S. J., 68, 232–233
Shia, 57, 61, 206, 229
Shinawatra, Prime Minister Thaksin (Thailand), 133, 174
Shinawatra, Prime Minister Yingluk (Thailand), 178–182, 188–189
shop-keepers, 84
Shrinivas, Aditya, 128, 130, 238
Shudra castes (India), 141
Siberia, 53, 56
Sibiryaks, 56
Siddique, Sharon, 80, 238
Sikhism, 6, 147
Silveira, Fernando, 118, 238
Silwal, Ani, 162, 235
Simpson, Brent, 5, 238
Simson, Rebecca, 46
Sindic, Denis, 60, 168, 238
Singapore, 32, 38, 41, 44, 154, 159, 229, 233, 236
Singer, Marshall, 163
Singh, Pooja, 38
Sinhalese (Sri Lanka), 21, 138–139, 161–167, 237
Sistema Único de Saúde (Brazil), 118

skepticism, 9, 11–12, 36, 136, 196–197, 200, 203, 216–218, 239
Skidmore, Thomas, 149
skills development, 82
Slemrod, Joel, 41, 231
Smith, Amy, 152
Smith, Edward, 71
Sniderman, P. M., 55
Snyder, Mark, 83, 239
Soares, Benjamin, 81, 239
Soares, Fabio, 96–97, 239
Soares, Sergio, 95
social engineering, 99, 101
social identities, 4, 61, 131
social identity theory, 52, 60–61, 64–66, 73, 142, 168, 186, 207, 209, 220, 237–238, 240
social norms, 64–65
social polarization, 131
social role theory, 70
social sector spending, 22, 103, 212
social welfare systems, 98
societal standards, 79
sociology, 61, 223
Solt, Frederick, 16, 239
Sommer, K. I., 59
sons of the soil claim, 19, 80, 165–166, 219, 223
Sordo Ruz, Santiago, 6, 227
South Africa, 106, 136–139
South Asia, 20–21, 27, 32, 46, 105, 173, 238
South Thailand, 174
Southeast Asia, 5, 20, 27, 44, 46, 56, 70, 158, 229, 240
Spears, Russell, 53, 237
Špolar, Vida, 121, 224
Sri Lanka, 4, 17, 21, 23, 34, 36, 38, 42–48, 135–136, 138–139, 145, 161–166, 168, 201, 205, 220, 222, 225–231, 235–238, 241
Sri Lankan Freedom Party (SLFP), 163, 167
Stampini, Marco, 97, 101, 234, 239
Standing, Guy, 99–101, 239
Steinberg, Chad, 173, 222
Stephens, John D., 117
stereotypes, 5, 9–10, 17–18, 65, 67–73, 76, 80, 82, 84–85, 94, 101, 111, 114–115, 117, 137–138, 140, 152, 165, 167, 170–171, 183, 187, 201, 206–208, 212, 215, 217, 219, 223–224, 231, 237, 241

Index

Stewart, Frances, 37, 206
Stiglitz, Joseph, 34, 39, 229
Stocks, Eric, 87, 239
structural adjustment programs, 92
Stürmer, Stefan, 83, 239
subcastes (India), 141, 143, 199
submissiveness, 19, 207
sub-national nativism, 83
Sub-Saharan Africa, 41, 105
subsidies, 13, 20–22, 93, 96, 98–101, 117,
    123–127, 130–132, 134, 155, 174,
    197, 234, 238
sufficiency economy doctrine (Thailand),
    185, 234
Sulawesi (Indonesia), 71
Sumner, Andy, 32, 239
Sundanese (Malaysia), 80
Sunnis, 61, 64
superego appeals, 208
supply-side policies, 34
suppression of individuality, 65
Suryadinata, Leo, 80, 238
  Swamy, Arun Ranga, 204
Syed, Murtaza, 173
symbolic racism, 114
sympathy, 63, 77–78, 206

Taber, Charles, 71–72, 239
Tajfel, Henri, 52, 56, 63, 68, 70–71, 73,
    231, 239–240
Tamil language, 73, 83, 129, 163–164, 167,
    225, 228, 231
Tamil Nadu (India), 73, 83, 127–129
Tamils, 38, 128, 136, 161–168, 201
Tamils (Sri Lanka), 161, 165
Tanzania, 55, 105–106
targeting of benefits, 22–23, 103, 196, 212
tax effort, 40–41, 48, 66, 100, 117, 232,
    236
tax reform, 69, 202
taxation, 11, 30, 40, 69, 101, 117–118,
    131, 193–194, 238
Taylor, Jim, 177
Techakesari, Pirathat, 74, 183, 240
technical occupations, 72
technocrats, 185
TeleSur, 151, 153, 240
Temphairojana, Pairat, 179
termination function, 132, 200, 203
Tetlock, P. E., 81, 239
Thai Rak Thai Party (Thailand), 176, 178

Thailand, 3, 5, 8, 16–17, 21, 23, 32–33, 36,
    42–43, 45–48, 57, 63, 116, 133, 159,
    170, 172–173, 175–180, 182–188,
    196, 198, 201, 203, 206, 217–218,
    221, 223–224, 226, 228–229,
    231–236, 238, 240–242
Thailand Development Research Institute,
    133, 224
Thai-Lao language, 185
Thaksin period (Thailand), 133, 174–178,
    180, 182, 236
Theparat, Chatrudee, 179, 237
Thibaut, John, 197, 231
thick democracy, 35–36
Thorat, Amit, 147, 240
Thyne, Clayton, 105, 240
Tilly, Charles, 39, 61, 240
Torche, Florencia, 105
Tornarolli, Leopoldo, 97, 101, 239
Townsend, Robert, 175, 230
Trabajar program (Argentina), 93
Treisman, Daniel, 40
Trejo, Guillermo, 99, 231
triple-appeal principle, 207, 232
tuition fees, 105, 132, 231
Turkey, 92, 171, 228
Turner, John C., 60, 64–65, 73, 229,
    240
Tversky, Amos, 67–68, 70, 196, 230, 240
tzadakah (charity), 6

Uganda, 105
Uighurs (China), 139
UMNO Party (Malaysia), 155–156, 158,
    160–161
UN Development Programme, 105
UNDP International Poverty Centre, 95
unions, 52, 57, 111, 119, 129
unit relation, 68
United National Party (UNP) (Sri Lanka),
    162–163
United Nations, 24, 241
United States, 16, 56, 72, 98, 138, 150, 235,
    240
universities, 105, 137–138, 140, 142,
    145–146, 150–151, 153, 161, 164,
    166, 183, 200, 208, 228, 238, 241
Upadhyay, V. S., 147, 241
Upmeyer, A., 71, 241
Uribe Mallarino, Consuelo, 130–132, 241
Urpelainen, Johannes, 125, 127, 228

Index

Uruguay, 27, 41, 94, 117, 233
Uruiola, Miguel, 132
utility rates, 22, 130–131

Vaishyas castes (India), 140
value-expressive attitudes, 59–60
Venezuelans, 65
Verba, Sidney, 221
Verkholantseva, Alexandra, 113, 241
vicarious retribution, 18–19
victimization, 10, 136, 167, 170
villager stereotype, 180
Vodopivec, Milan, 107, 241
Vogt, Manuel, 55, 223
Volpe, Michael, 182
Vorauer, Jacquie, 74, 183, 241
vouchers, 132, 231

Walter, Henrik, 86
want criterion, 79
wealth, 7, 16, 20, 22, 30, 55, 57–59, 70, 78,
     81, 152, 177, 185, 206, 208, 236
Weber, Dara, 71, 117, 223
Weber, Regine, 128, 231
Weinreich, Peter, 177, 241
welfare values, 208
well-being value, 6, 208, 218
Wenger, Jeffrey, 76, 81, 242
West Africa, 72, 81
West Bengal (India), 129
West Kalimantan (Indonesia), 72
Western Europe, 16
Whah, Chin Yee, 159

Whitt, Sam, 63, 66, 241–242
Wickremasinghe, Seeth, 34
Widianto, Banbang, 93, 241
Wilkins, Vicky, 76, 81, 242
Willer, Robb, 5, 238
Wilson, Rick, 63, 66
Winant, Howard, 150
Wjuniski, Bernardo, 105, 242
Wolgemuth, Darin, 132
Workers Party (Brazil), 96, 119–120, 150, 153
World Bank, 4, 16–17, 24, 28–30, 33, 36,
     42–43, 45–47, 95, 98–99, 104, 108,
     118, 121, 173, 201, 221, 226, 228,
     231–232, 235–237, 242
World Bank Group, 104
World Values Survey, 194

xenophobia, 138

Yadav, Ashok, 144
Yadav, Yogendra, 145
Yadavs (India), 142–145, 226, 242
Yakimova, Sonya, 74, 224
youth education, 217
Yu, Wusheng, 127, 242
Yusof, Zainal, 155–156, 242
Yzerbyt, Vincent, 74, 224

zakat (charity), 6, 213
Zambia, 41, 105
Zhang, Tiedao, 121, 224
Zimbabwe, 37, 41, 105
Zobbe, Henrik, 127, 242

Printed in the United States
by Baker & Taylor Publisher Services